Pedagogical Economies

The Examination and the Victorian Literary Man

Pedagogical Economies

CATHY SHUMAN

Stanford University Press
Stanford, California 2000

Stanford University Press
Stanford, California

© 2000 by the Board of Trustees of the
Leland Stanford Junior University

Printed in the United States of America, on acid-free,
archival-quality paper

Library of Congress Cataloging-in-Publication Data

Shuman, Cathy.
  Pedagogical economies : the examination and the Victorian
literary man / Cathy Shuman.
    p. cm.
  Includes bibliographical references and index.
  ISBN 0-8047-3715-0 (alk. paper)
  1. English prose literature—19th century—History and criticism.
2. English prose literature—Male authors—History and criticism.
3. Examinations in literature. 4. Men in literature. 5. Literature
and society—England—History—19th century. I. Title.
PR468.E93 S48 2000
828'.80809355—dc21   00-059533

Original printing 2000
Last figure below indicates year of this printing:
09 08 07 06 05 04 03 02 01 00

Designed by James P. Brommer
Typeset in 11.5/14 Centaur

ACKNOWLEDGMENTS

As readers, critics, supporters, and friends, the following people have contributed their invaluable time, goodwill, and intelligence to make this book possible: Nancy Armstrong, Jill Campbell, Michael Dietz, Frank Donoghue, Ian Duncan, Andrew Elfenbein, James Fredal, Margaret Homans, Audrey Jaffe, Sumiko Kagei, Marlene Longenecker, Sandra MacPherson, James Phelan, Kathy Psomiades, David Riede, Cristina Ruotolo, Clare Simmons, Susan Williams, the anonymous (and amazingly helpful) readers at Stanford University Press, my husband Philip Rupprecht, and my parents Peggy and Earl Shuman. My editors at Stanford, Helen Tartar and Kate Warne, and my copyeditor, Ruth Steinberg, have done a wonderful job from initial contact to final editing. Thanks are also due to two remarkable reading groups who helped found and develop my thinking: the Group at the Foundry Cafe and the Yale English Department's Marxist Reading Group. I received valuable institutional support from the Mrs. Giles Whiting Foundation and the Department of English at The Ohio State University under its chairs Morris Beja and James Phelan. An earlier version of Chapter 4 appeared in *Novel: A Forum on Fiction* 28, no. 2 (1995). Copyright NOVEL Corp. © 1995. Reprinted with permission.

Contents

1. Only a Test:
   The Social Functions of the Examination ... 1

2. Public Money, Private Subjects:
   HMI Matthew Arnold ... 29

3. Laborer and Hire:
   Trollope, Northcote–Trevelyan,
   and 'The Three Clerks' ... 76

4. "In the Way of School":
   Dickens's 'Our Mutual Friend' ... 123

5. "Preached to Death By a Mad Governess":
   Ruskin's Anti-Exam ... 170

   Epilog:
   Money for Nothing ... 213

   Notes ... 219
   Works Cited ... 237
   Index ... 251

Pedagogical Economies

Chapter One

ONLY A TEST:
THE SOCIAL FUNCTIONS OF THE EXAMINATION

1. Desire and Invigilation

> *For some reason my most vivid memories concern examinations. Big amphitheater in Goldwin Smith. Exam from 8 A.M. to 10:30. About 150 students— unwashed, unshaven young males and reasonably well-groomed young females. A general sense of tedium and disaster. Half-past eight. Little coughs, the clearing of nervous throats, coming in clusters of sound, rustling of pages. Some of the martyrs plunged in meditation, their arms locked behind their heads. I meet a dull gaze directed at me, seeing in me with hope and hate the source of forbidden knowledge. Girl in glasses comes up to my desk to ask: "Professor Kafka, do you want us to say that . . . ? Or do you want us to answer only the first part of the question?" The great fraternity of C-minus, backbone of the nation, steadily scribbling on. A rustle arising simultaneously, the majority turning a page in their bluebooks, good teamwork. The shaking of a cramped wrist, the failing ink, the deodorant that breaks down. When I catch eyes directed at me, they are forthwith raised to the ceiling in pious meditation. Windowpanes getting misty. Boys peeling off sweaters. Girls chewing gum in rapid cadence. Ten minutes, five, three, time's up.*
>
> —Vladimir Nabokov, *Strong Opinions*

I've always found it fascinating to watch my students take exams. As Nabokov's vivid rendering of invigilating at Cornell University suggests, it is an absorbing sight, involving the observer in a highly charged network of gazes—"forbidden," "pious," of "hope and hate," of suspicion, amusement, affection, assessment. Unexpected identifications and strange alignments emerge: test-takers and test-givers are alike gripped by a ritual whose theatricality inheres in both the unmoving overseer and the frantic performance he oversees. The invigilating instructor is treated to the voyeuristic pleasure of seeing (and displaying) activities—thinking, reading, writing, watching—which are essentially unspectacular, indeed, almost invisible. She can watch her expertise and power splendidly on view in the form of rows of heads bent over her questions and rows of pens reproducing her ideas. Also on display, however, is the extent to which her expertise and power are detachable from her person, which is reduced to the proletarian (yet somehow deeply satisfying) task of writing the time on the blackboard every ten minutes. While it epitomizes pedagogical power structures, the examination also loosens them: from consumers of discourse, students become producers; from the watched, the teacher becomes the watcher; power is no longer literally invested in her, but in the sheets of paper that make up the examination itself. The "source of forbidden knowledge" is no longer stable—"Professor Nabokov" can be renamed the more appropriate "Professor Kafka," for example.

With its nod to "the great fraternity of C-minus, backbone of the nation," Nabokov's mocking description hints at additional sources of contradiction and drama. Modern education systems perform a kind of double sorting for capitalist societies. Through a number of mechanisms, foremost among them the examination, they create, and find a market for, distinctions among both people-as-consumers and people-as-workers. C-minus names a kind of person, already recognizable while still "scribbling away," whose career and purchasing habits can be predicted. In his brilliant analysis of labor in university English departments, Evan Watkins argues that as student populations circulate through the education system, evaluations from that system circulate in the culture at large (6)—all the more powerfully for relating to the economy only through "discontinuity, indirection" (91). There is a far-from-perfect fit between the classroom and the markets it supplies; indifferent performance on literature exams is fully compatible with forming "the backbone of the nation." Educational testing both bridges and deepens the gap between the education system and the labor market by endowing knowledge with exchange value in the form of the grade—but without making it at all clear for what it is to be exchanged. This does not, however, completely explain the extent to which academic judgments are diffused and complicated. As Nabokov's possible pun on "fraternity" suggests, the exam is always already impinged upon by the school's many other rituals of consensus and differentiation occurring simultaneously inside and outside the classroom (see Eggleston).

We can find a precursor to Nabokov-the-invigilator's "vivid memories" of twentieth-century higher education in the famous classroom examination that opens Dickens's *Hard Times*. Nothing could be more sterile and predictable than the exchanges of Mr. M'Choakumchild's domain, set in contrast to the novel's "real-life" testing of the Gradgrind family. The most Utilitarian aspects of this examination, however, are also what allow it to be a site of drama and meaning. The ranked and divided schoolroom, an "inclined plane in two compact bodies, divided up the centre by a narrow interval," may be arranged in the service of disciplinary surveillance, but also directs the "ray of sunlight" that enters the classroom so that it links the angelic Sissy and the coldly calculating Bitzer and illustrates the difference between them (11–12).[1] We leave M'Choakumchild examining his array of pupils "not unlike Morgiana in the Forty Thieves: looking into all the vessels ranged before him, one after another, to see what they contained" and filling "each jar brim full" of his "boiling store" (15). Like Nabokov's, Dickens's examination is "vivid," registering not just its "sense of tedium," but also its sense of "disaster" and drama: the nineteenth-century examination (with its roots in the catechism and perhaps even the confessional still showing) can never, any more than its twentieth-century counterpart, shake its tacit association with the Day of Judgment.[2] And though *Hard Times* quickly abandons M'Choakumchild's classroom, it retains the thundering theatricality of the examination until novel's end: Stephen Blackpool's tragic death and Mr. Bounderby's comic humiliation are both ornately theatrical "last judgments," played to sellout crowds.[3]

In *The Bertrams* (1859), Trollope provides a textbook example of the ridiculous sublime inseparable from literary descriptions of examinations, as he imagines the feelings of runner-up and winner of

> our grand national struggle [the Mathematics Tripos] at Cambridge.... The youth who is second, who has thus shown himself to be possessed of a mass of erudition sufficient to crush an ordinary mind to the earth, is ready to eat his heart with true bitterness of spirit. After all his labour, his midnight oil, his many sleepless nights, his deserted pleasures, his racking headaches, Amaryllis abandoned, and Neara seen in the arms of another—! After all this, to be beaten by Jones!... He could have been contented to have gone out in the crowd; but there is nothing so base as to be second—and then second to Jones!
>
> Out of the whole lot, Jones alone is contented; and he is told by his physician that he must spend his next two winters at Cairo. The intensity of his application has put his lungs into very serious jeopardy. (*The Bertrams* 4–5)

Trollope's hyperbolic language here is only partly in fun. In fact, Victorians often worried quite seriously about the effect of cramming for exams on mental and physical health (see Roach 277) and the candidate eliminated from the lists by "brain fever" became a stock comic —or tragic—figure. The application of principles of competition to knowledge seems to be at once genuinely absurd and genuinely life-threatening. The examination brings together the incongruous, separates the indissoluble, and, as I will argue, thus provides "imaginary solutions to real contradictions" (Jameson 79) in relations between the subject and knowledge, the person and the state, the worker and his work, masculine self-discipline and feminine self-sacrifice, and intellectual and money economies. It is therefore a central ritual of nineteenth-century discourses of subject formation and value.

In *Pedagogical Economies* I analyze the figurative work done by the examination and the resistance to it in a set of literary texts written during the 1850s and 1860s, when it began to structure a whole range of British institutions from the factory school to the government of In-

The Social Functions of the Examination

dia. Although Western literature has always been fascinated by testing rituals, the Victorians first give a central cultural role to the *examination*—not simply an ordeal, but (as I define it for the purposes of this study) an ordeal of questions and answers about acquired knowledge or skills, sanctioned by an institutional framework and resulting in some kind of assessment. Victorian literary men (like late-twentieth-century literary critics) routinely criticized and resisted the spread of the examination. Their work nonetheless reveals a fascination with its ability to make intellectual labor visible, to remap institutional power relations, and to endow cultural capital with exchange value.

While actual Victorian examinations play a role in this book, I am primarily concerned here with the exam as an element in literary discourse—as topos, as plot structure, as figurative intersection. The following chapters explicate four versions of the examination as imagined by Victorian literary men: Matthew Arnold's official reports on his inspections of government-funded primary schools, the trials of Anthony Trollope's *Three Clerks* under the pressure of a reforming Civil Service and an unregenerate limited-liability economy, the qualifying exams set by professional men for the class-climbing heroines of Charles Dickens's *Our Mutual Friend*, and John Ruskin's battle against the examination's exchanges in favor of a Socratic identification with the pupils at a private girls' boarding school. All four of these literary men dealt with literal examinations in one way or another in their professional lives. As poet, critic, and school inspector, Arnold's professional identity was profoundly concerned with examination and assessment. Trollope's crusade against competitive examinations for Civil Servants is well known, as is his career as a postal inspector. Dickens was a visitor and patron of all kinds of schools, and Ruskin put his pedagogical theories to work in lessons at Winnington Hall School. These men also stand out not only as some of the Victorian era's best (and best-known) writers, but as very vocal participants in Victorian markets of literature and education when examination fever was at its height. The many differences among them will, I hope, illustrate the adaptability of the examination trope to a range of midcentury problems and positions. For example, Arnold and Trollope are conservative liberals writing from the heart of the Victorian examination system—the Civil Service. Dickens and Ruskin, whose reputations depend to a certain extent on their being iconoclasts, write from positions defined as outside the state. And yet, all four writers use the figure of the examination to invent ideal versions of the state, capable of conflating moral and economic assessment. The examination trope proves useful for all four authors in depicting the relation between surface expression and psychological interiority. But while Arnold and Dickens use their versions of the exam to stabilize this relationship, Trollope and Ruskin use theirs to question it.

Despite recent and growing interest among Victorianists in pedagogical issues, there has been virtually no work as yet on the examination as an element in literary language.[4] The examination as a cultural phenomenon has been explicated, however, by two of the theorists whose work has most influenced current left literary criticism, Michel Foucault and Pierre Bourdieu. Foucault grants the exam a central place in the technology of discipline, as it "combines the techniques of an observing hierarchy and those of a normalizing judgement, . . . the ceremony of power and the form of the experiment, the deployment of force and the establishment of truth" (*Discipline* 184). Bourdieu suggests that in its sheer obviousness, the spectacle of the examination decoys us from equally constitutive aspects of the education system, "masking, behind the opposition between the passed and the failed, the relation between the candidates and those whom the system has de facto excluded from the ranks of the candidates, and so concealing the links between the school system and the structure of class relations" (Bourdieu and Passeron 159). My own account of the exam's role in Victorian literature owes a great deal to these figures, and I will outline briefly the way I have used them to supplement each other as well as suggesting what they leave out.

Foucault maintains that "[t]he perfect disciplinary apparatus would make it possible for a single gaze to see everything constantly. A central point would be both the source of light illuminating everything, and a locus of convergence for everything that must be known: a perfect eye that nothing would escape and a centre towards which all gazes would be turned" (173). But a glance back at Nabokov's, Dickens's, and Trollope's descriptions suggests that this is not the ideal expressed in the examination. I will argue in this book that the examination does *not* fix the gaze, but calls attention to its mobility and contingency. Further, the terms Foucault cannot avoid using in his discussion of the exam—terms like "ritual of power" (186) as well as "judgement" and "ceremony" (184) suggest that this paradigmatic moment of disciplinarity hearkens back to earlier forms of power. Indeed, the exam's power as a figure for the nineteenth century owes as much to its association with display and drama as with surveillance and normalization. In *The State Nobility*, Bourdieu also refers to a "rite of institution," and "ceremonies of consecration" (73), but far more self-consciously than Foucault. He not only concedes, but emphasizes, the "state magic" performed by the exam—its association with all that is most irrational and passionate. In fact, this is part of its function: "[T]he wonder of satisfied love is the most undeniable expression of the success of an educational enterprise that is never so miraculous, in a sense, as when it manages to take what is actually the most likely destiny and turn it into the anticipation of a miracle" (108). Bourdieu argues that the passion as well as the "rationality" associated with the exam have the same function: concealing "the efficiency of social mechanisms ordinarily associated with the most archaic societies" (376).

If Bourdieu is more aware of the historical contradictions of the examination, Foucault reasons more subtly about power: he insists that discipline is power itself, not simply that which hides it. In *Pedagogical Economies* I will argue that both the "normative judgment" and the "state magic" wielded by the examination are working parts of its power in Victorian culture, and that they hide surprisingly little from test takers and givers. The examination's persistence itself proves this. Foucault writes in *The History of Sexuality* that "power is tolerable only on condition that it mask a substantial part of itself" (86), and in *Dis-*

cipline and Punish that "[d]isciplinary power" in particular "is exercised through its invisibility" (187). Bourdieu agrees: "Domination must... be known and recognized for what it is not" (383). It takes only a cursory glance at Victorian writing on education, however, to see that the examination's advocates as well as its detractors were fully aware of its range of repressive social functions (see Vallance).

After the "very sudden and very sweeping victory won by the examination idea within some two decades—roughly between 1850 and 1870,... there were very few parts of public life or educational effort upon which the examiner had not laid his hand" (Roach 3–5). Not only the Oxbridge prizeman, but the ragged-school urchin, was expected to be a subject interpellated by questions and answers about acquired knowledge or skills in an institutional setting. The examination has been both controversial and ubiquitous in Britain ever since. "If... I were asked what, in my opinion, was an essential article of the Victorian faith," E. E. Kellett maintains in his 1936 memoir, "I should say it was 'I believe in Examinations'" (Roach 3). Improving standards of universities, public schools, and grammar schools were seen as tied to this belief (Roach 194). And yet, the Northcote–Trevelyan Report's recommendation in 1853 that competitive exams be required for Civil Service candidates was extremely controversial (Fielding 5). Such an eminent Victorian as Disraeli distrusted examinations, complaining in the 1870s that they gave "no moral security" for applicants to government posts (Roach 30). Even supporters of exams in the nineteenth century tended to open their appeals by referring to a fallen human nature and the necessity of making the best of a bad business: "I cannot see how examinations can be avoided" muses one such writer and another admits that "[e]xaminations... are often necessary evils" (Gordon and Lawton 187). Its tendency towards arbitrariness and cultural bias, its association with rote learning, and its ridiculous attempts to quantify what cannot be quantified have been obvious to generations of British authors, educators, and even bureaucrats—and yet the examination still dominates the British education system. In fact, as the following chapters will show, opposition to educational testing has been as important to its history as examinations themselves.

We tend to think of the Victorian examination, whether in the university, the Civil Service, or the classroom, as either a capitalist tool (a symbol of pedagogical quantification, professionalization, and democracy) or an element in a regime of truth dependent on the internalization of discursive power structures. But it can as easily be seen as capitalism's grand exception. It was—and is still—a moment of spectacularization without commodification and of display without loss of agency, a scene surrounded by elaborate ritual, superstition, mysterious and sudden illnesses, and hyperbolic imagery of violence and confusion. And yet, it is a ritual where value circulates: a market. The examinations Victorian authors describe are strategies for making reading and writing visible as labor and the classrooms they create are above all workplaces. They are also emphatically public places, where bureaucratic techniques of subject formation are *openly* privileged over familial ones. Like other Victorian social solutions, from "self-help" to innovations in childrearing, the examination depends on a logic that sees identity as constructed and contingent—indeed political. Victorians re-imagine the market as a classroom (and vice versa) not because the latter is somehow distant from capitalism, but because it can make value both visible and stable in ways unavailable to private money or domestic intimacy. To this end the mid-Victorian culture of testing helped to establish the flexible and powerful idea of an unspecific "ability" or "talent," from the first associated with aristocratic privilege, which was eventually to become "intelligence." As I will argue, this idea is able to contest birth and income as social dividers not so much because, as Bourdieu and Foucault suggest, it is less easy to see as arbitrary, but because it is better at enforcing distinctions between different *kinds* of labor. In the writing of Victorian literary men, testing, not possession or surveillance, is, as often as not, the paradigmatic relationship between subject and object, allowing value to float (almost) free of supply and demand, free of discipline. Instead of wanting, or watching, these texts suggest, we grade.

2. The Pedagogical Economies of the Victorian State

> *In 1853 the India Act opened appointments in the Indian Civil Service to competitive examination. In November of the same year the adoption of the same principle for appointments at home was recommended by the Northcote–Trevelyan Report.... Limited competition began in 1855 and open competition was introduced by Gladstone in 1870. External examinations at the secondary level for both grammar schools and private schools were begun by the College of Preceptors after 1850 and by the Universities of Oxford and Cambridge in 1857 and 1858. In 1854 a scheme of examination designed for adults studying in Mechanics' Institutes was published by the Society of Arts, and after 1859 the Science and Art Department began to make grants on the basis of examination performances in scientific subjects. Finally, in 1862, the Revised Code imposed examinations in reading, writing and arithmetic upon all elementary schools receiving government grants.[5]*
>
> —John Roach, *Public Examinations in England, 1850–1900*

As a public mechanism placed between the government and the citizen, the examination brings into view continuities between Victorian discourses of politics and economics and the gender-inflected language of Victorian pedagogy and professionalization. Because it found favor with bureaucrats and pedagogues as a way of assigning exchange value to cultural capital, the examination established a relationship between the subject and the state mediated by exchange and managed by professional intellectual laborers. The mid-nineteenth-century craze for exams documented by Roach owed much, of course, to the huge network of bourgeois campaigns to reform and rationalize British institutions, from Parliament to the Church of England. Support for examinations, however, by no means equaled support for democracy or other middle-class values. Historians of Victorian education agree that, for the most part, examinations legitimated older class and gender hierarchies, rather than transforming them.[6] As Gladstone, an eager advocate of exams for the Civil Service, wrote on the eve of the Northcote–Trevelyan Report, "I do not hesitate to say that one of the great recommendations of the change (to open competition) in my eyes would be its tendency to strengthen and multiply the ties between the higher classes and the possession of administrative power" (Hart 79). The Committee of Council on Education was formed independently of Parliament, and state intervention in education was the product not of parliamentary debate, but of administrative action. As one of its prime movers, James Kay-Shuttleworth, admitted, Victorian education reform "did not spring from the people, it originated with the Government" (Hunter, *Rethinking* 47–48)—or rather, with the well-connected, university-trained bureaucrats of the Education Office.

Victorian education, inspection, and examination systems worked to form not only classed, gendered, and British subjects, but also what Foucault calls "governmentality," a "form of power, which has as its target population, as its principle form of knowledge political economy" (Foucault, "Politics" 102). The place of the individual in a governmental state begins to be determined not by her role in a family or community, but by her demographic status. Children, for example, are no longer primarily offspring, but primarily young. The definition of "child" becomes more and more an institutional one, linked to school-leaving age. Women's domestic capacities are seen as less a matter of their family responsibilities, and more as a matter of innate gender characteristics. Men are contracting agents not as heads of families, but as individuals. Foucault identifies the techniques of governmentality as "Christian-pastoral and diplomatic-military" ("Politics" 104), and he gives many examples in *Discipline and Punish* of schools run by the Church and the military developing the techniques of disciplinary power, including the examination, for the modern state. Nineteenth-century governmentality thus allows for the simultaneous "intensification of the personal sphere and ... expansion of public administration" (Hunter, *Culture* 41). State and subject meet in governmentality's "quest for a *social government*" (Gordon 23). This quest brings the state to what Denise Riley calls the "social" sphere, the location developing in the nineteenth century for issues related to "health, education, hygiene, fertility, demography, chastity and fecundity" (Riley 50), "a blurred ground between the old public and private, voiced as a field for intervention, love, and reform" (49). The state makes itself heard in this field, most often, in the form of an examination, whether that be the questioning of witnesses by parliamentary commissions, statistical interviews, official inspections, or a whole range of educational tests taking place in schools, universities, and government offices. At midcentury, the key to the governmental relationship between "an ethical persona for the administrator... and ... a public... to be the *subjects* of this particular kind of administrative rule ... was to be the examination" (Osborne 305).

As the preferred method of state involvement in British education during the nineteenth century, the examination distances and focuses the relationship between state and citizen: the former can shape the life of the latter in increasingly precise ways, without resorting to direct legislation (Montgomery 42). This transaction does not hide the relationship of domination between state and subject, but seems to open it up, give it breathing room, by likening the choices demanded by the examination to those offered to the consumer.[7] John Stuart Mill, for example, saw "annual public examinations" as an alternative to a state education system, one that would prevent the "infringement of individual liberty and ... deadening uniformity" (Gordon and Lawton 180). The authors of the Northcote–Trevelyan Report claimed that

> we need hardly allude to the important effect which would be produced upon the general education of the country, if proficiency in history, jurisprudence, political economy, modern languages, political and physical geography, and other matters, besides the staple of classics and mathematics, were made directly conducive to the success of young men desirous of entering into the public service. Such an inducement would probably do more to quicken the progress of our universities, for instance, than any legislative measures that could be adopted. (14)

Brian Simon shows that even when "no direct financial support was provided by the state..., state intervention... was directly concerned with a redistribution (and the use) of actually existing financial resources" (24). At once domestic haven and elite origin of social change, the Victorian state nevertheless constitutes what I call a pedagogical economy. The examination's mediation of the governmental state's role in the lives of the people causes goods to be "exchanged between subjects as... quantifiable value[s]" (Guillory, *Cultural* 299). Education produces educated citizens, for which the state is willing to pay. And perhaps even more importantly, from the point of view of the authors I study here, the state pays an increasingly influential group of workers to run this system.

The "avenue of communication between schools and society" (Broadfoot 11), the examination is the medium by which the cultural currency of evaluations, and also the literal currency of government money, circulate in nineteenth-century Britain. As the century advanced, government grants, salaries, and appointments were increasingly dependent on test scores. Roach even describes college servants laying bets on the Senior Wrangler competition at Cambridge (8). The Revised Code "payment by results" method of funding primary schools "initiated the concept that accountability for the use of public funds could and should be reckoned in terms of the academic performance of the scholars" (Broadfoot 51): public money is translated by this means into the working class's progress in literacy. Through the mechanism of the exam, subject formation is figured as an economic process, a set of equivalencies and exchanges. A "constant exchanger of knowledge" (Foucault, *Discipline* 187), the examination brings into play both the figure and the reality of monetary exchange, allowing the economic transaction—like the economic reward granted an unmercenary character in a Victorian novel—to figure that which is valuable because it transcends the economic.

Money's role in the state's pedagogical economy, then as now, troubled critics of the exam. In 1888, "over 400 leading figures, including over 100 Members of Parliament" signed a "manifesto" against "The Sacrifice of Education to Examinations" (published in *The Nineteenth Century* and expanded to a book the following year):

> Children... are treated by a Public Department; by managers and schoolmasters, as suitable instruments for earning Government money; young boys of the middle and richer classes are often trained for

scholarships, with as little regard for the future as two-year-old race horses are trained for races; and young men of real capability at the Universities are led to believe that the main purpose of education is to enable them to win some great money prize, or take some distinguished place in an examination. (Gordon and Lawton 186)

It is the idea of "real capability" or priceless childhood finding an equivalent in *public* money that disturbs the manifesto's authors. Even by the 1880s the notion of children earning money was far from scandalous, though it was controversial, and the belief expressed in a generalized "real capability" that is somehow measurable was held by advocates of examinations as well as their opponents. The outrage here, evocative of late-millennial dismay at the extension of market values and tactics into public schooling and university management, is at the intrusion of the economic domain into the social, an intrusion the examination symbolizes over and over again for both its critics and its advocates.[8] For example, Robert Lowe, Secretary of Education, defended the introduction of the Revised Code examination in 1862 by making explicit its adaptability to high-capitalist economic principles: "Hitherto we have been under a system of bounties and protection. Now we propose to have a little free trade" (Midwinter 38). Despite the horror they display at the exam's ability to price people and mimic work, opponents of exams also figure the benefits of education in economic terms: as the compensation, or price, for a range of social ills. Evan Watkins shows how literary education, for example, "transmitted across the generational discontinuities of a democracy," was seen as compensation for the noise, nastiness, and stress of nineteenth-century American industrial capitalism (95). James Kay-Shuttleworth made the distinction between state and "free trade" education explicit in 1833 when he compared the inevitable fluctuation of capitalist incomes with the stability of public money in order to support his arguments for state-funded education. But he cannot resist describing education as a good investment, claiming that money spent on education would be money saved on police and prisons: "Is society to continue to pay upwards of two millions, annually, for the repression of crime, . . . [when] a remedy for these chronic social disorders [might be] purchased by the same means?" (Digby and Searby 84–85).

The idea that the educational system is to compensate society for the ravages wrought by capitalism grows paradoxically out of liberal theory's dissociation of state and civil society, and the identification of "economy" with the latter. As historians of the state have long argued, however, this dissociation was never a reality; capitalism includes the state and vice versa[9]: "[L]abour in production had to be free(d) to be exploited; as labour in society it had to be moralized, normalized, individualized" (Corrigan and Sayer 117–18). The academic title brings the state education system into day-to-day conflicts in the workplace over job descriptions, conditions of labor, and pay scales (Bourdieu 121). The state is itself an economic entity:

> No modern government can *not* influence economic life, because the mere existence of government must do so: the "public sector," however modest, is nearly always a very large "industry" in terms of sheer employment, and public revenue and expenditure form a significant portion of the national total. Even at the peak of British *laissez-faire*, around 1860, government expenditure amounted to several percent of the national income. (Hobshawm 226)

If the governmental state has its own internal politics, its own logic of growth, its own conflicting desires, it also has its own internal economy. School inspectors and civil service examiners are not paid by those who take their tests—but they are paid. The exchanges that take place in the examination are literally as well as figuratively economic: money changes hands as well as information. The indirect paths taken by money in this economy may make it appear analogical to and completely separate from, rather than cooperative with, the money paid by the capitalist to the worker, but it is money nevertheless.

In his crucial work on Victorian education, Ian Hunter makes the Foucauldian claim that the governmental state does not operate in any class's interest; it cannot be dismissed as a "mere instrument" of a "sovereignty lying elsewhere" (*Rethinking* 46). He wants us to see the state-as-institution as an entity in its own right, acting in its own interests:

"The interest of the state in popular education ... was less the result of the logic of the relations of production and more the product of these 'special measures' of investigation which gave rise to that specific sphere of political interest and rationality which we call 'social welfare'" (*Culture* 55). But this sphere, as Dorice Williams Elliott among others has noted, is not only staffed, but produced, by cultural workers. Citing Carlyle, Hunter remarks on the paradox that "'do-nothing' liberalism was in fact at the centre of a new and powerful apparatus for investigating and regulating social life" (*Culture* 92). This paradox is easily solved if we remember that early reformers like Kay-Shuttleworth and Chadwick were essentially bureaucratic entrepreneurs, energetically engaged in carving out and colonizing the social sphere. Maintaining this sphere, keeping watch over its products, is also work, as Foucault himself recognizes: "[S]upervision became ... a special function," demanding a "specialized personnel" (*Discipline* 174). The "investigating and regulating social life" Hunter refers to is performed as paid labor by this group. Hunter's analysis, by both insisting on the primacy of intellectual labor's tasks and refusing to notice it *as* labor, begins to look surprisingly like those of the nineteenth-century cultural workers themselves (see Perkin 118).

The division between capitalist state and capitalist economy is not, however, simply an ideological smokescreen. It stands for real struggles over the economic construction of the nineteenth-century subject and the ideological line between exchange value and use value. These struggles may not always be fought along class lines, but they are certainly fought along the fractures in a fragmenting ruling class—between intellectual labor and industry, money capital and cultural capital—in Bourdieu's terms, between the dominant and the dominated within the field of domination. The legislative controls put on factories, mines, schools, food, and so on, can be seen as "one long campaign orchestrated by ... the professional class against the vested interest of the propertied class" (Perkin 121). As the nineteenth century progressed into its second quarter, a new set of workers—engineers, statisticians, analytical chemists, medical men—wielded a new kind of power in the state, encouraging, monitoring, and staffing its involvement in Victorian social life. Their loyalties were mixed, to professional as well as governmental ethics, and their role in governmental innovations was correspondingly strong. A "cycle of expertise" within the state itself began to propel change (Macleod 10).

Whether working inside or outside the state, professionalizing intellectual workers were, of course, heavily dependent on, as well as creating, its institutions of inspection and evaluation. We cannot ignore the "collectives and associations" created by "English professionalism ... which changes what can be understood by the term 'middle class'" (Cohen 8). In order to "constitute *and control* a market for their expertise," nineteenth-century professionals had to struggle both to create boundaries between different kinds of labor and to police those boundaries by exerting control over who is to be included within them (Larson 14). Although the new professionals of the nineteenth century took advantage of precapitalist associations, "the constitution of professional markets which began in the nineteenth century inaugurated a new form of structured inequality; it was different from the earlier model of aristocratic patronage, and different also from the model of social inequality based on property and identified with capitalist entrepreneurship" (Larson xvii). Professional labor is not quite "residual" nor "emergent" (to use Raymond Williams's terms), neither feudal, capitalist, nor socialist.

An uneasiness about the role they play in capitalist relations still haunts the self-examination of intellectual laborers. One of the most significant problems in Marxist thought after Marx has been the need to account for the phenomenon of the professionalization of intellectual labor and its disturbance (real or apparent) of nearly all the crucial concepts of historical materialism: the class struggle, the historical succession of modes of production, and the relation between the economic and the extraeconomic (or base and superstructure). We are still arguing about Gramsci's question of the 1930s: "Are intellectuals an autonomous and independent social group, or does every social group have its own particular specialized category of intellectuals?" (301). Do intellectuals form a class, complicating or even challenging the centrality of the struggle between capital and labor? Or does the role intellectual labor plays in that struggle depend on its identification with one class or another? As Ehrenreich and Ehrenreich argue, intellectual labor problematizes the division of significant social action as either capitalist or working-class. As Larson indicates, it complicates the division of past and present into feudal and capitalist modes of production. And as Block and Hirschhorn claim (in their perhaps overoptimistic account), intellectual labor can be seen as the force which destroys the possibility of differentiating between work and leisure, public and private, base and superstructure—the force which will render Marxist critiques of capitalism obsolete by destroying capitalism.

For Bourdieu, both problem and solution, both mystification and demystification, inhere in the double nature of cultural capital as both complicit with and antagonistic to material capital:

> This struggle over the power to dictate *the dominant principle of domination*, which leads to . . . a *division in the labor of domination* (at times intended and conceived as such, and explicitly negotiated), is also a struggle over . . . the legitimate mode of reproduction of the foundations of domination. (383)

The "foundations of domination" cannot be reproduced without intellectual labor's playing this double role, destabilizing the analogy between money and cultural capital on which the system depends. The historian Harold Perkin critiques any easy analogies between money and cultural capital by describing the necessary step in translating one into the other as rhetorical:

> [S]pecialized training of itself yields only earned income . . . , which may even fall below the cost of production if the service is oversupplied and undervalued [as in the case of academic Ph.D.'s today]. It cannot, except accidentally, create property in the form of vested income without some device to transform it into a scarce resource. . . . The transforming device is professional control of the market. When a professional occupation has, by active persuasion of the

public and the state, acquired sufficient control of the market..., it creates an artificial scarcity in the supply which has the effect of yielding a rent, in the strict Ricardian sense of a payment for the use of a scarce resource. (Perkin 7)

The traditional professions of medicine and law were, predictably, the first to take this route, forming professional associations, developing occupational standards and qualifying procedures, and so on (Reader 71). But "the middle years of the nineteenth century saw the proliferation of qualifying associations which monitored the qualifications and practice of engineers, actuaries, pharmacists, architects, and others" (Burstyn 124). Obviously, the examination is a crucial ingredient in the process of transforming specialized training into a scarce resource. It provides the necessary medium of translation—but also of differentiation—between money and cultural capital.

3. Literary Men

At the same time that Marx and Engels were beginning to analyze ideology's role in reproducing relations of production, British intellectual workers were discovering in themselves a responsibility for this reproduction and the development of institutions that would administer it. Like their bureaucratic colleagues, Victorian authors were fully aware that their proper work was the reproduction of social relations—and that the reproduction of social relations was work. The great interest in defining writers' social and professional status in midcentury periodicals, fiction, and writers' groups (see Feltes 5–6; Poovey, *Uneven* 101–2) can be seen as a less fully institutionalized version of more traditional forms of professionalization, establishing and policing the boundaries of professional authorship. If the nineteenth-century professional is the paradigmatic giver and taker of tests, figurative examinations are equally necessary to the literary man, as he articulates literature's place vis-à-vis its most significant rivals in the social sphere: the public legislation enacted by the state and its institutions, and the private influence wielded by bourgeois femininity.

There is a good deal of overlap between the mission of Victorian literature and that of the Victorian state and its professional employees. From the Romantic period, literature has taken a strong interest in the state's educational role, and "literary representations of schooling... increasingly color debates on education as the century progresses" (Richardson 8). Critics and novelists, as well as government inspectors, spent much of the nineteenth century establishing and evaluating complex yet coherent structures of moral and material equivalencies and standards of cleanliness and godliness as well as professional competence and artistic merit. Conversely (and pace Dickens), the moral energy and rhetorical omniscience of bureaucratic reformers make many a blue book—whether on education or factory reform—read like a Victorian novel. Dickens himself might have penned Joseph Fletcher's remark to the Committee of Council on Education that "no sane individual, in any conceivable state of society, can escape education in every branch, either to truth or error, to good or evil... the choice to be made for them is *not* between 'education' and 'no education,' but between 'good' and 'bad' education" (*Parliamentary Papers* 299–300). G. W. Hastings, the first secretary of the Gradgrindesque National Association for the Promotion of Social Science, describes the state's function in ways reminiscent of the wonderfully extensive claims of Victorian realist fiction. Like the omniscient narrator in a Dickens or Eliot novel, the reforming state reveals "that each one of the social problems we have been at any way at pains to unravel strikes its roots into the substance of the nation, ramifying through 100 secret crevices into classes apparently the most removed from its influence" (Corrigan and Sayer 135; see also Arac).

The authors I consider in *Pedagogical Economies* represent a range of interaction with the Victorian state's education reforms. I will argue in the ensuing chapters that, whatever his place in this system, each invokes the figure of the examination to imagine and enforce a particular relation between literature and government. Arnold's version of the inspection, for example, simply does away with this relation: literature is constitutive of the state, as government is constitutive of literature—

"the best that is known and thought in the world." In Trollope's *Autobiography*, far from being identical, they are opposed: the state is a place where, in marked opposition to the craftsmanlike author's workshop, work transcends quantification and commodification. Dickens and Ruskin, whose extraliterary lives were further removed from official government, both imagine literature as containing the state. In *Our Mutual Friend*, a version of the state education system expands to cover all of society in the form of a "real world" examination room, but one only possible within the embrace of the novel. Ruskin's state, like Arnold's, is synonymous with art, but only when it is imagined as a "moveless" statue enshrined in the minds of girl readers of his prose.

Bargain and sale threaten to devalue the literary man's intangible products, while placement beyond the market threatens to deny him access to consumers of these products (see Larson and Duncan). But although lawyers, doctors, and pharmacists can demand "that society should accept their own valuation, guaranteed by exclusive education and certification" (Perkin 16), authors cannot. Literary men are drawn to the examination's dramatic rendering of intellectual labor partly because of their own lack of professional certification mechanisms. As I have argued, educational testing (like the cultural capital it measures) can function either as a replacement for the market or as an alternative. A fear of losing connection with the market economy prompts the former (as in today's defunded academy's increasing reliance on "raising standards"), while a fear of becoming overwhelmed by the market prompts the latter. For example, the Northcote–Trevelyan report stresses the need for some kind of character-building substitute for exposure to real-world competition. It contrasts the stagnant career of a civil servant to the education provided by the market to those in "open professions," where "a man's success . . . depends upon his obtaining and retaining the confidence of the public." In the legal or medical professions, "[t]he able and energetic rise to the top; the dull and inefficient remain at the bottom. In the public establishments, on the contrary, the general rule is that all rise together" (5). Instead of the rough and tumble of the professional marketplace, civil servants, the report complains, are subjected to the feminizing coddling of a home education: "their course is one of quiet, and generally of secluded, performance of routine duties, and they consequently have but limited opportunities of acquiring that varied experience of life which is so important to the development of character" (5), evoking not the life of duty and effort of the exemplary middle-class son, but the sheltered life of the exemplary middle-class daughter. By excelling on an examination, the candidate for promotion or appointment can bring manliness, choice, agency, competition, and progress to the overly familial Civil Service. In contrast, Carlyle's unpublished response to the report claims an authoritative expertise that is even further from the marketplace than the middle-class home:

> Merit by merit: Oh Heavens, that were truly the Millenium, neither more nor less, that everybody were rewarded and punished according to his merit! But it will need much cunninger methods than the [Northcote–Trevelyan] one to find out the merit at all. It will need —Shall I tell you? No, I will not tell you, lest you rise in too furious a manner and perhaps do a mischief to yourselves and me. Enough to say, it will need a reform not of Oxford university only, . . . but of the Brit[ish] Nat[io]n generally to an extent which it is painful to contemplate at the moment. (Fielding 9)

In Victorian literature, then, we find the privileging of examinations (whether literal or figurative) that oppose rather than ape the test administered by supply and demand. Arnold's resistance to the cut-and-dried exchanges of the Revised Code in the name of a self-reproducing inspection ritual, Trollope's to academic cramming in the name of work-as-display, Dickens's to the "banking model" of education in favor of a "midwife model," and Ruskin's attempt to erase the quid pro quo of the exam itself all emphasize the way the exam can be made to evaluate and display intellectual labor without commodifying it.

In her study of the contradictions of nineteenth-century professional authorship and the gendered separation of public and private, Mary Poovey has shown that Victorian intellectual workers rely on the extraeconomic authority granted the domestic woman by the doctrine of separate spheres in order to resolve the contradictions of their place in capitalist relations of production: they may then depict themselves as policing the line between the public and private spheres rather than challenging it (*Uneven* 89). Sawyer notes that the authority of Victorian non-fiction is generically androgynous, "powerful precisely in its mingling of feminine sweetness and masculine authority" (130). Hence, the authors I examine in *Pedagogical Economies* rely on a range of carefully managed feminine identifications. Arnold, for example, builds his ethic of inspection on an opposition to a figure who bears traces of femininity as well as Philistinism. When the masculine intellectual laborers of *Our Mutual Friend* administer tests to the novel's class-climbing heroines, knowledge and value are trapped safely and permanently within feminine bodies.[10] But masculine self-discipline has to be separated from, as well as allied with, feminine self-denial (Adams 8–9). James Eli Adams writes of the "anxious conjunction of discipline and performance in middle-class Victorian constructions of masculinity" and the need to manage the "intractable element of theatricality in all masculine self-fashioning" (Adams 10).[11] Normative middle-class masculinity is inevitably on show, but literary men must purge display of its associations with feminine vanity and aristocratic excess (Adams 27).

The hyperbole that surrounds the examination both expresses this anxiety and contains it. Whatever version of the examination these literary men invoke, it invariably articulates a question about interiority[12]: testing requires a division between surface and depth, so that it may bring that which is within to the surface. The examination asks us to put up *and* shut up; knowledge must be displayed *and* contained. The examination ritual provides a uniquely satisfying solution for these writers because in the exam display *is* discipline: performance is not a problem, but a necessity—the proof of labor. The examination can thus be used to replicate situations that allow the nineteenth-century gentleman to display, out of stern necessity rather than vanity, that which he has hidden within him (Bizup 55). But it can also serve as an implicit argument against realism's reliance on the opposition between surface and depth. In Trollope's *The Three Clerks*, tests that involve the passage from inside to outside are silly and trivial; the only real tests are those that collapse surface and depth, advertising the identity of intellectual labor and its display. And Ruskin resists the inside-to-outside logic of the exam with the Carrollian mirror-logic of an erotically charged identification between questioner and answerer, student and object of study.

The examination displays intellectual work without commodifying, feminizing, or rendering it obsolete, and thus performs a crucial, yet dangerous, service for literary men. The professional intellectual laborer's autonomy is put at risk by this spectacularization: as the century grew old and the culture of testing grew strong, bureaucratic professionals were forced into spending longer hours on view in the office, and their freedom in the field decreased—as did their extra-official research and publishing (Macleod 17). But then, that very autonomy is itself risky in a cultural climate placing ever-increasing moral value on hard and persistent labor. Productivity, not humility, is becoming the measure of virtue and the proof of docility (see Foucault, *Discipline* 138; Cohen 7). The ostentatious industriousness of the classic Victorian author owes a great deal to the shame beginning, by midcentury, to be associated with work that doesn't, somehow, *show*. The examination calls attention to the intellectual laborer's work *as* work, and makes this identification self-evident, staringly obvious, for all to see. It is here that the examination's greatest value as a figurative device lies for Victorian literary men. But the artificial situation of the exam—the clouds of archaism and femininity it trails behind its up-to-date virility—risks an inevitable slippage into irony, even parody. The examination *mimics* work, and thus risks mocking it, not just showing intellectual labor, but showing it up as a performance: self-conscious, visible, artificial, scripted. Judith Butler writes that *"In imitating gender, drag implicitly reveals the imitative structure of gender itself"* (137). The examination is drag work, labor impersonation.[13] And to take this perhaps dangerous analogy further, the impersonation of labor can destabilize it as a category of human action. Laden as it is with "tedium and disaster," the exam is always farcical, but also always an opportunity to see intellectual work's ideological construction, and thus, perhaps, for intervening in the conditions of our own labor.

In a passage from Trollope's *Autobiography*, these contradictions are both acknowledged and managed, as he combines in his own person the private author writing in public and the public official asking after private letters. While traveling far and wide as a postal official, he tells us, he decided to make use of the time in novel-writing:

> I made for myself therefore a tablet, and found after a few days' exercise that I could write as quickly in a railway-carriage as I could at my desk. I worked with a pencil, and what I wrote my wife copied afterwards.... My only objection to the practice came from the appearance of literary ostentation, to which I felt myself to be subject when going to work before four or five fellow-passengers. But I got used to it, as I had done to the amazement of the west country farmers' wives when asking them after their letters." (103)

Trollope displays himself "going to work" to his readers as well as to his fellow passengers, calling our attention to the physical aspects of writing that mark it as labor ("after ... exercise ... I could write as quickly"), requiring a laborer's tools ("tablet ... pencil"). To prevent our seeing it as merely physical, however, Trollope gets the assistance of the gendered division of labor. His wife's "copying" *is* merely physical, providing a much-needed contrast to his "writing." The passage also raises and quenches the other fear associated with the display of intellectual labor—others might see it as "literary ostentation." This danger is also averted by recourse to "wives" when he likens the passengers watching his display of labor to the "west country farmers' wives" whom he examines in the interests of the nation. Trollope writing his novels on the train shares the theatricality of the test-giver and -taker, while the gendered division of labor keeps this display from sliding over into merely physical or merely parodic work.

In the following chapters, I will move from Arnold's championing of one version of the examination, through the various forms of ambivalence Trollope and Dickens display, to the erasure of the examination altogether by Ruskin. Arnold dismisses the sterility of the Revised Code payment-by-results examination only to celebrate its near relative, the inspection, and Trollope retains its form and function while insisting that it must equal rather than represent labor. Dickens turns the examination upside down, rewarding ignorance rather than knowledge, and Ruskin rewrites the exam plot to establish identificatory relationships within institutional structures. Despite this implicit narrative, the following chapters are meant primarily as a set of case studies in the literary use of the examination; a full-scale study of the trope's development over the nineteenth century is beyond the scope of this project. In this book, I use what might be called a political formalism to detail the social significance of discursive strategies within a small number of specific texts rather than setting these texts in relation to others. It is, by now, a given that literary texts function within specific institutional practices. Powerful work has already been done that traces the network of nineteenth-century discourses of subject formation and exchange within which the texts I examine make sense.[14] Consequently, this is not my goal here. I define my object of study not as, on the one hand, a specifically literary history, or on the other, literature in relation to social facts occurring, somehow, elsewhere—but, rather, as social history occurring *in* literary texts. Thus, while my arguments are firmly rooted in the wonderful subtleties and contradictions of high-Victorian literary prose, I am committed to reading these subtleties and contradictions politically.

In the next chapter, on Matthew Arnold's *School Reports* (1852–1882), I trace Arnold's depiction of the heroic bureaucrat, a figure whose administration of working-class subjectivity and opposition to bourgeois subjects denaturalizes the construction of the subject and makes a spectacle of the work of ideology. Far from the privacy of the bourgeois primal scene, the interpellation of the working-class subject is figured as public, institutional, bureaucratic—a stage for the display of professional, masculine, intellectual labor.

Like Arnold, Trollope imagines a subjectivity embodied in the conflation of the display of labor with labor itself. Throughout his career at the Post Office, Trollope opposed the introduction of competitive examinations. I argue in Chapter 3 that in the early novel *The Three Clerks* and in his posthumously published *Autobiography*, this opposition can be read as part of his more general resistance to the typically Victorian projection of a space *beyond* quantification or even articulation. To put it another way, one of the most prominent exemplars of Victorian realism rejects realism's construction of interiority and its insistence on a cause-and-effect relationship between child and man, education and work.

The Dickensian school, from *Nicholas Nickleby* to *Our Mutual Friend*, is one of his most memorable contributions to nineteenth-century fiction. In Chapter 4, I argue that *Our Mutual Friend* appropriates the examination to provide a model of professional expertise, as valuable and invaluable as domestic power, yet freed from its fragility and contingency. This novel depicts the retreat from the market to domesticity as impossible, so instead the retreat is into the classroom—albeit a classroom where gender remains the governing discourse. Dickens's ideal examination features a feminine student who evaluates and places the masculine intellectual laborer by producing and containing a reified knowledge immune from the risks of exchange.

In my final chapter, I turn from literary men who rework the trope of the examination to one whose pedagogy depends on its erasure. In Ruskin's *Sesame and Lilies*, *Ethics of the Dust*, and letters to the schoolgirls on whom he based the latter's characters, educational narratives put gaps or paradoxes in the place of credentialing or testing moments, and girls' education is figured as the productive consumption of knowledge of which they must not take possession. Ruskin's fascination with the systems of exchange operating in and around the young girl's classroom thus sets the context for a revisionary reading of his identification with the schoolgirls he addresses, as well as the anxieties associated with this identification.

In very different ways, then, each of these literary men use the figure of the examination to explore and control contradictions in the relation between literature and the state, in that between marketplace and intellectual exchange, and between an interior energy and an exterior self-control. In the literal and figurative classrooms created by these authors, the examination is a strategy for making reading and writing visible as value-able labor.

Chapter Two

PUBLIC MONEY, PRIVATE SUBJECTS: HMI MATTHEW ARNOLD

> Briefly, th[e abstract labor form of literary criticism] is the following: A accomplishes a task of speaking or writing; B evaluates the performance of that task; and B reports the evaluation to A and/or C.
> —Evan Watkins, *Worktime: English Departments and the Circulation of Cultural Value*

1. Ideology Works

Ideology works. To begin with the most obvious meaning of this statement, it defines the thinkable and the unthinkable and resists (sometimes even gains strength from) demystification. It is, however, equally certain that it contains the seeds of its own destruction, available for misappropriation and contradiction. The study of literature has long been a site for such transformations, as each culture rewrites the ideological work of the past in its own image. No critic is more eager in this cause than Matthew Arnold, who promises in "The Function of Criticism at the Present Time," that "whoever sets himself to see things as they are will find himself one of a very small circle; but it is only by this small circle resolutely doing its own work that adequate ideas will ever get current at all" (274). Evan Watkins also suggests, in *Work Time*, that we use the teaching of literature as a site for social change by taking advantage of the inevitability of ideology's self-destruction, making literary texts available for revolutionary reappropriation. He provides an array of alternative strategies: use the dialectic as opposed to demystification to structure analysis, adopt a Gramscian "politics of positionality," encourage the subversive use of unexamined cultural givens. To what extent are these strategies descended from Arnold's strategies in making literary texts available to working-class children because the "animation of mind, the multiplying of ideas, the promptness to connect, . . . and to illustrate one thing by another, are what is wanted, just what *letters*, as they are called, are supposed to communicate" (*Reports* 1874)? Of course, the differences between these pedagogies are profound: Arnold essentializes the ideological effectiveness of literature, while Watkins stresses its contingency and constructedness. Arnold's ideal students are formed by literature, while Watkins's re-form it. But both theorists imagine—albeit in very different terms—the possibility of an alliance-through-acculturation between professional-class teacher and working-class students in opposition to bourgeois hegemony. Just as Watkins, deliberately and polemically, ends his book by evading the logical completion of his argument, substituting instead a series of anecdotes, Arnold (deliberately? polemically?) famously evades and thus critiques logical argument everywhere in his prose works, substituting instead his famous repetitions and tautologies.[1] John Holloway notes of Arnold's style in general: "It suggests an approach; or it is deliberately negative and inconclusive, or where positive its statements are deliberately commonplace and familiar" (204). He does not attempt to "inculcate . . . a set of ultimate beliefs . . . but simply certain habits and a certain temper of mind" (203). If Watkins may be said to substitute a relationship of serendipitous solidarity between the intellectual laborer and the working class for "a set of ultimate beliefs," I will argue in this chapter that Arnold substitutes an *inspectorial* relationship between them.

Both Watkins and Arnold make this move as a way of begging the same question: What is the social utility of reading, teaching, and learning about literature? Arnold's major essays return over and over to the validity and social role of criticism, forging links between literature and social value that literary critics still find useful: "Arnold is above all a diagnostic critic who uses literature instrumentally, to advance social health and human wholeness" (Dickstein 16–17). As poet, critic, professor, and above all as one of Her Majesty's Inspectors of Schools, Arnold's professional identity is profoundly concerned with rituals of assessment. And, as Ian Hunter reminds us, like most literary critics today, Arnold was a professional agent of a state educational system (*Culture* 3), in which, as the "son of Dr. Thomas Arnold, brother-in-law of Gladstone's Education Minister William Forster, slum school inspector, and Oxford Professor, all at once" (Baldick 60), he took an overdetermined place. In his annual *General Reports* on his school inspections (1852–1882), Arnold's analysis of the explicitly political power wielded through inexplicit acculturation makes it clear that he sees himself and his fellow School Inspectors as producing and supervising something very close to Althusser's "School Ideological State Apparatus."[2] In other words, Arnold *shows* ideology working, insisting that ideology *is* work, and that the purveyors of ideology are workers. This insistence works for Arnold (and continues to work for us). It allows him (as it allows us) to claim social agency for literature, literary pedagogy, and literary criticism.

The Nonconformist-run primary schools that Arnold inspected during the 1850s and 1860s were actually a step up from "slum schools." Their clientele, as he reminds his Education Committee superiors frequently, blur the distinction between the working and the middle class; they are the sons and daughters of "small farmers, small tradesmen, skilled mechanics" (*Reports* 1853). The system by which these schools were funded was notoriously complex. Until 1870, state-funded schools were strictly "Voluntary" schools, receiving government grants but founded and administered by the Church of England's National Schools Society, the Nonconformist-administered British and Foreign Schools Society, and eventually similar societies founded by other religious bodies. The rivalry between the two main providers of schools to the working class may have kept a state education system from developing in Britain, but it also aided its growth by encouraging the opening of more and more schools (Smelser 95), preventing narrative, fostering proliferation. In the 1850s and 1860s, 70 percent of English children under ten were enrolled in Voluntary schools (Smelser 255–60) and they continued to compete with the government-run "Board" schools until late in the century. Most of these schools taught the three R's, religion, and sewing (to girls), but "model schools" existed where children were also taught geography, elementary science, English history, grammar, domestic economy, and more ambitious needlework (Purvis 92). Parliament's yearly grant to the Education Committee in Council supplemented funds provided by the Societies, donations from local worthies, and student fees, by allocating money for school buildings and other supplies, and (after 1846) for pupil-teachers,

> who were apprenticed to schoolmasters and mistresses, and further grants were made to students at training colleges. The whole process was managed and the grants allocated through annual examinations conducted by Her Majesty's Inspectors of Schools, which were the first large-scale examinations held at a number of different centres in the country. (Roach 22–23)

In 1870 the first state-run schools were created, run by local boards of education and funded by rates. Primary education was not compulsory until 1876, not free until 1891, and not reorganized on a national level until 1902 (Smelser 141).

In its Victorian infancy as a school subject, English literature was the study most encouraged of populations seen as generative of social problems: women, the working class, and colonized peoples (see Purvis, Eagleton, Viswanathan). In his *Reports*, as elsewhere, Arnold is a vigorous promoter of this study for working-class and petit-bourgeois primary-school students.[3] As my reading of the *Reports* will demonstrate, he imagines English literature as a kind of examination on a grand scale, with the power to sort people into classes and set up relationships among them. As an Inspector, Arnold himself embodies this power: throughout the *Reports*, the figure of Her Majesty's Inspector of Schools underwrites a set of relations that amount to a mode of production and an economy of knowledge. In this pedagogical economy, working-class subjectivity is, first and foremost, that which can be administered by the intellectual worker—just as bourgeois subjectivity becomes, first and foremost, that which resists him. Arnold's *General Reports* thus furnish a perfect (if almost anachronistically early) example of Ehrenreich and Ehrenreich's claim that the self-definition of intellectual labor depends equally on its invasion of working-class culture and its ideological opposition to the bourgeoisie. As a literary man, Arnold uses literature to lay the foundations of the edifice we still inhabit as ideological workers and agents of the state.

David Riede suggests that Arnold "*assumes*," rather than arguing for, "the power in words to cultivate the mind" (21). The power in words renders each one irreplaceable, not subject to exchange—hence Arnold's habit of repeating words and phrases instead of substituting pronouns (Tillotson 95). Words are not simply media of knowledge, but invaluable objects in their own right. While Arnold may condemn certain kinds of verbal interchanges (the Revised Code Examination, for example) as mechanical and inert, words themselves are at once solidly material and vitally animate. This means that, for Arnold, while language is ultimately only language, this does not detract from its effectiveness as a tool of social control. The hesitation Riede notices between Arnold's faith in language's referential power and a conviction of its arbitrariness (21) is precisely what makes literature so valuable a lesson for him. In the *Reports*, he specifies working-class children's "excessive scantiness of vocabulary" as "the signal feature of their mental condition, [which] constitutes their real inferiority to the children of the cultivated classes." If a child suffers from "want of words" he will inevitably lack "the ideas which go along with the words" (1878). He advocates the teaching of simple grammar to primary-school pupils, suggesting that parsing a sentence or learning the parts of speech can teach a child a kind of "elementary logic" (1878), but with an extralogical bonus. As Arnold notes in a discussion of examining pupil-teachers:

> [G]rammar . . . is not only exact—it not only compels the pupil examined in it to show himself clearly right or wrong, as knowing the rule or as ignorant of it—but it also compels him, even more than

arithmetic, to give the measure of his common sense by his mode of selecting and applying, in particular instances, the rule when he knows it. (1861)

Grammar is preferable to arithmetic because it forces the student to transcend logic with his "common sense" as well as obeying it with his knowledge. Arithmetic, with its tradesman-like insistence upon the establishing and exchange of equivalent values, is not as effective as the study of language, which is different from all other school subjects because it is at once natural and learned, already known to schoolchildren, and yet still to be taught: "Indeed, all that relates to language, that familiar but wonderful phenomenon, is naturally interesting if it is not spoiled by being treated pedantically" (1876).

"Everyone has noticed Arnold's habit of repetition" and of self-quotation, notes Timothy Peltason; he is "a tradition in himself" ("Function" 754). It is as if he were attempting a new form of reproduction, free of the taint of factory or bedroom. Literature, like "all that relates to language," is useful in the primary school because it awakens young minds in a way that reproduces them in their invigilator's image, awakening them to examination as well as to being examined:

> [T]he remedy will be found to lie, not in attempting to teach the rules of taste directly—a lesson which we shall never get learnt—but in introducing a lesson which we can get learnt, which has a value in itself whether it leads to something more or not, and which, in happy natures, will probably lead to this something more. The learning by heart extracts from good authors is such a lesson. I have often thought of it as a lesson offering an excellent discipline for our pupil-teachers. (1861)

Students provided with the chance to evaluate a text are themselves rendered evaluable—capable or not of making the text into "something more," possessed of more or less "happy natures." As I will argue in this chapter, evaluation per se is Arnold's pedagogical economy, not the production or exchange of information or value.

2. Unpedagogical Economies

Figurative and literal economic systems proliferate and collide in all kinds of Victorian writing on the Voluntary school system. Sometimes the National and British and Foreign Societies are figured as competing producers—but of what for whom? Of education, subjects, class privilege, the school itself? For the people, the state, the Inspector, the churches? Students may be figured variously as buyers, sellers, workers, and commodities in these systems, as are their parents, their instructors, and the state (see Smelser 24–25). In his *Reports* Arnold depicts three pedagogical economies competing in the grant-earning primary schools: the first an unregulated free-trade economy based on the "private" money of bourgeois managers and petit-bourgeois parents, the second a "payment-by-results" economy based on the Education Department's 1862 Revised Code, and the third a redemptively "public" economy based on the inspector's evaluation.

Private money infects schools wherever government influence is least powerful. Treated by Arnold with a predictably contemptuous hostility, this system threatens to equate educators with stock-jobbers and petty tradesmen on the one hand, and well-meaning but silly amateurs on the other. In the *Reports*, the free play of the market is depicted as lethal to the free play of the mind. Free-trade education proves an easy target for Arnold, but the second system he describes, the policy of "payment by results" instituted by the Revised Code of 1862, is based on an examination and mandated by Arnold's own superiors at the Education Committee Office, and thus requires a more elaborate attack. Here the threat is not that educators will become entrepreneurial sharks or reckless spenders, but drudge-like wage laborers. Arnold resists the payment-by-results system by exposing it as a sham, the production of nothing by teachers and managers masquerading as the production of knowledge by pupils. In fact, Arnold refused to reduce grants to schools according to the Revised Code examination's "results" (Montgomery 41), as if not recognizing them as genuinely binding transactions. The third economy Arnold describes in the primary-school classroom, identified with the figure of the Inspector, will occupy us most: an economy of evaluation, where an explicitly inexplicit ideological exchange backed by government money and expertise frees student, teacher, and Inspector from the unchecked whirl of speculation as well as the deceptive quid pro quo of "payment by results." Before exploring his inspectorial economy, however, I will show how Arnold resists its competitors.

Early in his career, Arnold notes the absurdity of applying market values directly to the transaction between pupil and teacher:

> [T]hose who pay least are to be taught least; consequently, scholars perfectly capable of taking their place with the highest class, but unable to make the highest payment, are thrown back into the lower classes, and comparatively neglected.... [T]hose children who make the highest payments are put into the highest class, whether fit for it or no. (1852)

One of the reasons that some schools' preference for children from wealthier families worries Arnold is that the higher the percentage of the child's education paid for by fees rather than the government or the Societies, the more likely parents are to view themselves and their children as customers, and thus always right. For Arnold, the connection between business methods and pedagogical incompetence is automatic. For example, to prove that "school managers . . . are hardly capable . . . of remedying by their own efforts and inventiveness any weakness against which the Department does not directly provide," he mentions that they "are in general business men" (1867). Ultimately, though, the problem with the system of supply and demand in education is its dealing in commodities at all. When he praises the Prussian education system's reliance on "experts of recognized expertness," he condemns the British reliance on free-market exchange in the same breath: "It would surely be well if we followed this example, instead of . . . suffering private speculation to have unchecked play" (1867).

Nevertheless, it is impossible for Arnold to imagine education as other than an object of some kind of exchange. In "A French Eton," his

1864 essay comparing French and English secondary education, he maintains that while "the mass of mankind know good butter from bad, and tainted meat from fresh, and the principle of supply and demand, may, perhaps, be relied on to give us sound meat and butter,"

> the mass of mankind do not so well know what distinguishes good teaching and training from bad; they do not know what they ought to demand, and therefore, the demand cannot be relied upon to give us the right supply. Even if they knew what they ought to demand, they have no sufficient means of testing whether or no this is really supplied to them. Securities, therefore, are needed. (101–2)

While beyond the judgment of the average shopper, teaching and training are still versions of butter and meat—objects of exchange—and in both the classroom and the marketplace the viability of this exchange depends on the viability of "testing," whether putting one's nose to a carcass or putting a child through the multiplication table. Arnold's pedagogy makes it necessary to posit the classroom as some kind of market, but one with as little as possible in common with the butcher's shop. "[E]xperts of recognized expertness" must provide "securities" against the chaos of consumer choice, and ensure that private money is purified by its indirect passage through public hands.

HMI Arnold, however, faces a more serious threat. The Education Committee's Revised Code of 1862 established "the notorious principle of payment by results. In order to encourage high and regular attendance and keep a careful fiscal check, ... grants, instead of being of a more general nature, should be based on attendance plus examination" of each student by the HMI according to a pre-set rubric (Midwinter 37–38). In other words, if a student could not pass the exam set by the Department, her school lost a certain amount from its grant that year. In 1862 the examination was limited to reading, writing, and figuring, but by the 1880s grant-earning examinations existed in a whole range of subjects (N. Morris 8). The Revised Code was touted as streamlining, cost-cutting, and putting teachers in their place (Smelser 124). Although it lasted for thirty years, it was controversial from its inception because of its emphasis on basic skills, rote learning, and memorization. Arnold was one of its fiercest critics, claiming that the Revised Code transferred power from educational buyers and sellers to an increasingly demonized examination itself. He complains that "when, practically, the substantive result of the inspector's proceedings in a school is the grant for this examination, it will, whatever the Department may say, efface everything else" (1869). Despite the characterization of the code by its originator, Robert Lowe, as introducing "a little free trade" (Midwinter 38) into state-funded education, Arnold depicts the Code as a parody of free trade, one that in fact blocks any kind of educational exchange. Even Arnold's scorn for privately funded education, elsewhere in the reports so marked, gives way to his antipathy to the Code, when he characterizes schools with better-off clientele, where "the instruction . . . is in great measure independent of Government action [and thus of the damage done by the Revised Code], and is maintained at a high standard by the demands of the parents, in general of a class quite removed from poverty and fairly intelligent" as "the best schools in my district" (1867).

Two crucial differences were instituted with the Revised Code: government grants were based on attendance levels and exam results rather than on the inspector's more general and less quantitative evaluation, and grants were handed directly over to school managers, to spend as they wished, rather than being directed toward specific items (Smelser 126–27). From 1846 to 1861, grants had been available for materials, salary augmentation, training colleges, and pupil-teacher stipends (Smelser 90), and Arnold notes the disastrous effects of the Code on pupil-teachers in his *Reports* (payments were restored for them in 1867 [Smelser 128]). Lowe's hostility to teachers was well known (Smelser 402), and Montgomery describes the code as marking a "rift between teachers and inspectors" (40) who mostly, unlike Arnold, supported the Code (Edmonds 76–77). Smelser echoes Arnold's rhetoric when he declares: "The act amounted to a devaluation of teachers by removing them from their quasi-civil-servant status and by making them more like technicians, training children in the basics and turning them out as 'results'" (Smelser 128). As Arnold complains, the Code's inclusion of a clause that returns the responsibility for paying all teachers to school managers means that it has "withdrawn from teachers all character of salaried public servants" (1867) and demoted them from bureaucrats to wage laborers.

Certainly the Code's economic "results" suggest that Arnold had plenty to complain about. From the Code's introduction in 1862 until 1870, the majority of funding for the Voluntary schools came from private rather than public sources, and the main increase was in school pence, excluding more and more of the poorest children from the possibility of attending. The Code's replacement of the pupil-teacher subsidy with an unregulated system of hiring and paying pupil-teachers left many of the graduates of the government's teacher-training programs without jobs or underpaid (N. Morris 15). The tying of grants to children's performance on the exams meant that children not likely to pass the examinations were a very low teaching priority (Smelser 129). And the Code caused certain schools to lose all government support because they were too poor to afford to meet Government standards for the certification of teachers, building regulations, and so on (Edmonds 79).[4]

The author of an anonymous attack on the Code ("The Twice-Revised Code"), Arnold in his 1863 *Report* risks his superiors' displeasure and battles with Lowe's characterization of payment by results as "free trade" by stressing the *pre*-Code inspection's "freedom, interest, and communication" (Edmonds 67). He objects that the Code exam matters too much, that it is boring for the inspector, and that it allows power to be transferred from expert to speculator, that is, from Government Inspector to Philistine school managers (1863). He depicts himself as cramped both physically and intellectually by having to examine each child on a prearranged topic:

> The new examination is in itself a less exhausting business than the old inspection to the person conducting it; it does not make a call as that did upon his spirit and inventiveness; but it takes up much more time, it throws upon him a mass of minute detail, and severely

tasks hand and eye to avoid mistakes.... Few can know how much delay and fatigue is unavoidably caused before one can get one's 600 communications [grades in reading, writing, and arithmetic for each pupil in a school of 200] fairly accomplished. (1863)

Once demanding "spirit and inventiveness," the inspection is now a mere matter of "hand and eye." In "A French Eton" Arnold worries about the Philistine proletarianization of the state, which becomes "a mere tax-collector and policeman—the hewer of wood and drawer of water to the community" (131–32). The Revised Code seems to make that threat a reality for the state's representative in the education system, the HMI. Rather than "making a call" on the Inspector, or speaking to him on equal terms, it merely throws a "mass of minute detail" at him, to be processed by the Inspector-as-factory-worker.

In order to resist proletarianization by the Code, Arnold must distinguish the functions of Inspector and examiner: "It will be remembered that the Duke of Newcastle's Commission attached great importance to leaving *inspection* just as it was, the new capitation grant examination being therefore kept subordinate to it, and committed to a subordinate functionary" (1869). When he himself conducts exams, he codes his work as investigation rather than drudgery (a kind of testing of the test): "I have not hitherto applied to your Lordships for any help in conducting these examinations in my district, but have, so far, accomplished them all myself, because I was anxious fully to observe their working." His conclusion is that "without a very large increase in the body of inspectors, and a strict discrimination of their separate kinds of function," the Education Department cannot do both old-style inspections of "intellectual life" and Revised Code examinations of every student (1863). He insists upon (and suggests the use of public money to enforce) a hierarchy in which a challenging and rewarding "inspection ought... to be disjoined from" a dull and routinized "examination":

> Inspection under the old system meant something like the following. The inspector took a school class by class. He seldom heard each child in a class read, but he called out a certain number to

read, picked at random as specimens of the rest; and when this was done he questioned the class with freedom, and in his own way, on the subjects of their instruction.... [T]he examination ... often acquired much variety and interest. The whole life and power of a class, the fitness of its composition, its handling by the teacher, were well tested; ... a powerful means of correcting, improving and stimulating them was thus given....

The new examination groups the children by its standards, not by their classes.... The examiner, therefore, does not take the children in their own classes. The life and power of each class as a whole, the fitness of its composition, its handling by the teacher, he therefore does not test. He hears every child in the group before him read, and so far his examination is more complete than the old inspection. But he does not question them; he does not, as an examiner under the rule of the six standards, go beyond the three matters, reading, writing, and arithmetic. (1863)

In the monitorial schoolroom, a thoroughly panoptical hierarchy of pupils, pupil-teachers, and masters is topped by the inspector, or visitor, "whose scrutinizing eye must pervade the whole machine, whose active mind must give it energy, and whose unbiased judgment must inspire confidence and maintain the general order and harmony" (Andrew Bell, qtd. in Edmonds 16). The Inspector is not simply needed to ensure quality in the classroom, he is the figure on which the whole system depends—logically, symbolically, and financially. For Arnold, the good classroom is the inspectable classroom: he suggests that "mechanical alteration leads to moral effect" when it makes the schoolroom more "comprehensible" (1855). But with Lowe's Code, and the necessity of examining children one by one, the Inspector may not confine himself to surveying his subjects calmly from the center; he is constantly put at risk by traveling out to them at the margins. Performing the Code examinations, Arnold complains of the

> difficulty of access to children's places, difficulty in seeing clearly in the obscurer parts of the school-room, difficulty of getting children to speak out—sometimes of getting them to speak at all—difficulty

of resisting, without feeling oneself inhuman, the appealing looks of master or scholars for a more prolonged trial of a doubtful scholar. (1863)

Not only is the Inspector having trouble seeing, but he himself becomes subject to the powerfully "appealing looks" of those he is supposed to examine. The Code brings governmental center and local margin too close to each other, squeezing the Inspector's agency as well as his body: "Suppose the inspector were to produce a book out of his pocket, and to pluck all the children who could not read fluently from it, would the Department sustain him? The managers would appeal to the Code" (1869) and override the Inspector's authority.

Arnold, whose own record on examinations was mixed,[5] grudgingly accepts the certifying or competitive examination as an exchange system, one governed by the ideology of the contract: "If a man wants a certificate or diploma of you, you say you will give it him if he learns this and that, which you prescribe.... Certainly, if a man wants a certificate, or a diploma, or honours of you, you must fix just what he shall get them for" (1869). For government places, university prizes, or job certification, the examination can function as a way of pricing such commodities as diplomas and honors—or prizes and jobs—consistently and fairly. However, as Arnold points out, this is not the function of the Revised Code examination:

> But, at any rate, to make a narrowing system of test examinations govern the whole inspection of our primary schools, when we have before us, not individuals wanting a diploma from us, but organizations wanting to be guided by us into the best ways of learning and teaching, seems like saddling ourselves with a confessed cause of imperfection unnecessarily. (1869)

And so, "to refuse [a child of seven] his grant for a timidity which is not, in his case, a school fault, seems to be going beyond the intention of your Lordships, who designed the refusal of your grants to be a punishment for school faults" (1863). The state's transaction here is not with the recipient of education (the schoolchild), but with the provider of education (the school, or its teachers and managers). The teacher, like the Inspector a victim of proletarianization, falsely represents his students as laborers producing facts (with which they have merely been crammed) for a government wage: "[T]he teacher... tries to cram his pupils with details enough to enable him to say, when they produce them, that they have fulfilled the Departmental requirements, and fairly earned their grant" (1869). But because the pupil is not involved in any transaction, she gains nothing from the Revised Code grant, not even an education: "[I]t is found possible, by ingenious preparation, to get children through the Revised Code examinations in reading, writing, and ciphering, without their really knowing how to read, write, and cipher," and "the circle of the children's reading has thus been narrowed and impoverished all the year for the sake of a *result* at the end of it, and the *result* is an illusion" (1869).

Albeit unwittingly, Arnold approaches a crucial issue here: working-class resistance to Society schooling was often owing to the slowness with which the knowledge and certification provided by these schools acquired exchange value in the society at large. Parents sensed that they, like the Inspector, were getting nothing for something. Attendance at a Voluntary school, unless one had ambitions to become a schoolteacher oneself, was not likely to raise one's income or class status (P. Miller 140–41). The Code exam may seem to put a price on pupils' heads, but it does so in a way that reveals the arbitrary falseness of this commodification of knowledge. The emptiness of the exchange prompted by the Revised Code puts the school at the mercy of entrepreneurs with no concept of enlightened self-interest. In 1876 Arnold urges the imposition of

> a penalty on parents withholding their children from school without good cause on the day of examination. At present they are frequently withheld, sometimes from vindictiveness, oftener from mere caprice, and nothing can well be more vexatious or more unfair to teachers and managers.

This hoarding of children is reminiscent of the orphan-market in Dickens's *Our Mutual Friend*:

> [T]he instant it became known that anybody wanted the orphan, up started some affectionate relative of the orphan who put a price upon the orphan's head.... The market was "rigged" in various artful ways.... Genuine orphan-stock was surreptitiously withdrawn from the market. It being announced... that [the clerical couple delegated to find an orphan for a childless couple] were coming down the court, orphan scrip would be instantly concealed, and production refused, save on a condition usually stated by the brokers as "a gallon of beer." (*Our Mutual Friend* 244)

But while Dickens's novel depicts a world where even familial relations cannot escape the cash nexus, and where "affectionate relatives" are attempting to get as much profit as possible out of available infants, the parents Arnold describes exercise an economic power that has nothing to do with the main chance. Of course, by far the most common reason for student absence was solidly economic: parents needed the income their children could produce as workers, or as child-minders while parents worked. And quite logically, when (as in 1861) jobs were plentiful, Voluntary schools were empty, and when (as in 1862) job opportunities closed up, Voluntary schools filled (Smelser 261). But Arnold implies that rather than being too thoroughly interfused with market values, the Code encourages their perversion. While teachers and managers will lose income if children miss the Code exam, there is no corresponding gain for the parents, who rig the pupil-market out of extraeconomic "vindictiveness" and "caprice," not greed.

Arnold suggests further that, if the Code *is* involved in any exchange, it is not one taking place in the classroom, but in a debased public sphere showing early symptoms of mass culture:

> [T]he ideal of payment by results was just the idea to be caught up by the ordinary public opinion of this country and to find favour with it.... But the question is, not whether this idea ... suits ordinary public opinion and school managers; the question *is* whether

it really suits the interests of schools and of their instruction. (1867)

Instead of an exchange system itself (having to do with relations among the working-class child, the Society school, and the state), payment by results functions for the "public" as either a slogan or a commodity *in* an exchange system (having to do with the relation between the state and the middle class) and ensuring the latter that it is getting the efficient education system it pays for by taxes and rates. The Revised Code examination, far from being too strict or confining, is in fact too easily manipulated by cheating teachers, stingy politicians, capricious parents, and a gullible public.

Early in his career, Arnold cites with approval an alternative to state funding chosen by a Welsh mining company:

> [A] weekly deduction is made from the wages of every person employed in the works, whether married or single, to form a fund to defray the expenses of the school, of the library, and of medical attendance.... [I]t becomes the direct interest of the population to avail themselves of an institution to which they are in any case forced to contribute. (1852)

Workers' money may not be directly exchanged for intellectual labor, but it serves as the incentive for the production and exchange of cultural capital. Arnold will not let go of the law of supply and demand of a market system entirely, but insists that it be filtered through a central institution. With the arrival of the Code, Arnold's suggested alternative keeps a similar role for money: make a larger proportion of the grant dependent on the Inspector's more general judgments about "intelligence," "proper extent" of instruction, and the "form and style" of the work performed (1867).

Before the Revised Code, the Inspector had more control over the grant and thus more control over the school. After all, schools saw the inspection, as much as the payment-by-results exam, primarily as a way of getting public money. But Arnold suggests that the Inspector's strategy of control is less dependent on money than is the examination's.

He both admits and denies the fact that, in either case, the school's incentive is monetary:

> The whole school felt, under the old system, that the prime aim and object of the inspector's visit was, after insuring the fulfillment of certain sanitary and disciplinary conditions, to test and quicken the intellectual life of the school.... The scholars' thoughts were directed to this object, the teachers' thoughts were directed to it, the inspector's thoughts were directed to it. The scholars and teacher co-operated therefore with the inspector in doing their best to reach it; they were anxious for his judgment on their highest progress, anxious to profit by this judgment after he was gone. (1863)

The "old system" provides a "quickening" judgment: it is, like all good criticism, reproductive, in marked contrast to the sterile limits of the Code examination. Arnold's typically "redundantly redundant" (Peltason, "Function" 754) language here stresses the relationship between this ideological reproduction and a univocal hierarchy, as the same goals are replicated in a great chain of being reaching from "scholars" to "inspector." Under the Revised Code, in contrast,

> the centre of interest for the school when the inspector visits it is changed. Scholars and teacher have their thoughts directed straight upon the new examination, which will bring, they know, such important benefit to the school if it goes well, and bring it such important loss if it goes ill. On the examination day they have not minds for anything else. (1863)

The shifting of the inspector from the "centre of interest" breaks the grammatical unity between him and students and teachers, and the examination limits, rather than quickens. It does not guarantee gain, as does the inspection, but brings the school into the realm of profit and loss, of needless risk. The Revised Code examination thus bears the same relation to the old-style inspection as the critic's "mere judgment and application of principles" do to his "communicating fresh knowledge, and letting his own judgment pass along with it." It is "like mathematics, ... tautological, and cannot well give us, like fresh learning, the sense of creative activity" (Arnold, "Function" 283).

While his resistance to private money and the Revised Code remains consistent throughout the *Reports,* Arnold's position on the literal economics of education does change slightly as conditions change and the state's level of participation rises. As his opponents change, and government control of education expands, Arnold's resistance takes the form of attempts to diminish the causal role of public money rather than redirecting its course. As I have argued, in the Code's early years, Arnold accuses it of falsifying exchanges between school and government, but once state-supported education is a reality, he depicts blocking exchange as the best hope for both Voluntary and Board schools. In 1880 he urges teachers worried about the complexities of the Code's requirements: "The Code does not *compel* you ... it offers you a few shillings.... If in this respect the intricate arrangements of the Code conflict with the due following out of a good programme, disregard them and sacrifice the few shillings of grant." He tells school boards, who are less dependent on grants than Voluntary school managers, that

> their first object should be a sound programme of instruction simply followed out; if our over-complicated machinery for grants ... is found to interfere with the due following out of a sound programme, that machinery is likely in process of time to be amended, and meantime the programme should not be sacrificed to it. (1880)

Now, Arnold's alternative no longer involves the use of money to bolster state power, but shows him distancing himself (and recommending that schools distance themselves) from the state apparatus. Whereas in the 1860s the Revised Code was blamed for allowing teachers, students, and managers to cheat the Inspector and the government, the Inspector now ranges himself with teachers, local school boards, and managers against the central government and its Code, urging them to look beyond its sterile ineffectiveness to the more fruitful, though less well-defined "good" or "sound programme." This vacillation between alliance with the central and with the local is, as we shall see, characteristic of Arnold's Inspector.

3. L'etat, c'est Lui: The Inspector

> "[T]he State, or organ of our collective best self, of our national right reason..."
> —Arnold, *Culture and Anarchy*
>
> [I]t was as an ethically exemplary personage that the cultivated man like Matthew Arnold entered the social sphere.
> —Ian Hunter, *Culture and Government*

The first governmental inspections in Britain were of factories, and part of the factory inspectors' task was to supervise the factory schools, in which some instruction was required from 1802. By 1833, factory schools were provided with paid, professional inspectors (Edmonds 25–26), and by 1844 government Inspectors of Voluntary Schools were armed with a 150-page questionnaire, covering "'mechanical arrangements,' school building and plans, 'means of instruction,' 'organization and discipline,' and religious instruction" (Edmonds 39–40), and emphasizing the maintenance of conformity, improvement of standards, and gathering of information (Edmonds 42). When Arnold became an Inspector in 1851, he "was joining a small but rather distinguished body of men with a pioneering job to do" (Hopkinson 31). Victorian Inspectors, with their high degree of professional autonomy, are described by Corrigan and Sayer as a vanguard of a revolutionary class of intellectual workers (125). Freelance bureaucrat, nineteenth-century knight-errant, the Inspector is "virtually a literary figure—a person who formed the 'human' link between government and the people, who became the repository of central knowledge, wisdom and tradition...a skilled adviser, a beneficial mediator as well" (Macleod 13).

The Inspector's authority rests on his disinterested freedom from power structures, but he also functions as a link in the chain of power between central and local institutions, serving as the perfect conduit for truly public money and the perfect basis for an evaluative economy. In the *Reports* Arnold imagines an Inspector who maintains and embodies the relationship between the state and the child as one of creative examination. In order to do so, the Inspector must command the professional autonomy necessary to wield a criticism that transcends localized religion and localized politics. Arnold's last, best pedagogical economy therefore begins with the Inspector's central location in the Victorian state bureaucracy. Baldick comments that "[I]t might seem odd that the unmediated leap so often made in [*Culture and Anarchy*] between the heights of state power and the depths of the psyche is passed off so calmly as common sense" (35–36). But of course the School Inspector makes that leap every day, and, in fact, personifies the bringing together of state apparatus and individual subject.

One obvious reason for Arnold's distaste for the Revised Code examination is that it forces him to deal with the rather grubby and inarticulate children one by one rather than inspecting the school as a totality. Arnold's impatience with the individual pupil expresses his wish to find the individual in the institution, and vice versa. His comments on Nonconformists in *Culture and Anarchy* reflect this view of their schools: "narrowness, one-sidedness, and incompleteness is what they most suffer from; in a word, that in what we call *provinciality* they abound, but in what we may call *totality* they fall short." Like Hegel, Schiller, and the other German thinkers he admires, Arnold sees civil society's particularism as posing a threat to the totalizing "best self," the state, "our national right reason" (see Hunter, *Culture* 82–83; Habermas 118–20; and Culler 124). And yet, political power in the nineteenth century continued to be situated locally. Despite the growth of the nineteenth-century national bureaucracy, local "magistrates continued to be, in large measure, 'the state' until the later nineteenth century" (Corrigan and Sayer 157). And when the state finally did take over British education, it did so not on the national level, but in the form of local school boards (N. Morris 9–10). Under Britain's Voluntary-school system, the working-class citizen/soul was educated by an uneasy alliance between institutions claiming jurisdiction over either British citizen or denominational soul. It required a structure of "funding and inspection" (Hunter, *Rethinking* 75) to stabilize this alliance as hierarchical and invigilatory.

Like the National Schools Society and the British and Foreign Schools Society, Arnold makes use of the rhetorically flexible concept of the nation to mediate between an ideal of centrality and a locally situated reality.[6] As local and limited, the geographical Britain and the racial British are frequently singled out in the *Reports* (as elsewhere in Arnold's writing) as lacking the universalizing tact and taste of more centralized states (see, for example, *Culture and Anarchy* 50, or *Reports* 1863). In the report for 1867, which is full of negative comparisons with Germany and France, Arnold draws on his own expertise as "an ex-professor of poetry" to characterize a poem from a school reader titled "My Native Land" as "especially bad" (it *is* pretty awful). As central and universal, however, the British Government can act as other governments do and as a result protect the nation from local entrepreneurs (see *Reports* 1860 and 1867). As in *Culture and Anarchy*, in the *Reports* Arnold identifies the task of critical evaluation with a Victorian state which depicts itself as neutral, above sectarianism and party politics (Corrigan and Sayer 123), dispensing grants to Anglican and Nonconformist schools alike, in an inspection ritual that places the state serenely above the debate over secular-versus-religious schooling. When he advocates making parts of the Bible an examinable subject in his Report for 1869, he claims that such a step

> could raise no jealousies; or, if it still raises some, let a sacrifice be made of them for the sake of the end in view. Some will say that what we propose is but a small use to put the Bible to; yet it is that on which all higher uses of the Bible is to be built, and its adoption is the only chance for saving the one elevating and inspiring element in the scanty instruction of our primary schools from being sacrificed to a politico-religious difficulty.

Arnold suggests that institutionalizing the Bible will at once secularize and sanctify it; it can be "elevating and inspiring" only if its moral and literary virtues are to be separated from its status as a "politico-religious" document. The secular state's role as humanizer-from-above can also be seen, however—as many Victorian religious groups did see it—as a far-from-neutral competitor rather than an umpire. As he continues, Arnold hints with no sense of conflict at the replacement of a religious with a nationalist approach to the Bible that begs the sectarian question: "There was no Greek school in which Homer was not read; cannot our popular schools, with their narrow range and their jejune alimentation in secular literature, do as much for the Bible as the Greek schools did for Homer?" (1869).[7]

The Inspector's importance in the professional revolution owed much to "the slowness with which inspectorial norms were routinized and how long it took for the victory of the central office over the circuits of the inspectors" (Corrigan and Sayer 125). Inspectors often rebelled against their bureaucratic superiors; their assistants were frequently reprimanded or fined (Edmonds 27–28). School inspection was professionalized very gradually. Before 1844, when Inspectors' responsibilities were clarified and codified, they were virtually independent agents, with little guidance and no training provided (Edmonds 20–37). Like many of his colleagues, Arnold had an uneasy relationship with his superiors in the Education Department. His fear that the Revised Code was planned as a way of keeping the HMI in check was far from paranoid: the Department indeed considered that the pre-Code Inspector was allowed to make too many subjective, unpredictable decisions, and held too much ambiguous power. Education Minister Robert Lowe was suspicious of his Inspectors and complained of their reports' irrelevant generalizing. He saw their yearly meetings as a threat to his control and rejoiced when what he called "a sort of Parliament in the office" was "put a stop to" (Edmonds 72). By the 1870s, the HMI—like his colleagues in other government departments—had been reined in by growth in staff, structure, and control (Macleod 15).

If central-office bureaucrats like Lowe saw Inspectors as representing an invasive autonomy, inspectors like Arnold saw the office as posing a threat to their agency. The Inspector's anxieties about his place—

at center or margin? in classroom or government?—complicate his role as a link between center and locality. The HMI's visit to the elementary school enacts both the extent of the state's (and the intellectual worker's) control over the minutiae of working-class life—and the limits of that control. Arnold's complaints about the whims of parents and managers and the constricting absurdities of payment by results show him chafing at those limits. The Inspector, qualified to quantify the unquantifiable, serves as a border—and also a conduit—between the state and the working class.

Marginal as well as central, conduit as well as free agent, the Inspector must function as object as well as subject in order to do his job properly, as Arnold's reliance on the figure of the expert indicates. In the *Reports*, Arnold's resistance to both managers and Department is most often sustained by an appeal to expertise. Unlike central-office bureaucrat or local-school manager, the expert will not be led away by slogans: "[I]t is eminently a question for educationists, since the general public has neither care nor skill for it, and is sure to be perfectly satisfied as soon as it hears of *paying by results*" (1869). He notes with enthusiasm that "nothing is more remarkable in the school administration of Germany than the care with which every branch is confided to experts, and experts of recognized expertness" (1861). Arnold's "redundantly redundant" language raises the expert above the tension between center and locality: he is self-certifying, able to function as both a subject—of expertise, and an object—of "recognized expertness." He depends not only on acquired knowledge, but also on essential personal qualities, which often turn out to be tied to class or gender categories. For example, when, in the mid-1870s, sewing became a grant-earning subject, Arnold refers once again to the "jealous care with which, in Germany, the regulation of the several matters of instruction is reserved to persons of known expertness in them" in order to maintain:

> The new grant for needlework requires female help for the proper award of it. No one will seriously maintain that a set of men are the fit judges either of plans on which to teach needlework or of results of examination in it.... I myself am so strongly averse to make-be-

lieve examinations and matter-of-course certificates that . . . even now, . . . I refer the approval of the needlework programme, and the certificate of creditably passing the needlework examination, to the award of experts of the other sex. (1876)

Of course, Arnold is not suggesting that gender is the only factor in the credibility of an inspector of needlework, but it seems to be the crucial factor, more important than credentials or official appointment. And great care was taken to choose cultured, tactful, creative men as HMIs (Edmonds 81), who came for the most part from the "gentry, professional, or merchant classes" (Corrigan and Sayer 128). As Hunter notes, "The inspector had to be a 'liberal man' shaped by a discipline permitting him to withdraw from competing social and religious doctrines, subjecting them to a more balanced and impartial judgement" (*Culture* 103–4). And despite the Inspector's allegiance to a state above class interests, such barbarian criteria as breeding and manner, and such philistine criteria as income level, enter into the determination of his expertise. In direct contradiction to the developing notion of an aristocracy of merit, inspectors were to be paid (at least in part) for what they were (and what they might stand for) rather than for what they knew or could perform. As members of a professional bureaucracy rather than a hereditary aristocracy, however, what they were to signify would be determined in part by how much they were paid. In 1844, early in the Inspectorate's history, its members themselves reminded the Department that their "usefulness depended upon their being able 'to occupy respectable positions in society,'" and thus demanded a rise in salary (Edmonds 29).

While it seems logical to assign the task of determining the value of different kinds of education to an educated person, and of assessing examples of needlework to a needlewoman, to choose a poet to judge the importance of poetry in relation to other school subjects verges on the absurd. When Arnold supports his high estimate of poetry by referring to the expertise of his old family friend Wordsworth, he collapses the opposition between untransferable essence and acquired expertise:

> Some people regard this my high estimate of the value of poetry in education with suspicion and displeasure. Perhaps they may accept the testimony of Wordsworth with less suspicion than mine. Wordsworth says, "To be incapable of a feeling of poetry, in my sense of the word, is to be without love of human nature and reverence for God." And it is only through acquaintance with poetry, and with good poetry, that this "feeling of poetry" can be given. (1880)

While for Wordsworth a natural "capability" suggests that the best elements of poetry grow out of unlearned and necessary human qualities, Arnold claims that studying poetry can "give" these qualities to the primary-school student. His reasoning here embodies the contradictions of his pedagogical economy: the importation of inherent qualities is, after all, how interpellation by ideology does its job. Arnold advocates the teaching of literature in primary schools because literature, when it is understood as ideology, teaches the student how to be, and thus erases the difference between that which is learned and that which simply is.

When, near the end of his career, Arnold begins to shift his ground, he attacks not just centralized government money, but bureaucratic expertise, and ranges himself on the side of the "sensible teacher." It is clear that he finds late-century experts suspect because their expertise is not essential, but purely theoretical: "[H]ow is a sensible teacher likely to effect most practical good. Is it by betaking himself to the scientific teachers of pedagogy, by feeding on generalities...?" Arnold answers his own question by suggesting a remedy familiar to readers of his other work: "The best thing for a teacher to do is surely to put before himself in the utmost simplicity the problem he has to solve" (1878). Not surprisingly, Arnold's pedagogy is identical to Arnold's criticism. In *Culture and Anarchy* he comments on the difference between Crown patronage of schools in Prussia and the piecemeal system of support for secondary education in Britain:

> I suppose, in the matter of schools, *one may call* the Licensed Victuallers or the Commercial Travelers ordinary men...; and a Sovereign with the advice of men like Wilhelm von Humboldt or Schleier-

macher may, in this matter, be a better judge, and nearer to right reason. And *it will be allowed, probably,* that right reason would suggest that, to have a sheer school of Licensed Victuallers' children, or a sheer school of Commercial Travelers' children, and to bring them all up, not only at home, but at school too, in a kind of odour of licensed victualism or of bagmanism, is not a wise training to give these children. (79–80, emphasis added)

On the one hand, Arnold expresses here his well-known preference for a universally acknowledged authority in educational matters. But undermining this appeal to rule from above is a more rhetorically consistent appeal to the rule of the individual reader's taste, what "one" already "calls," "allows"—even what one smells—as the vocation of his first group of school founders invites "one" to literalize his reference to the "odour of licensed victualism." The linking of the right reason that comes from above with aesthetic sensibilities that come from within is spelled out even more clearly in "The Function of Criticism," where "the prescriptions of reason" which "are absolute, unchanging, of universal validity" turn out to be "proposition[s] of which everyone, from here to the Antipodes, feels the force" (264). The government Inspector's job, then, is to find out and disseminate as "right reason" that which "one" already knows. Criticism accomplishes the first part of this task. For the second, Arnold turns to literature: "The grand work of literary genius is a work of synthesis and exposition, not of analysis and discovery; . . . dealing divinely with these ideas, presenting them in the most effective and attractive combinations" ("Function" 261). In other words, criticism and literature combined are themselves the best inspectors.

4. Ideology Working

The Inspector's "redundantly redundant" expertise in literary criticism qualifies him as an examiner that can transcend the local influences of private money and the pressures emanating from the Education Office. If the free-trade exam merely tests the quality of butter and meat, and the Revised Code exam is an illusion, how does the inspection Arnold opposes to these exams put these transcendent qualifications to work? Late in his career, Arnold comments on mental breakdowns among candidates for the Indian Civil Service (the first government service to rely heavily on examinations):

> The mind is less strained the more it reacts on what it deals with, and has a native play of its own, and is creative. It is more strained the more it has to receive a number of "knowledges" passively, and to store them up to be reproduced in an examination.... [T]he character and quality of mental exertion required for [composition in classical languages] is more healthy than the character and quality of exertion required for receiving and storing a number of "knowledges." And the candidate whom the former test brings to the front is likely to be a healthier man in body and mind. (1882)[8]

The amassing of knowledge involves a dangerous passivity; "receiving and storing" must be counteracted by the work of productive play only possible in literary study. Like physical games (becoming more and more popular as the century progressed), playing hard at reading proves more profitable than the drudge-like work of "receiving and storing," yielding profits which cannot be alienated because they are embodied. It takes this play to perform the work of evaluation. Like the Civil Service candidate, the working-class student must be trained to literary work in order to keep his mind in a healthy body:

> [T]o know the laws of health ever so exactly, as a mere piece of positive knowledge, will carry a man in general no great way. To have the power of using, which is the thing wished, these data of natural science, a man must, in general, have first been in some measure *moralised*; and for moralising him it will be found not easy, I think, to dispense with those old agents, letters, poetry, religion. (1876)

In order to judge the value of, and thus use, facts, the working class must first be trained in the evaluation of literary and religious texts. In other words, in order to understand the real point of health regulations, an individual must be able to perform the labor of a literary critic. Arnold may sound naive here, but this evaluative economy is nevertheless recognizable as the ancestor of our own pedagogical economies, which rely on that same labor to decode the relations of capitalist production. We know that ideology works—and so did Arnold. His job, like ours, is managing it.

Despite canon debates and theoretical revolutions, the literary text is still the text we *work* to read. As Watkins argues, "the organization of work in English is enormously inefficient to *purvey* anything at all.... English must produce a labor process available to be monitored for proficiency" (Watkins 253). But for Arnold at least, as his views on the Revised Code indicate, this "labor process" must not be *too* "available," and its evaluation must not be too straightforward, lest both be subject to fraudulent imitators. What is needed is a nameless expertise in judging an unquantifiable entity. In 1878, Arnold returns yet again to his campaign to bring "good poetry" to the primary school:

> [T]o serve in any way to form the pupil in addition to giving him the mere power of reading, no serious person would maintain that our reading books are at present fitted. But good poetry is formative; it has, too, the precious power of acting by itself and in a way managed by nature, not through the instrumentality of that somewhat terrible character, the scientific educator. (1878)

Here we see inspectorial economics in action: a figure whose authority is undefined, yet powerful (the "serious person") makes self-evident but unspecified judgments that, when brought to bear on the reading of working-class children, will protect them from those "terrible characters" whose credentials are not always already in place. Only poetry can perform the reciprocal function of evaluating while granting the power of evaluation and provide a single model for the labor of scholar, teacher, and inspector. Profitable lessons are those that are both calculable and incalculable, that can be memorized, and the results inspected, but that also provide the power of creative play. Memorizing poetry is exactly this kind of lesson:

[it] must be learnt right, or it has no value; a lesson of which the subject matter is not *talked about*, as in too many of the lessons of our elementary schools, but *learnt*.... Then, in all but the rudest natures, out of the mass of treasures thus gained (and the mere process of gaining which will have afforded a useful discipline for all natures), a second and more precious fruit will in time grow; they will be insensibly nourished by that which is stored in them, and their taste will be formed by it, as the learning of thousands of lines of Homer and Virgil has insensibly created a good literary taste in so many persons, who would never have got this by studying the rules of taste. (1863)

This process—ideology working through literary language—is natural, productive, indirect. It breaks down the division between creating and storing, work and leisure, passivity and agency, for knowing a poem is all of these. The memorization of English poetry by working-class children and of Homer and Virgil by public schoolboys provides an examinable body of *embodied* (and thus untranslatable—it can't be "talked about") knowledge, the acquisition of which will indirectly and mysteriously provide the examinee with an unexaminable and unalienable quality.

The HMI's inspection of the government-funded primary schoolroom brings together three different subjects of examination: the professional intellectual laborer whose work, located at the border between the economic and the extraeconomic, must be made visible; the working-class schoolteacher, who must rise through the certification rituals of pupil-teaching in order to re-place himself vis-à-vis, rather than in alignment with, his class of origin; and the working-class or petit-bourgeois child, who must be brought into Victorian economic life by being taught to read, write, figure, and sew for the state and its representative, the Inspector. In the rest of this chapter, I will show how Arnold uses his inspectorial economy to fold these varied tasks into one.

While in *Culture and Anarchy* Arnold's famous threesome, Barbarians, Philistines, and Populace, face each other with more or less equal capacities to act and be acted upon, the *Reports* depict class relations quite differently. The public schoolboys to whom Arnold occasionally compares his examinees are learning not to become Barbarians, but civilized human beings. They are "our children," the children of educators and bureaucrats (as Arnold is himself, as Arnold's children are). When Arnold declares that the early payment-by-results examination of a Voluntary school's upper classes "is as inefficient as if Dr. Temple..., when he goes to inspect his fifth form, were just to hear each boy construe a sentence of delectus, conjugate one Latin verb, and decline two Greek substantives" (1863), he is translating the working-class child into a language his public-school-and-Oxbridge-educated audience of upper civil servants will understand. In the *Reports*, as we shall see, to examine is to humanize, and to be human is to examine. So the first class struggle we find there is that of an easily identified (and identified-with) elite of evaluating subjects, struggling to reach and transform a shadowy mass incapable of evaluating, and thus unavailable to inspection.

The working-class origins of the vast majority of pupil-teachers must thus be mitigated somehow. Arnold claims that his inspections construct a causal chain leading from his own critical disinterestedness through that of the teacher to that of the student. "More free play for the inspector," he promises, means "more free play, in consequence, for the teacher" (1867). In order to support this perhaps rather dubious claim, Arnold attempts to show that it is possible to reclass the schoolmaster, aligning him with the Inspector as public servant and evaluator, just as he hopes to reclass his students: through an identification with humanizing, civilizing literature. Hunter describes the process: "It was in his own formative passage through the moral regime of the training college that the working-class teacher acquired the attributes of friend, parent and ethical exemplar; ... the purpose-built personality in whose 'moral observation' [working-class pupils] would discover their 'true characteristics and dispositions'" (*Culture* 64). In Arnold's discussions of pupil-teacher training, his championing of poetry suggests that it can become a weapon in aligning working-class consciousness with a critical consciousness that is passive and disengaged:

> I am sure that the study of portions of the best English authors, and composition ... would tend to elevate and humanize a number of young men, who at present, notwithstanding the vast amount of raw information which they have amassed, are wholly uncultivated. (1852)

Discussing the curriculum for training pupil-teachers, he campaigns relentlessly for the importance of literature, or

> the side [of education] through which it chiefly forms the character; the side which has perhaps been too exclusively attended to in schools for the higher classes ... would have the great social advantage of tending to bring them [pupil-teachers] into intellectual sympathy with the educated of the upper classes. (1852)

Whereas many Victorian educators recommend that the teachers of the working class remain in the working class, Arnold associates the elementary school teacher's rise above "a drudge's spirit" with a rise in class above his pupils. Responding to critics of the rigorous training of pupil-teachers, Arnold points out that

> it is now sufficiently clear, that the teacher to whom you give only a drudge's training, will do only a drudge's work, and will do it in a drudge's spirit: that in order to ensure good instruction even within narrow limits in a school, you must provide it with a master far superior to his scholars, with a master whose own attainments reach beyond the limits within which those of his scholars may be bounded. (1855)

It is not the cultured human being whose mental labor transcends the inspectorial eye of the state, but the mindless labor of the drudge that eludes judgment. Arnold claims that when the Revised Code makes "the work of teaching in school ... less interesting and more purely mechanical" (1863), this proletarianizing of the teacher's job makes him into a potential ally of the working-class student in a conspiracy against the state: "The school examinations ... are ... a game of mechanical contrivance in which the teachers will and must more and more learn how to beat us" (1869), by getting their students to cheat on the exam for the sake of the grant.

By the mid–nineteenth century, the growing need for working-class consumers of mass-produced goods was beginning to call for their construction as desiring, "consuming subjects." The bourgeois public sphere, accessible to all subjects, in a culture where subjectivity is based on the possession of property, served many nineteenth-century reformers as a model for this transformation (Habermas 113). In his *Reports*, Arnold (like other nineteenth-century liberals) advocates an extension to the propertyless of that subjectivity, in the form of the literary education that had traditionally served as a key to that sphere. This move made it possible to imagine a hierarchy of "culture," independent of source or amount of income, one that could be used to oppose a growing class-consciousness among the proletariat, already in place before the full development of the British state education system (Smelser 255). As the nineteenth century progressed, bourgeois public opinion went from imagining working-class education as dangerous to the security of the state, to (by the 1830s or 1840s) imagining it as necessary to the creation of working-class citizens. Corrigan and Sayer argue that nineteenth-century state formation itself represented a "concerted moral revolution, an attempted organization of consent and incorporation, which culminates in a certain kind of admission—sponsored, protected, conditional, and profoundly disruptive of labor's own forms of social organization and expression—of labor into society" (115; see also Poovey, *Making* 4). In order for education to reduce the threat posed by unassimilated groups, then, these groups must be imagined as otherwise than a threat—whether potential or vitiated. They must be imagined as subjects.

Most Victorian educators were perfectly aware that increased governmental support of the Voluntary schools not only provided the working class with new skills, it also replaced traditional forms of working-class education. The expansion of standardized education for the working class through Society schools threatened an already existing working-class educational system (Digby and Searby 5). The vigorous effort made to stamp out working-class private "dame" schools indicates that they did represent some form of resistance to the Society schools, though this resistance was probably allied with "residual rather than emergent" working-class cultures (Gardner 4, 8). During the 1850s and 1860s, the middle class grew increasingly worried about working-class children who were "neither at [paid, legitimate] work nor at [government-inspected] school," contained in no stronger institution than the "dame school" or working-class family, loose on the street, unavailable to culture (Smelser 133). Despite middle-class educators' awareness of these alternatives to the Voluntary school, the inspectorial project of containing the working class within the school relies on an assumption that there is nothing beyond it. Arnold's nervousness about the inaccessibility of the working-class child extends to his comments on classroom fittings: "The general rule on which I insist is this;—*the scholar, to get on, should have a fixed place, and that place at a desk*" (1855; Arnold's emphasis). He just barely recognizes the presence of self-conscious class affiliation in the pupils he examines,[9] but frequently complains of their lack of any presence at all—whether figurative or literal, mental or physical:

> The system of weekly payments joined to the touting of rival schools for scholars, and joined also, I must say, to the pernicious notion fostered among parents by our present mode of making our grants, that a child confers a favour on the school managers by earning money for them; all these combine to create an insecurity in our elementary schools, a slightness of hold upon the school children, and an inversion of the proper relations between them and their teachers, which has no parallel anywhere else. (1867)

Once again, this traffic in children is not a sign of the commodification of family relations or the pricing of priceless pedagogy, but of working-class indifference to both public and private systems of exchange. Arnold's solution is once again not a retreat from the economic. Despite his anxiety, he does not advocate the legislation of compulsory attendance, claiming in the *Reports* that it would be unenforceable. Instead, he returns to the manipulation of public money: refuse grants to student-poaching schools. When the Inspector figures himself as a colonizing explorer, held back by the "difficulty of access to children's places, difficulty in seeing clearly in the obscurer parts of the school-room . . . sometimes of getting them to speak" (*Reports* 1863), he figures schoolchildren as recalcitrant and well-hidden natives of the "dark" continent/schoolroom. Such images aid Arnold's attack on the Revised Code, which, he suggests, can get at teachers, inspectors, and managers, but not the working-class child, who is quite literally beyond the reach of the state:

> The truth is, what really needed to be dealt with in 1862 as at present, was the irregular attendance and premature withdrawal of scholars, not the imperfect performance of duties by the teachers; but it was far easier to change the course of school instruction and inspection, and to levy forfeitures for imperfect school results upon managers and teachers, than to make scholars come to school regularly and stay there a sufficient time. (1867)

Hidden from HMI Arnold in the obscure corners of their ill-constructed classrooms, from government with its reliance on economic sanctions for those who have no money, from the interpellating bourgeois family romance, and from Victorian middle-class writers who are unable to figure a working-class subjectivity, the working-class child must be forced into publicity in order to be "private"—in order to become an evaluating subject.

While in *Our Mutual Friend* Dickens presents the ragged school Charley Hexam attends as the site of competing knowledges (with that of the street a sure winner over that of the school), Arnold presents the schools he inspects as sites of a battle between knowledge and ignorance. Arnold asks the Department not to blame teachers for the schools' poor results, because "the weakness is in the unawakened and uninformed minds of the majority of our school children, even of those who can pass the examination" (1874). If the working-class child arrives at school a tabula rasa, surely instruction will fill it in—but this very blankness is described by Arnold as "an obstacle of the most fatal kind to instruction" (1874). The only way to eradicate ignorance—instruction—is made impossible by the very ignorance it is intended to eradicate. The state cannot discover and disseminate the self-evident to those who do not know it already. Arnold frequently refers to the education of upper-class boys, and almost always as a way of suggesting that, through the invigilatory power of poetry, working-class children might receive the same benefits from their education as the former do from theirs. But this implication is attended with considerable ambivalence. For example, comparing pupil-teachers to their more privileged counterparts, Arnold provides no answer at all to the following speculation:

> It would be extremely interesting to make a raid among the youth of the wealthier classes, whether at their schools and universities, or at their scenes of amusement, to catch five or six hundred of them from the age of eighteen to that of twenty-five and to subject them to the same test of their general intelligence to which, by this passage of poetry to be paraphrased, the general intelligence of the candidates from elementary schools is subjected. It would be most interesting, and opinions may differ as to the results which such an application of the test would show. (1874)

Significantly, the objects of this experiment are not depicted as blank slates, but as already occupied (although with instruction or amusement, not with employment or useful action)—the suppositious "raid" will know where to find them. Testing is not depicted here as civilizing, but as violence. Will the civilization of the working class—and the consequent loosening of the tie between education and class status—threaten or maintain the power of the intellectual worker?

The imagining of working-class ignorance as both unreadable blank page and stubbornly solid obstacle suggests that it supports the intellectual worker's cultural authority in two contradictory ways. The inspectorial examination makes human beings out of Britain's poor children, and thus promises to bring them into the cultural fold. But it also denaturalizes humanity, makes it visible as a process, the elementary school visible as its site, and the Inspector as its agent: "[T]he ideal which we should propose for ourselves for the school-course in these schools is . . . the ideal admirably fixed long ago by Comenius. . . . 'The aim is,' says Comenius, 'to train generally all who are born men to all which is human'" (1880). In other words, the inspection not only makes the working-class subject's interpellation by ideology visible, it puts it on display (even at the expense of keeping the student's agency offstage). Far from the privacy of the bourgeois primal scene, it is public, institutional, bureaucratic: the state-funded elementary school is the ideal theater for this performance, and the Inspector is the star of the show.

A crucial function of nineteenth-century social legislation (and the bureaucracy that administered it) was establishing a specific and intimate relationship between governmental institutions and the working-class individual. As the bourgeois public sphere collapsed and "state and society permeated each other, the institution of the conjugal family became dissociated from its connection with processes of social reproduction" (Habermas 151–52) in all classes of society. But at first this dissociation served as a way of fixing class lines: "The new form of patriarchal gender order constructed within the middle class then depended, for a time at least, on the impossibility of constructing a similar gender order among the majority of workers" (P. Miller 133). Despite the many leveling suggestions in Arnold's writing on education, in "A French Eton" he suggests a hierarchy of metaphors for the school:

> For the wants of the highest class . . . not *school a family*, but rather *school a little world* is the right ideal . . . the grand aim of education should be to give them . . . the notion of a sort of republican fellowship, the practice of a plain life in common, the habit of self-help. To the middle class, the grand aim of education should be to

give largeness of soul and personal dignity; to the lower class, feeling, gentleness, humanity. Here, at last, [the] ideal of the *family* as the type for the school, comes in its due place. (113)

We are back to the class system of *Culture and Anarchy* here, with each class needing specific qualities which only a compensatory education system can supply. The implication here is that providing Barbarians with "the habit of self-help" and fellowship, Philistines with "largeness of soul," and Populace with gentleness, will make the class differences less distinct. But the passage also structures analogies and oppositions among classes. While Arnold maintains the time-honored analogy between state and family (the republican classroom is to the public schoolboy as the domestic classroom is to the Voluntary school student), he also undermines it by instituting a class hierarchy of relationships between state and family, from the public school as aristocratic state to the state school as family for the working class. For the middle-class child, Arnold hopes for spiritual expansion beyond local interests and appropriately enough, the future rulers of the empire are assigned the most global institution ("a little world"), but the public institution in which Arnold hopes to place the "lower class" (the school as family) must represent that which is local and private, counting and accounting for the evasive working-class child. Arnold was, of course, not alone in seeing the school as the working-class substitute for the bourgeois home; it was a common trope at midcentury and later.[10] Few writers, however, can have applied it as systematically as he. It is not contemplating a mother's self-sacrifice, but memorizing poetry, that Arnold imagines teaching humanity and compassion to the working-class child. It is not the family romance, but the teaching of grammar to boys and sewing to girls, that produce them as gender-differentiated subjects. It is not excessive mothering, but excessively familial schooling, that threatens gender differentiation. In "A French Eton," for example, Arnold warns of the "danger" to working-class "energy and manliness" that "lies in pressing the spring of gentleness, of confidence, of child-like docility . . . a little too hard" (113–14).

It is thus not only in its provision of a humanizing "culture" that the school promises the proletarian and petit-bourgeois child an escape from class. It is also in its mimicry of the haute-bourgeois domestic sphere, as the special attention paid to girls' needlework in government-assisted schools demonstrates. For Kay-Shuttleworth and others, the poor's problems could be blamed—at least in part—on working-class women's ignorance of domestic skills (Gomersall 42, Purvis 84). After 1862 grants were awarded only to schools that taught "plain sewing" to girls (Gomersall 45); sewing is the only individual subject, other than literature and grammar, on which Arnold comments at length. He notes that "in girls' schools... there is, there must always be, a branch of industrial instruction... —instruction in needlework" (1855). Classes in needlework provide preparation for labor as a servant or sempstress but also for domesticity as a wife. The line between the domestic labor of the working woman (a form of labor resisted by female pupil-teachers as demeaning) and the domesticity of the middle-class lady begins to blur (Gomersall 48–49).

In redrawing that line, Arnold replaces the desiring subject of consumption with the evaluating subject of inspection:

> [T]he only kind of needlework which the parents admire, and which the children are anxious to practice, is crochet-work and ornamental needlework.... The importance to a poor family that the daughters should be skilful in plain needlework is obvious to all; yet their ignorance of it is something incredible. I heard the other day in a Lincolnshire village of a pauper family, in which were several daughters living at home; the family were actually in receipt of parochial relief; their debts were collected, and among them was found a considerable one to a dressmaker, who, it appeared, made all the clothes of the female part of the family. (1853)

With this anecdote, Arnold implies that while for the students and their parents, ornamental sewing at home and purchasing clothing from a dressmaker symbolize ladyhood, their lack of critical judgment causes them to misread. While the working-class family is only too successful in creating desiring subjects of consumption, it fails in creating critical subjects of evaluation, capable of seeing that it is not the uselessness of embroidery and macramé that fit them for the bourgeois woman, but their location: inside the bourgeois home and outside the market. Far from raising their class status, then, the preference for these forms of sewing merely indicate working-class idleness and improvidence. In order for the working-class household to become a home, uncommodified (but useful) plain sewing must replace ornamental sewing.[11]

Under the eye of Her Majesty's Inspector, this replacement is possible. By 1858 Arnold notes with approval the growing willingness of parents to have their children taught plain needlework, implying a shift from an ideology of consumption to one of evaluation. He credits this shift to a publicly managed reversal of familial roles, a "progress" that literally and, most importantly, *visibly*, undoes the past. The *Reports* celebrate a remarkable negotiation between public and private, family and state, mother and daughter, past and present:

> I was informed, on remarking the excellence of the needlework in the girls' Lancastrian school at Loughborough, which I inspected the other day, that the girls in that school now often bring to school with them work done by their mothers, in order to pick it out and to do it better, and that this takes place with the full approbation of their mothers, who are delighted with their daughters' progress, and no longer remain satisfied with the clumsy needlework which would a few years ago have perfectly contented them. For until lately, in the homes of these girls little care was felt for excellence in plain useful needlework; their daughters' proficiency in ornamental needlework alone excited the pride and interest of the mothers. (1858)

One of the most intimate as well as the least class-specific of feminine tasks, sewing here becomes public, and this public space is shared between the mother's domestic failure (at home) and the daughter's domestic success (at school). The school becomes the location of domesticity, not only teaching domestic tasks, but regulating and organizing—even reversing—the relationship between generations. And the result is that, once again, Arnold presents us with a classroom whose task it is to denaturalize the construction of the subject and spectacularize the work of ideology.

The importance of this performance makes even the Victorian school's well-documented role in maintaining class hierarchies take second place. In the *Reports*, Arnold's most important battle is not over who ought to be educated, or even how. It is not over who ought to pay for that education, or how. It is over who ought to *oversee and judge* education, and thus over who can be trusted to make ideology visible as work. For example, the difference in Arnold's remarks about different classes of children seems to be connected not so much to the actual children in question, but to the different emphases he wishes to give to different kinds of resistance to the inspectorial examination at different times. Early in his career he praises parental involvement in schools attended mainly by petit-bourgeois students:

> The conveniences [of higher fees] are—the better and more instructed class of children frequenting these schools as compared with that frequenting cheaper ones; the greater intelligence of their parents, and greater sense of the advantage of having their children educated, with consequently greater disposition, as well as greater means, to keep them longer at school. (1852)

But a different agenda causes him to blame lower-middle-class parents for school difficulties in discipline. Here, the problem is not the lack of an imaginable domestic sphere, as it is for working-class children, but the intrusion of an unacceptable version of it into the schoolroom. It is as if the girls brought their school-sewing home and had it redone by their mothers. For example, while "the children of the upper classes are generally brought up in habits of regular obedience because these classes are sufficiently enlightened to know of what benefit such a training is to the children themselves," and the

> children of very poor parents receive a kind of rude discipline from circumstances, if not from their parents.... [T]here is no class of

children so indulged, so generally brought up ... without discipline, that is, without habits of respect, exact obedience, and self-control, as the children of the lower middle class in this country ... in consequence ... if they are not disciplined at school, they will, while young, be disciplined nowhere. (1852)

The relationship between the working class and intellectual labor in the primary-school classroom is complicated by a different kind of class struggle: the literary man's battle with the bourgeoisie, part of what John Kucich calls "the rabid struggle for cultural authority ... between [the middle class's] professional and nonprofessional factions, ... that appears to have become more intense from the 1860s on" (613). Throughout his writing on education, Arnold inundates Nonconformist Philistines with energetic abuse, despite their important role in supporting the schools he inspects, whether as managers, patrons, or parents. The *Reports* maintain a constant and inflexible opposition between such terms as "impartial," "educated persons," "experts," "proven qualifications," and "plainness" and such terms as "common run," "unchecked private speculation," and "charlatanism," opposing the disciplinary expertise of the bureaucrat to the undisciplined supervision of the middle class. Indeed, one of the most pressing reasons for educating the poor is that the poor are getting richer, and may be tomorrow's Philistines:

> Parents who pay 6d a week for the instruction of their children are apt to criticize nicely, though not always judiciously, the institution where that instruction is given. They desire this and that for their child, and they object to this and that, and being often not very reasonable persons, they greatly embarrass a teacher. (1852)

Arnold's struggle in the *Reports* is thus not only with the wilderness of working-class consciousness, or the need of the working class for parenting, but with rival colonizers—or other forms of education provided by the middle class. After all, the HMI is not the only inspector of the elementary-school classroom. He is joined (albeit in decreasing numbers as the century progresses) by a constant stream of bourgeois and professional visitors: managers, volunteer teachers, lady-visitors, and clergy. The Societies (in addition to Church of England dioceses) had their own inspectors too—the Voluntary school was a space where a near-chaos of administrative methodologies raged. It is here that professional, masculine bureaucracy must make a stand against its traditional enemies: money capital, private charity, religious sectarianism, and bourgeois femininity.

In this battle as well, showing off the ideological work of the Inspector is Arnold's best weapon. In 1867 Arnold quotes a charmingly open and vivid letter from a girl at a state-funded school:

> DEAR FANNY,—I am afraid I shall not pass in my examination; Miss C—— says she thinks I shall. I shall be glad when the Serpentine is frozen over, for we shall have such fun; I wish you did not live so far away, then you could come and share in the game. Father cannot spare Willie, so I have as much as I can do to teach him to cipher nicely. I am now sitting by the school fire, so I assure you I am very warm. Father and mother are very well. I hope to see you on Christmas day. Winter is coming; don't it make you shiver to think of? Shall you ever come to smoky old London again? It is not so bad, after all, with its bustle and business and noise. If you see Ellen I—— will you kindly get her address for me. I must now conclude, as I am soon going to my reading class; so good bye.
>
> From your affectionate friend,
> M——. (1867)

He contrasts it with scarcely any comment to a hilariously florid production by a boy at a private, middle-class academy:

> MY DEAR PARENTS,—The anticipation of our Christmas vacation abounds in peculiar delights. Not only that its "festivities," its social gatherings, and its lively amusements crown the old year with happiness and mirth, but that I come a guest commended to your hospitable love by the performance of all you bade me remember when I left you in the glad season of sun and flowers.
>
> And time has sped fleetly since reluctant my departing step crossed the threshold of that home whose indulgences and endear-

ments their temporary loss has taught me to value more and more. Yet that restraint is salutary, and that self-reliance is as easily learnt as it is laudable, the propriety of my conduct and the readiness of my services shall ere long aptly illustrate. It is with confidence I promise that the close of every year shall find me advancing in your regard by constantly observing the precepts of my excellent tutors and the example of my excellent parents.

We break up on Thursday the 11th of December instant, and my impatience of the short delay will assure my dear parents of the filial sentiments of

Theirs very sincerely,
N———. (1867)[12]

Arnold does not imply that the engaging simplicity of the first letter and the pretentious rhetoric of the second are due to the schools' sources of income, the children's class status, or that of their teachers. Rather, what is at stake is the certification of their inspectors. The government school is overseen by "impartial educated persons," the purely private school is overseen by "the common run of middle-class parents." In typically Arnoldian fashion, Arnold spells out the moral of the comparison by not spelling it out. After displaying the difference the Inspector's examination makes by displaying the two letters, he makes a single remark before closing the report: "To those who ask what is the difference between a public and a private school, I answer, *It is this*" (1867).

Ian Hunter opens his 1988 study of the rise of English in British schools by citing Arnold's use of these two letters. He comments: "[T]he remarkable thing is that Arnold attributes the sincerity and 'freedom from charlatanism' of the popular scholar's letter not to the effects of literature or to the spread of culture, but to the fact that it was produced in a governmental apparatus organised by a certain supervisory function" and critiques the notion that "the educational system is nothing more than the (true or false) social realisation of the ideal values of culture and criticism" (*Culture* 2–3). Arnold's expression of governmental values is, in this case, complicated by the fact that the paired letters seem to be included as an attempt to soften the *Report* for 1867 after a long and energetic attack on the Revised Code. But more importantly, as I have argued, Arnold draws no distinction between "a governmental apparatus" and "literature and the spread of culture." He firmly identifies culture's mission with that of the state (see Baldick 37): for Arnold the bureaucratic literary man, bureaucracy *is* literature, and both have as their highest function the work of ideology. For better or worse, one of Arnold's most important legacies to literary criticism has been this seamless connection between literature and the state through the Inspector's examination.

Arnold, then, cannot completely abandon the examination, broadly conceived, but restricts his hostility to the exam as a direct conduit of public money. What he prizes about the inspectorial examination is the very thing that his fellow civil servant Anthony Trollope critiques about competitive examinations in the Civil Service: they depend on the transference of a unique and essential identity. Trollope's target is thus not a sterile exchange system like Lowe's Revised Code, but the same indefinable certitude about the integration of labor and education that Arnold celebrates in his heroic figure of the Inspector.

Trollope was a model Colonial Administrator, bringing British efficiency, order, and honesty to Ireland, Egypt, Malta, Gibraltar, and the West Indies—not to mention the rural areas of England and Wales themselves (see Super and *Autobiography*). After retirement, he continued to visit post offices all over the world and give free advice:

> Wherever I go I visit the post-office, feeling certain that I may be able to give a little good advice. Having looked over post-offices for thirty years at home I fancy that I could do very good service among the Colonies if I could have arbitrary power given to me to make what changes I pleased. My advice is always received with attention and respect, and I have generally been able to flatter myself that I have convinced my auditors. But I never knew an instance yet in which any improvement recommended by me was carried out. (*South Africa* (1878), qtd. in Super 84)

The comic self-deprecation is significant here, as is the marked *lack* of "attention and respect" in the local postmistress's account of an inspection in *A Small House at Allington*:

> There was a man here yesterday with his imperence. I don't know where he come from,—down from Lun'on, I b'leeve: and this was wrong, and that was wrong, and everything wrong; and then he said he'd have me discharged the sarvice.... So I told 'un to discharge hisself, and take all the old bundles and things away upon his shoulders. (661)

Like Arnold, Trollope believes in a powerful, morally superior Inspectorate, venturing out from the center of the state to domesticate England school by school, postal route by postal route: "During those two years it was the ambition of my life to cover the country with rural letter-carriers" (*Autobiography* 89). But Trollope's inspections are not so clearly separated as are Arnold's from the empty exchanges of speculation or payment by results:

> I was paid sixpence a mile for the distance travelled, and it was necessary that I should at any rate travel enough to pay for my equipage. This I did, and got my hunting out of it also. I have often surprised some small country postmaster, who had never seen or heard of me before, by coming down upon him at nine in the morning, with a red coat and boots and breeches, and interrogating him as to the disposal of every letter which came to his office. And in the same guise I would ride up to farm-houses, or parsonages, or other lone residences about the country, and ask the people how they got their letters, at what hour, and especially whether they were delivered free or at a certain charge.... In all these visits I was, in truth, a beneficent angel to the public, bringing everywhere with me an earlier, cheaper, and much more regular delivery of letters. But not infrequently the angelic nature of my mission was imperfectly understood. (90)

Is the Inspector a comic pedant, a genteel parasite, or an avenging angel? Trollope accepts and yet deflates the Arnoldian heroicizing of the Inspector, the "negotiation between the mundanity of the administrative life and its ethical romanticization; ... a condition of possibility for the transformation of officialdom into a composite ethical calling" (Osborne 302). Midcentury examination advocates, like Arnold, imagined the Inspectorate as a secular clerisy (see Gowan and Osborne on Coleridge's influence on Gladstone at this time), simultaneously perfecting and uniting the nation. As we will see, in his 1857 novel *The Three Clerks* as well as in *An Autobiography*, Trollope links the extraeconomic glamour of the Inspector not only to the arrogant self-interest of the aristocrat who gets his gentility paid for by the state, but also to the pedantic self-importance of the bureaucratic number cruncher.

Chapter Three

LABORER AND HIRE: TROLLOPE, NORTHCOTE–TREVELYAN, AND 'THE THREE CLERKS'

1. The Gentleman and the State

> *The general principle, then, which we advocate is, that the public service should be carried on by the admission into its lower ranks of a carefully selected body of young men, who should be employed from the first upon work suited to their capacities and their education, and should be made constantly to feel that their promotion and future prospects depend entirely on the industry and ability with which they discharge their duties, that with average abilities and reasonable application they may look forward confidently to a certain provision for their lives, that with superior powers they may rationally hope to attain to the highest prizes in the Service, while if they prove decidedly incompetent, or incurably indolent, they must expect to be removed from it.*
>
> *The first step towards carrying this principle into effect should be, the establishment of a proper system of examination before appointment.*
>
> —Sir Stafford Northcote and Charles Trevelyan,
> *Papers on the Re-Organisation of the Civil Service*

Anthony Trollope began his career in the Post Office as a clerk in 1834. In 1841 he moved from London to Ireland to take an assistant surveyorship, and thus (according to his own account) was transformed from incompetent filing and copying clerk to dashingly efficient inspector. He went on to establish and reform postal routes all over Great Britain, and conduct postal treaty negotiations around the world, retiring in 1867. Throughout his career and long after retirement, Trollope was bitterly opposed to the introduction of competitive examinations for entry and promotion in the Civil Service, speaking and writing against them in official communications, unofficial talks, in the press, and in his fiction. As I will argue, the actual sources of this opposition are, rather surprisingly, a good deal more obscure than those of Arnold's distaste for the Revised Code.

Midcentury civil service reforms began—although they did not end—in a middle-class movement for "financial reform." A series of scandals (notoriously, the handling of the Crimean War) moved "criticism ... from the targets of excessive numbers and excessive salaries [of Civil Servants] to mismanagement and maladministration" (Hart 69). Liberal Party leaders in the 1850s agreed on advocating governmental reform as the key to "winning the rising middle classes away from any class coalition with the radical democrats among the workers" (Gowan 19). But while the Prime Minister Lord Russell saw the solution in "franchise reform" and the extension of working-class education, then-Chancellor of the Exchequer Gladstone, M.P. for Oxford, argued for the reform of the patronage system of government appointments. "Civil Service Reform would have come in any case at some time," Roach argues, "but it need not have taken the very academic and intellectualized shape which it did.... There can be little doubt that at this crucial time public opinion was being influenced by a small group of men who knew one another well and who were quite clear what they wanted.... Oxford, Cambridge, India ... were the roots of the new system" (33–34). One of the most important of this small group of men was the classical scholar Benjamin Jowett, Oxford tutor of many distinguished civil servants, and he was "quite clear" that he wanted competitive examinations. In 1853, Gladstone chose Treasury chief Charles Trevelyan, who had been strongly influenced by Jowett in recommending reforms to the Indian Civil Service, to put together a proposal for reform at home. He produced with Sir Stafford Northcote perhaps the most famous mid-Victorian declaration of faith in examinations, *On the Organisation of the Permanent Civil Service*, otherwise known as the Northcote–Trevelyan Report. In 1855, it was published with reactions from a number of civil servants and educators, most prominently Jowett. Northcote and Trevelyan describe "the objects which we have principally in view" as "a proper system of examination, for the supply of the public service with a thoroughly efficient class of men ... [and] ... To encourage industry and foster merit, by teaching all public servants to look forward to promotion according to their deserts, and to expect the highest prizes in the service if they can qualify themselves for them" (22–23). The Report's emphasis on examinations—a late addition—was controversial. Middle-class financial reformers in particular were not impressed—they reacted tepidly to the report, deeming that its suggestions required too much (probably expensive and useless) education for civil servants (Hart 71).

Trollope's literary critique of the Northcote–Trevelyan Report begins with a scathing review in the *Dublin University Magazine* in 1855 and the 1857 novel *The Three Clerks*, which includes a caricature of Trevelyan in "Sir Gregory Hardlines," of Northcote in "Sir Warwick Westend," and of Jowett in "Mr. Jobbles." It lasts his entire career—and beyond. In his *Autobiography*, written after his retirement, and after competitive examinations in the Civil Service had become a fait accompli, his opposition prompts one of Trollope's famously coy allusions to "'Gentlemen'":

> As what I now write will certainly never be read till I am dead, I may dare to say what no one now does dare to say in print,—though some of us whisper it occasionally into our friends' ears. There are places in life which can hardly be well filled except by 'Gentlemen.' ... The gates of the one class should be open to the other; but neither to one class or to the other can good be done by declaring that there are not gates, no barrier, no difference. The system of competitive examination is, I think, based on a supposition that there is no difference. (39–40)

In the late novel *Marian Fay* (1882), too, the comic vulgarity of the ungentlemanly civil servant Samuel Crocker eventually has serious consequences for the more genteel characters. On the surface, Trollope's opposition to Northcote and Trevelyan seems like a perfectly predictable resistance to the bourgeoisification of government, thoroughly in line with Arnold's resistance to the Revised Code, by a member of the professional class eager to uphold the concept of gentility and to claim for it an intrinsic, indefinable, untransferable expertise. But both Trollope's contemporaries and twentieth-century historians would disagree with this view of the Northcote–Trevelyan Report. For as Peter Gowan and others have argued, while Northcote–Trevelyan uses the examination as a symbol of educational free trade and technocratic bourgeoisification, it does so in the service of extending an explicitly genteel power in the state.

Although "in the first half of the nineteenth century more and more of the high places in public life were being taken by men who had enjoyed successful careers at the university—that is, successful in the great test of public examinations" (Roach 14), factors other than formal education had hitherto set class hierarchies in public offices. Even political patronage wielded by a reformed Parliament ensured that there was a "fairly high social qualification for office in this period"—Home Office clerks, for example, seem to have moved in the same social circles as the politicians who appointed them, if less well educated and less well off (Donajgrodzki 97). In general, too, older departments had more social status, even if their work was more routine and formal, and even if they were not as well paid (Donajgrodzki 104). Trollope's friends' disapproval of his 1841 move from clerk in London to surveyor in Ireland reflects the status attached to the more established and centrally located job, even though it was also more boring and ill-paid (Donajgrodzki 103). The location of one's office might be as significant for a young clerk as the location of the London house of a social-climbing couple. In his *Dublin University Magazine* review, Trollope warns Northcote and Trevelyan that their attempt to distribute the best candidates equally throughout the Service will fail, a victim of the rules of the social geography of officialdom. The candidates, he claims, will "all want to frequent the West End" and will "eschew the Customs and Excise, and unduly hanker after the glories of Downing-street" ("Civil" 1855, 412).[1] In *The Three Clerks*, the prestigious Weights and Measures Office is housed in a "handsome edifice... which stands so conspicuously confronting the Treasury Chambers," and contains all the proper furniture and fittings, while the déclassé Internal Navigation Office is slatternly and disorganized, with irregular hours, no proper waiting room, and "has little else to redeem it from the lowest depths of official vulgarity than the ambiguous respectability of its material position" in Somerset House (10).

It was not so much the social hierarchy that needed change, from the Oxford point of view, as the way that hierarchy was signified. The shift from these time-honored social signifiers to a new dispensation dismays and bewilders the head of the Internal Navigation Office, Mr. Oldeschole, when he is brought before the Civil Service Commission: "They would ask him to sit down in a beautiful new leathern armchair, as though he were really some great man, and then examine him as they would a candidate for the Custom House, smiling always, but looking at him as though they were determined to see through him" (*Three Clerks* 528). But, Oldeschole that he is, he is incapable of realizing that "beautiful leathern arm-chairs"—which anyone can buy—are good enough for a civil servant in disgrace because they are no longer capable of signifying high social status. A university education, however, could remain a more carefully guarded commodity. Northcote–Trevelyan was strongly influenced by a letter from Gladstone to Trevelyan shortly before its original release:

> I have a strong impression that the aristocracy of this country are even superior in natural gifts, on the average, to the mass; but it is plain that with their acquired advantages their *insensible* education, irrespective of book-learning, they have an immense superiority. This applies in its degree to all those who may be called gentlemen by birth and training. (Hughes 228–29)

Inspired by Gladstone, Northcote and Trevelyan "provided a new and powerful instrumental rationale for the dominance of 'liberal education' and therefore of Oxbridge and the top public schools" (Gowan 33) in order "to demonstrate that [a gentry-identified] governing class deserved its control over the state on the grounds of superior capacities" (Gowan 21–22). Apparently, this strategy worked: the introduction of competitive examinations did actually produce more expensively educated and socially superior candidates for government posts until late in the century (Roach 192).[2] Recognizing that continuation of political patronage meant accepting the control of Parliament's middle- and working-class constituencies after the Reform Bill of 1867, top-level civil servants abandoned their resistance and agreed to the uniform administration of examinations in 1870 (Gowan 31).

Northcote and Trevelyan's report, as Trollope and many of its other critics noted, is extremely ambitious, suggesting examinations in political economy for posts at the Treasury and the Board of Trade, languages, history, and law for the Foreign Office, and advanced mathematics for accounting offices: "Whether immediately wanted for the daily work of the office or not, all such attainments tend to give an official a higher interest in his employment, and to fit him for superior positions. They may also be regarded as reflecting honour on the service" (27). But like Arnold, they stress the importance of "general ability"—the "*insensible* education" Gladstone associates with the aristocracy—and urge the recruitment of those possessed, not of expertise, but of "capability" tied to a liberal education:

> [T]he great advantage to be expected from the examinations would be, that they would elicit young men of general ability, which is a matter of more moment than their being possessed of any special acquirements. Men capable of distinguishing themselves in any of the subjects we have named, and thereby affording a proof that their education has not been lost upon them, would probably make themselves useful wherever they might be placed. (Northcote–Trevelyan 14)

Northcote and Trevelyan make the apparently self-contradictory claim that "[i]t is only by throwing the examinations entirely open that we can hope to attract the proper class of candidates" (13). As in the "open professions," like law and medicine, that they contrast with the backwater of the Civil Service, the openness of open competition is in the service of social closure. The best man who will inevitably win will have the high social status necessary for a flexible relationship between cabinet ministers and the Civil Service:

> [T]he Government of the country could not be carried on without the aid of an efficient body of permanent officers, occupying a position duly subordinate to that of the Ministers who are directly responsible to the Crown and to Parliament, yet possessing sufficient independence, character, ability, and experience to be able to advise, assist, and, to some extent, influence, those who are from time to time set over them. (3)

Northcote and Trevelyan's depiction of "administration as an autonomous ethos or art, separated both from the pull of political patronage and from narrow, specialized expertise" (Osborne 294) sounds a good deal like Arnold's defense of the state from the ravages of the Philistines. "Political patronage" suggests the middle-class constituencies controlling Parliament as well as the Nonconformist managers of the schools Arnold inspected, and the training-school graduate's "specialized expertise" is closely linked to the kind of learning Arnold associates with the "scientific educator" and the Revised Code. Like Arnold's ideal inspector, this "administrator was not simply to be a faceless official . . . but was to enjoy a certain discretionary autonomy" (Osborne 294). Arnold's resistance to the Revised Code is thus not so far from Northcote–Trevelyan's championing of examinations.[3]

In his commentary on the Report, Sir James Stephen objects that "the successful candidate in such an examination would not usually be the kind of man wanted. You stand in need, not of statesmen in disguise, but of intelligent, steady, methodical men of business" (Northcote–Trevelyan 76). Trollope, whose strongest opposition is to competitive rather than qualifying exams, agrees, suggesting that by "throwing the examinations entirely open" the only ambitions satisfied would be those of the examiners: "Quantity would be there, though quality might be wanting; and Mr. Jowett would revel in his multiplicity of question-papers, and in the rapidity of his curt *viva voce* examinations" ("Civil" 1855, 413). In *The Three Clerks*, Trollope satirizes this heroicizing gentrification of administrative busywork by reducing the intellectual labor of the rabid examiner Mr. Jobbles to its visible component:

> It was beautiful then to see how Mr. Jobbles swam down the long room and handed out his examination papers to the different candidates as he passed them. 'Twas a pity there should have been but five; the man did it so well, so quickly, with such a gusto! He should have been allowed to try his hand upon five hundred instead of five. His step was so rapid and his hand and arm moved so dexterously, that no conceivable number would have been too many for him. But, even with five, he showed at once that the right man was in the right place. Mr. Jobbles was created for the conducting of examinations. (128)

And yet *The Three Clerks* is far from dismissing this kind of test. When the mathematical whiz Mr. A. Minusex breaks down under the pressure of Mr. Jobbles's examination, the event is as comic as his name: "[P]oor Minusex was ill, and sent a certificate. He had so crammed himself with unknown quantities, that his mind—like a gourmand's stomach—had broken down under the effort, and he was now sobbing out algebraic positions under his counterpane" (126–27). But when the sensitive and chivalrous Harry Norman cannot take the pressure, a major turning point in the novel's plot gets caught in Mr. Jobbles's petty tyrannies, and Harry plays the role of sore loser for the rest of the novel:

> Norman, put utterly out of conceit with himself by what he deemed the insufficiency of his answers, did the same. He had become low in spirits, unhappy in temperament, and self-diffident to a painful degree.... Mr. Jobbles... smiled with satisfaction.... It was an acknowledgement of his own unrivalled powers as an Examiner. (130)

Throughout, *The Three Clerks* registers the tension between the silliness and pedantry that surround the academic examination and the serious violence of which it is capable. The novel that gives most explicit voice to Trollope's objections to the examination system climaxes in a series of spectacularly effective displays of intellectual labor: examinations conducted by professional testers—a barrister and (ironically) a Civil Service Commissioner—as part of their jobs.

Critics of Trollope seem to agree that his work is structured by vacillation or unresolvable opposition, whether between romantic choices available to protagonists, the formality of comedy and the looseness of realism, main plots and subplots, or control and transgression.[4] The result, as Henry James declares, is that "[t]he thing is not so much a story as a picture" (106). The focus is on a single moral decision or battle of wills; our attention is never called to the outcome (usually, though not always, fairly predictable) or even the process of decision making. Trollope's characters may vacillate, but they rarely change their minds. They are far more likely, like Harry Norman, Lewis Trevelyan, Lily Dale, George Bertram, or President Neverbend, to become obsessive (Slakey 28–29). What matters, as on a multiple-choice test, is the repeated display of a set of options: "In repetition we see how crucial is the past to moral decision.... Repetition, which associates one with the past, puts a drag on the wheels" (Slakey 32; see also Kincaid, *Novels* 48; Riffaterre 283; D. Miller 145; and Rogers 94). In *The Three Clerks*, for example, Alaric Tudor's corruption is tragically predictable, drawing us instead to the image of the troubled relation between ambition and honesty (a common theme in Trollope, as Kucich demonstrates). Alaric's cousin Charley Tudor's story is even more static; his vacillation between dissipation and respectability, the barmaid Norah Geraghty and the delicate Katie Woodward, is replayed over and over. Harry Norman, once he has lost both promotion and bride to Alaric, has no choices to make, and for the rest of the novel is reduced to a character in the other two clerks' plots.

In *The Three Clerks*, the static and repetitive nature of civil service work blocks plot development. In order to have anything happen to them, the three clerks must all leave the service (whether completely or in part)—whether for squiredom, literary work, Australia—or only to visit the ladies at Surbiton Cottage every weekend. Like Trollope himself, each clerk vacillates between his government post and a second source of income—as does the hero of Charley Tudor's comic tale "Crinoline and Macassar," a devoted civil servant who cannot take enough time off from the Episcopal Audit Board to work up the courage to propose to his sweetheart, and thus marry and produce a child—the conditions he must fulfill in order to inherit his aunt's money. Like Macassar Jones making longer and longer stays in Lady Crinoline's drawing room, Harry Norman spends longer and longer leaves at the family estate in Normansgrove, until finally he inherits it from his dissolute older brother and retires from the Service. Charley begins by writing pulp fiction for the penny paper the "Daily Delight" and eventually becomes a novelist—a more wholesome and rewarding occupation than the time he wastes with his fellow "Infernal Navvies" at the office. Alaric gets involved in a tangle of dubious stock-jobbing to supplement his government work, which eventually robs him of that work, and of England itself, as after his release from prison he and his family are forced to begin their life again in Australia.

Kincaid, who argues that plot is too "gross" for Trollope (*Novels* 27), explains that Trollope's disapproval of exams fits in with his fictional structures, because exams are "compact and clear symbols of a cluster of values which is forward-looking, self-centered, contemptuous of tradition, and thus, finally, anti-comic. Because the examinations system is based on the judgement of results, its utility as a symbol for the simple-minded belief in ordered, patterned life is obvious" (60). The examination cannot coexist with the stationary vacillation that typifies Trollope's fiction. And yet if there is one thing upon which Trollope and Northcote–Trevelyan agree, it is that the Civil Service as it exists does not provide enough plot: "[V]aulting ambition cannot be expected to confine its youthful years to the art of copying fastly, and its maturer powers to writing letters for other people to sign. Ambition, we should say, had better, under existing circumstances, keep itself out of Government offices" ("Civil" 1855, 419). Examinations, Trollope insists, can't work without adequate rewards. He even goes so far as to ignore the Report's suggestion to open staff positions to clerks, who could then "expect the highest prizes in the service if they can qualify themselves for them" (Northcote–Trevelyan 22). In fact, Trollope claims that "[i]t is literally true, that not a word escapes Sir Charles as to the reward by which the ambitious, the gifted, and the educated, are to be brought up to these tremendous competing examinations" ("Civil" 1855, 411–12).

It would seem that Trollope himself shares, to an extent, the progressive ideology of Northcote–Trevelyan. In fact, in *The Three Clerks*, as in *The Bertrams*, far from working counter to the comedic spirit, the examination proves a useful complement. It sets up trajectories, pits protagonists against each other, and invites comparisons—important structural devices for the multiplot novel. And, oddly enough, although both novels explicitly denounce competitive examinations, they also privilege unquestioningly those who genuinely do well on exams. Harry Norman, "the most useful man" (63) in the Weights and Measures Office, first gets appointed by competitive exam, while the less scrupulous Alaric gets in through a loophole, and only wins the promotion competition after Norman drops out. We never know who would have won on "merit" (as defined by the Commissioners) alone, but it is implied that Norman would have. And despite the long protest against the scrapping of the losers of such highly competitive exams as the Cambridge tripos in *The Bertrams*,[5] the novel does just this, abandoning one of its two protagonists and his second-class degree to focus on George Bertram, the most senior of all the wranglers.

Like Northcote and Trevelyan, Trollope wanted the Civil Service to be composed of hard-working, intelligent gentlemen selected by merit, and deplored the practice of political patronage ("Civil" 1865, 616–17). And until 1870 the Civil Service Commissioners "merely administered qualifying examinations of a low standard" (Roach 27), subject to the approval of its official clients—exactly what Trollope himself advocates. Unlike Arnold, of course, Trollope was no product of Oxford—though he did attend Harrow and Winchester. But he was no Philistine either—as the son of a scholarly barrister and a novelist and the grandson of a clergyman, his antecedents and alliances were solidly professional-genteel. Why, then, Trollope's long-standing and vehement objection to the Report's view of the Civil Service?

2. Gentility and Genre

From contemporary reviews to current criticism, discussions of Trollope's writing have inevitably taken up the question of realism, and especially its relation to other genres. Christopher Herbert, for example, suggests a partial repression of comedy by realism in Trollope's writing, or a

> visible upper stratum, the realm of the realist verisimilitude that many of his readers have found to be uncannily realer-seeming than life itself and that historians now confidently draw upon for information about Victorian social structures; and the submerged stratum with its dense network of allusions to old plays and, more generally, its elaborate deployment of the artificial comic code. (8)

As critics have noted since Trollope began publishing, however, his novels contain frequent challenges to verisimilitude that are ostentatious rather than submerged—the fairy-tale-like title of *The Three Clerks*, for example. And as Kincaid notes, his realistic depiction of contemporary life is "more aural than visual.... There is often a sense of a crowd but very seldom a sense of a scene.... His materialism is really non-objective" (*Novels* 50). Classic realism relies on a narrative surface crusted with material objects that metonymically contain and define the penetrable depths beneath (see Jakobson 111, Levine 15, and Butler 136). In *The Vicar of Bullhampton*, Trollope describes one of his obsessive lovers, Harry Gilmore, trying to read the paper when he has just been rejected by Mary Lowther:

> It was the time of the year when newspapers are not very interesting, but he made a rush at the leading articles, and went through two of them. Then he turned over to the police reports. He sat there for an hour, and read hard during the whole time. Then he got

up and shook himself, and knew that he was a crippled man, with every function out of order, disabled in every limb. (158)

George Levine's comment on the passage hesitates in its description of the precise relation between action and emotion: "What Gilmore does is more important, for the moment, than what he feels—or perhaps the description of surfaces is an implicit description of feeling. The feeling itself is described in the same plain style as is the reading of the police report and settles easily within the time sequence" (193). As this hesitation suggests, feeling and action are depicted by Trollope as on the same plane, scarcely divided at all. Mary's rejection is certainly more important to Harry than the police reports, but this hierarchy is not indicated through the language of depth and surface, or speech and silence. We get no sense, in Trollope's fiction, as we do in that of virtually every other canonical Victorian realist, of a tension between surface and depth, or of a selfhood constituted by this tension. In Trollope, notes Kincaid, "values are countered but not subverted" (*Novels* 4)—repression simply doesn't figure in his fiction.

As Herbert notes, "realist fiction centers often on the fable of the slow discovery of some character's true nature that at first is obscured by conventional preconceptions ... a fable that projects the essence of the realistic imagination itself, always *finding things out*" (Herbert 106). But this is exactly what Trollope does not believe possible. The gentility of which Trollope wants to see civil servants possessed may be indefinable, but it is nevertheless patent: "A man ... saying in public that ... berths in the Civil Service should be given exclusively to gentlemen ... would be defied to define the term,—and would fail should he attempt to do so. But he would know what he meant and so very probably would they who defied him" (*Autobiography* 40). The Trollopian gentleman is instantly recognizable, requiring no plumbing of depths, no trial-by-examination to reveal his inner talent (see Gilmour and Pollard). The tongue-in-cheek references to indescribable gentility that dot Trollope's work insist that what we need to know about people we can know without testing them. Trollope resists, rather than embracing, the typically Victorian notion that the true self lies within, instilled in childhood and to be revealed in the process of maturation and testing. In its combining of an ostentatious subversion of realist conventions with a critique of competitive examination, *The Three Clerks* vividly demonstrates the connection between Trollope's opposition to Northcote–Trevelyan and his rejection of realism's construction of interiority and its plot of self-revelation and self-integration (see Bersani 52–66).

The development of a "psychological unity and intelligibility" (Bersani 61) is not a significant—or even a plausible—goal in *The Three Clerks*. Each clerk is tested in a number of contradictory ways and establishes multiple professional identities. So instead of falling prey to the repressive hypothesis, the novel, like a kind of Foucauldian morality tale, delineates a governmental relationship between state and individuals formed by a set of interacting discourses linked to specific markets, institutions, and generic expectations. As well as filling its traditional role of sorting characters by class, genre is also implicated in the novel's articulation of the role of the state in the plot possibilities open to Victorian gentility. Each clerk's entry to the Civil Service fixes the relationship between individual and state in the process of establishing a generic mode. For the aristocratic Harry, the exam is a kind of jousting match, for the bourgeois Alaric a speculation, for the parson's son Charley a gate to a safe haven. Harry's story of (somewhat priggish) academic achievement and self-sacrifice, Alaric's ability to take advantage of political chances, and Charley's miraculous emancipation from the results of his entrance exam, are each fully appropriate to the stories of archaic romance, tragic realism, and magical redemption to come.

Towards the end of *The Three Clerks*, its narrator pauses to remind us of the novel's generic complexities: "[W]e are soon to part company with the three clerks and their three wives. Their three wives? Why, yes. It need hardly be told in so many words to an habitual novel-reader that Charley did get his bride at last" (540–41). In fact, the novel's dependence on an almost ritualistic predictability makes good on its title's promise of a fairytale formula: three city clerks match up with three country sisters in three plots structured by testing and temptation. As is usual in such tales, the youngest and least promising protagonist gains the most sympathy and the most significant success, marrying the youngest, sweetest, and prettiest sister, and embarking on a career as a novelist.[6] The novel's melange of genres includes an interpolated burlesque on the novel's themes (the tale of "Crinoline and Macassar"), two serious essays (one on honesty in politics and one—a chapter long, though omitted in the one-volume version—on the Civil Service), mock epic descriptions (including a descent to the underworld of the Mary Jane Mine), social satire, domestic comedy, and tragic realism.

The "first clerk," the most aristocratic and wealthy as well as the oldest of the three, is "Harry Norman . . . the second son of a gentleman of small property in the north of England. He was educated at a public school, and thence sent to Oxford" but becomes a martyr to primogeniture, and must sacrifice his college career and "the chance of combining the glories and happiness of a double first, a fellow, a college tutor, and a don" to pay his elder brother's debts. Harry is then rigorously tested and determined to be "the least undeserving of the young men" (3–4) nominated to posts at the prestigious Weights and Measures. With his squirearchy background and brilliant academic career, Harry is exactly the kind of candidate for the Civil Service that Northcote, Trevelyan, and especially Jowett, dream of. But his flawless gentility suggests a ruling class that has lost contact with the world that surrounds it—he finally retreats from the Civil Service to become "Mr. Norman of Normansgrove" on his brother's death. When Alaric proposes to and wins Gertrude (who has rejected Norman) as well as the promotion competition at the Weights and Measures, Norman behaves like a parody of a knight who has won no prize to lay at his lady's feet, and must thus lose the lady as well. Examination anxiety—understood as a shameful supersensitiveness—is his downfall: "He had been schooling himself to bear a beating with a good grace, and he began to find that he could only bear it as a disgrace. On the morning of the third day, instead of taking his place in the Board-room, he sent in a note to Mr. Jobbles, declaring that he withdrew from the trial" (130).

The noble Harry Norman is provided with an obvious contrast in the canny Undecimus Scott. Both are "younger sons" representing two different, yet equally outmoded, ways of participating in a competitive economy. Undy's aristocratic background leads him to look to the public service for support, while Norman's achievement of squiredom separates him from his civil service job. Undy has the speculator's ability to distance himself from competition by taking advantage of it and betting on the results, just as his partner Alaric takes advantage of the political vagaries of the Civil Service in order to get hired in the first place. Norman, on the other hand, is utterly incapable of distancing himself from competition imagined in a thoroughly aristocratic way, not merely a fight for survival, but a fight—to the death—for honor. His plot peters out for the same reason he gives up on the promotion examination: because he takes competition too seriously. Harry is the nineteenth-century aristocrat as history's sore loser. Even two years after Alaric's marriage,

> Norman's feelings had by no means been quieted, nor his animosity pacified. He had loved Alaric with a close and manly love; now he hated him with a close and, I fear I may say, a manly hatred. Alaric had, as he thought, answered his love by treachery; and there was that in Norman's heart which would not allow him to forgive one who had been a traitor to him. (357)

Alaric Tudor's irregular appointment at the Weights and Measures prepares the reader not just for his irregular gentility (he has been educated at a private school and a German university, as opposed to Norman's public school and Oxford), but also for his seeing employment by the state not as the field of honor but as a kind of floating capital: "How it happened that he contrived to pass the scrutinizing instinct and deep powers of examination possessed by the chief clerk, was a great wonder to his friends, though apparently none at all to himself" (6). In fact, the chief clerk Mr. Hardlines has been lectured by his superiors on being too tough on candidates, and "the first apparent effect of the little lecture . . . was the admission into the service of Alaric Tudor" (7), who, with Undy's encouragement, continues to manipulate the chances of official life inside and outside the office.

Contemporary reviewers praised the depiction of Alaric's fall into speculation and embezzlement as soberingly all-too-realistic: "All the incidents belong to the present day; the terrors are those of Millbank, not of Otranto . . . this part of the novel is strangely true to life, and very much do we admire Mr. Trollope's treatment of these conspicuous aspects of our times" enthused the *Leader* in December 1857. The *Athenaeum* of that month declared that "Alaric, the defaulter, has too many prototypes in every day's newspaper; the gradual process by which the germs of worldliness and ambition choke his better nature, and the self-deception that leads him on from step to step till ruin overtakes him, is extremely well developed." But despite its adherence to the laws of tragic realism, Alaric's plot—a cautionary tale about the fate of ambition in a Civil Service with no prizes—subtly partakes of the static, fairytale quality of the rest of the novel as well. As Bareham points out, Alaric's story brings him full circle, and he ends the novel as he began it, as a foreign bank clerk (68). And as some critics opined, its predictability keeps this "realistic" plot static too:

> From the moment of the first transaction . . . we know what is to follow. . . . It is not very pleasant to follow the windings of such a story, in which we see the end from the beginning. . . . It would be more agreeable to think, if but for a moment, that there is some chance left—there is some loophole to be discovered for an escape. The author is inexorable. (E. S. Dallas in *The Times* review of May 1859)

Just as Norman is trapped in a plot of chivalry and revenge, inappropriate to the nineteenth-century state, Alaric is stuck in realism's "inexorable" plot of gradual corruption. Realism can be as timeless—as static—as unreal—as romance.

Of the three clerks, Charley Tudor's plot is the most static, an early version of the classic Trollopian vacillation plot: will he go to the dogs and marry the barmaid Norah Geraghty or will he get clear of his debts and dissipations and marry the celestial Katie Woodward? "One of

Trollope's most explicitly autobiographical characters" (Rogers 83), he enters the Civil Service in the same undignified and untested way, according to *An Autobiography*, as Trollope himself.[7] Like Trollope, Charley is asked to copy from a newspaper to demonstrate his handwriting—which is atrocious. He is then asked if he knows arithmetic, answering "some of it." Threatened with further trials of his skills the next day, he goes home to practice his handwriting and bemoan his utter ignorance of arithmetic, only to find that the threat never materializes (*Three Clerks* 13–15 and *Autobiography* 35–37). Doomed to the slovenly paternity of Mr. Oldeschole, Charley finds in the state an undeserved haven. Although Charley seems to spend most of the novel bemoaning his lot, fate is actually extremely kind to him. Not only is he miraculously admitted at the Internal Navigation despite failing their test, and unfairly protected there because Mr. Oldeschole thinks him handsome and well-bred (201–2), but when reform threatens Mr. Oldeschole's reign, Charley is miraculously plucked from under his wing and deposited, with Harry Norman's help, in the even safer (and far more respectable) haven of the Weights and Measures. Neither civil service sloth nor civil service reform pose a threat to the lucky third clerk: Mr. Oldeschole and Sir Gregory Hardlines both become his fairy godfathers, enabling him to land on his feet through no virtue of his own. He survives the disastrous "fate of the Navvies" (526–27) to be "admitted [to the Weights and Measures], without any examination or scrutiny whatever" (536). A similar process wins him his beloved Katie. Katie is unusual among Trollope heroines for her extreme youth, and inhabits a childlike world of fairytale and redemption. When Charley pulls her out of the Thames, she is sure he has saved her life and rewards him with a purse which he treasures as if it were a magic talisman or "amulet" (372). When he gets arrested for debt, she imagines him in chains for life (337), and when she falls in love with him, she nearly dies of it—only to recover miraculously at the last minute, once assured of his love.

Charley does gain one reward by his own efforts—though not through moral growth and self-discovery. It is rather by the relation he establishes between work and display in his literary, as opposed to his official, career. He thus proves a contrast to the extra-officio speculator, Alaric. Trollope's depiction of Alaric's non-stop criminal labor at his second job seems to prefigure his description of his own non-stop writing at *his* second job in *An Autobiography*:

> The rich labour now, and work with an assiduity that often puts to shame the sweat in which the poor man earns his bread. The rich rogue, or the rogue that would be rich, is always a laborious man. He allows himself but little recreation, for dishonest labour admits of no cessation. His wheel is one which cannot rest without disclosing the nature of the works which move it. (346)

Unlike Charley, Alaric is not idle. His illicit labor, however, is beset by a flaw with greater significance for Trollope's own authorship: it must be kept secret—it cannot be displayed. Charley's literary work, in contrast, is almost excessively open. To the irritation of many readers, it is displayed in the form of a chapter-long interruption to the novel, his story of "Crinoline and Macassar." Rogers argues that "Charley's credibility as an author is established, the presentation of domestic life in *The Three Clerks* is enhanced, and Trollope's views of fiction are indicated through contrast and example in 'Crinoline and Macassar'" (Rogers 92–93). Most importantly, its reading by Mrs. Woodward functions as a certification ritual, displaying Charley's intellectual labor at full length. In order for his authorship to pass muster, it must be put on display not only for the eagerly attentive Woodwards but also for the readers of *The Three Clerks*—as if to compensate for Mr. Oldeschole's lack of interest in Charley's handwriting or arithmetic. Alaric's hidden "authorship" merely emphasizes the extent to which tragic realism limits him. Charley, however, escapes the limits of the fairytale not by revealing hidden depths but by *showing us his work*, and thus his ability to negotiate the contradictions of incongruous generic expectations (see Rogers 86, 90).

The *National Review* of October 1858 would seem to have preferred the classical realist uncovering of a character's inner core to "one piece of bad taste ... which reaches its climax in *The Three Clerks*":

> [T]he extraordinary names imposed by Mr. Trollope upon all except the most favoured heroes of the tale,—names which... remind... us at every moment that we are reading a purely fictitious story.... Why must we be told beforehand by the titles assigned to each, of the respective parts to be played by Mr. Hardlines and Mr. Oldeschole?... We hope that Mr. Trollope has become ashamed of it. (qtd. in Smalley, *Trollope: The Critical Heritage*)

In fact, *The Three Clerks* does contain more than its fair share of such names, especially among characters who are not merely grace notes (like Harry and Alaric's colleagues, Messrs. Upinall, Minusex, and Alphabet Precis, or Charley's fellow-Navvies Scatterall and Corkscrew), but are fully developed: not only Sir Gregory Hardlines, Mr. Jobbles, and Mr. Oldeschole, but Captain Cuttwater, the wily and unscrupulous barrister Chaffanbrass, the moneylender M'Ruen, the dancing Miss Golightly, and the priggish Fidus Neverbend (a name Trollope reuses later for the monomaniacal narrator of *The Fixed Period*). And even the heroines' surname, Woodward, signifies on an obvious level in a novel so neatly divided between city and country. *The Three Clerks* even goes so far as to comment on its own "bad taste," blending layers of satire when Katie suggests that there is little difference between the comic names in Charley's story and those of her own uncle's "real life" naval cronies:

> "Crinoline and Macassar!" said Uncle Bat. "Are they intended for human beings' names?"
> "They are the heroine and the hero, as I take it," said Mrs. Woodward, "and I presume them to be human, unless they turn out to be celestial."
> "I never heard such names in my life," said the captain.
> "At any rate, uncle, they are as good as Sir Jib Boom and Captain Hardaport," said Katie, pertly. (240)

Why do emblematic names play such a prominent part in the comedy of *The Three Clerks*? In attacking the logic of the exam, the novel insists that a patent identity can be every bit as complex, interesting, and useful as one that reveals itself gradually, as demonstrated by the names of even the novel's "favoured heroes," the three clerks themselves: Harry Norman, Alaric Tudor, and Charley Tudor. Just as Charley reaches his goal not through inner growth but through his display of generic layering, the protagonists' names signal their status in the novel not by their opaqueness or subtlety, but by their overdetermined obviousness. The more plebeian Jones, Brown, and Robinson of the Weights and Measures Office, for example, have names that refer to no subject other than social distinction, because that is the only one they know. The overeducated and narrow Upinall, Alphabet Precis, and Minusex are more recent acquisitions to the Weights and Measures. The protagonists' names, however, signify in multiple ways. Bareham, for example, remarks on the appropriateness of the "grim" Norman for the priggish Harry and the "flamboyant" Tudor for the speculator Alaric and the dissolute Charley (74). On the other hand, the solidly British "Harry" and "Charley" do far more than hint at their possessors' old-fashioned worth when set against the name of a foreign invader, "Alaric." And both "Norman" and "Tudor" evoke the obsolescence, as well as the governing caste, of their originals. The royal names add to the story's fairytale aura, while reminding us that nineteenth-century reforms do not change the rulers, just the structure within which they rule. Trollope uses such overdetermined labeling rather than developmental plotting to attain a dense surface, which includes contradiction and desire rather than containing them in its depths. Charley Tudor is an obvious example of this. His royal name suggests an impossible (even utopian) combination of insider and outsider, reigning Tudor and reigning Stuart—making him the perfect embodiment of a controlled yet transgressive bourgeois avant garde (see Kucich 613).

3. "At the Bottom of a Cheque"

"Professions produce intangible goods," writes M. S. Larson, "their product, in other words, is only formally alienable and is inextricably bound to the person and the personality of the producer" (14). The intellectual laborer must be able (at least figuratively) to alienate his personality, or he has nothing to sell. Such is the logic of the certification-by-examination of intellectual labor: one must alienate one's expertise—bring that which is inside to the surface—rather than actually producing value by working. As I will argue, Trollope insists that, on the contrary, identity and value are metonymically rather than metaphorically related: a man may produce or possess value, but he may not represent it. In *An Autobiography* and *The Three Clerks*, he illustrates the risks of separating the representation of value in an examination from its production in visible labor.

In *An Autobiography* Trollope describes his parting interview with one of his publishers, Longman's, who has refused to meet his price for a manuscript:

> "It is for you," said [the editor], "to think whether our names on your title-page are not worth more to you than increased payment." This seemed to me to savour of that high-flown doctrine of the contempt of money which I have never admired. I did think much of Messrs. Longman's name, but I liked it best at the bottom of a cheque. (109)

It is not that Longman's name does not mean something. Trollope is happy to accept the name of such a solid business as a guarantee that the check won't bounce. But he resents having that meaning palmed off on him as a commodity. Longman's editor, he implies, misunderstands the relationship between personal identity and value. He assumes that identity is alienable from its owner and from the cash for which it is often traded, as when a gentleman gives his "name" on a promissory note (a disastrous step common in Trollope's fiction) or when a job applicant demonstrates his intellectual promise on an examination sheet rather than demonstrating his intellect by doing his job. The preference Trollope declares in *An Autobiography* for lump-sum payments rather than "a deferred annuity" and his experiments in anonymous publication also depict his defense of metonymic rather than metaphoric relations between author and value. In both cases, he detaches self from product as quickly and definitively as possible. The creditworthy gentleman, who trades labor rather than identity for money, is thus closer than he might seem to his alter-ego, the literary man as honest craftsman, symbol of a lost (because it never existed) economic system, where value is easily established and the claim that art transcends value is easily identified as a cheat:

> No doubt the author or the artist may have a difficulty which will not occur to the seller of cloth, in settling within himself what is good work and what bad,—when labour enough has been given, and when the task has been scamped. It is a danger as to which he is bound to be severe with himself—in which he should feel that his conscience should be set fairly in the balance against the natural bias of his interest.... But in this he is to be bound only by the plain rule of honesty which should govern us all. (108)

The author-as-craftsman sets up a moral accounting system, but only within himself. In his dealings with others, he cannot trade in "conscience" or "interest," only in labor. Both the gentleman's check and the artisan's autonomous work standards guarantee the exchange of an honest day's work for an honest day's wages.[8]

Set against the background of the unstable money markets of the 1850s, when laws of supply and demand seemed no longer to operate and there were more bills in circulation than banknotes (Weiss 26),[9] Alaric Tudor's dealings in *The Three Clerks* with the unscrupulous speculator Undecimus Scott illustrate vividly the difference between the alienable, invisible value of a prestigious name and the clearly visible value of that name at the bottom of a check. The classic portraits of Victorian speculators—Dickens's Mr. Merdle and Alfred Lammle, Trollope's own Ferdinand Lopez and Augustus Melmotte—are of outsiders, racial and social others. By contrast, we are introduced to "Undy" through his aristocratic (if Scottish) pedigree, flawless gentility, and government connections. His entire family are "fully alive to the fact, that a noble brood, such as their own, ought always to be able to achieve comfort and splendour in the world's broad field, by due use of those privileges which spring from a noble name" (81). The depiction of Undy suggests a natural link between the speculator and the aristocrat who thinks he can trade his gentility for a living. Undy himself sees no difference between drawing a salary for a Treasury job and making a profit on speculations involving government-influenced projects. It doesn't matter to him *how* he gets money out of the state: "The one strong passion of his life was the desire of a good income at the cost of the public" (88). Trollope assigns a very different role to his aristocratic civil servant from that imagined by Northcote and Trevelyan.

The Limited Liability Act of 1855, making the shareholder responsible only for his own shares, was engineered by and for the middle and working classes, small investors, small entrepreneurs, and those with ideas rather than money. But the literary world's severe, constant, and perhaps well-founded critique of the Act expressed some of the same anxieties that produced the "connecting" Victorian novel: fear of speculation, fraud, the weakening of "individual enterprise," and, above all, the separation of self and enterprise, identity and labor, promise and fulfillment (Weiss 137–38). Undy Scott's refusal to accept his financial and moral responsibilities, blithely unloading them on the not-quite-wicked-enough Alaric, is clearly meant to suggest the speculator's invoking of limited liability and the ease with which he can alienate his name and his identity from his person.

A spate of speculation scandals in the 1840s and 1850s involving members of parliament and civil servants (see Weiss 141–43 and *Three Clerks* 347) caused *The Times* to note "the parallels with Dickens's *Little Dorrit* in this spectacle of public officials using their positions for private gain" (Weiss 142–43). Opening with an assurance that the Weights and Measures Office "is exactly antipodistic of the Circumlocution Office" (1–2), *The Three Clerks* offers a more complex view than *Little Dorrit* of "public officials using their positions for private gain" in its analysis of the intimacy with which government regulation of the economy and economic exploitation of this regulation are inextricably entwined.[10] Northcote and Trevelyan imagined the Civil Service Commission helping to enforce the distinction between official and extra-official life:

those whom examinations have admitted will be wise and virtuous enough to keep government from exceeding its proper role (Osborne 307–8). But in the midst of exam fever, speculation and government are almost indistinguishable in *The Three Clerks*. The state's attempts to introduce moral standards in financial dealings (the introduction of examinations themselves, the inspection of a mine where crooked dealing is suspected, a commission to look into the construction of a bridge, attempts at reforming laws on married women's property) have no effect other than to provide Undy and Alaric with the raw material for speculation. Harry Norman gives up halfway through the competition for promotion, leaving its authentic results unknowable, and we never know if Alaric's positive report on the Mary Jane Mine is fraudulent or not. Undy writes to Alaric on the engagement of the latter's ward, Miss Golightly:

> It would ... be most scandalous if we were to allow [her fiancé] to get possession of her money. He would, as a matter of course, make ducks and drakes of it in no time.... You will of course see it tied up tight in the hands of the trustees.... Now that I am once more in [Parliament], I hope we shall be able to do something to protect the fortunes of married women. (342–43)

A reformed Trust law does finally catch up with Alaric for stealing his ward's money—although, as we will see, it takes the extralegal audacity of the barrister Chaffanbrass to catch up with Undy. Protecting the fortunes of married women, hiring intelligent and efficient workers, keeping mine owners from criminal actions, and preventing a useless bridge from being built, may be in themselves good limits to place on laissez-faire, but the limits themselves may be bought and sold, engulfed by the system they are supposed to contain. Trollope's critique of Northcote–Trevelyan in *The Three Clerks* warns that not even Arnold's "expert of recognized expertness" is immune to illicit reappropriation by the speculator. Trollope suggests that the greatest evil of Victorian capitalism is that it allows the speculator to profit from anything, whatever his relation to it, whether it is good or evil, whether it means loss or gain to others. The autonomy of the speculator is thus made to interact in dangerous ways with the autonomy both of the government inspector (most obviously in Alaric's simultaneous trips down the slippery slopes of the Mary Jane Mine and insider trading)—and that of the novelist (as I have suggested, Alaric's non-stop extra-officio speculation is paralleled in different ways by both Trollope's and Charley's extra-officio writing). The speculator, the inspector, the author—all make the real unreal and the unreal real in profiting from the sorrows of others.[11]

One of the most troubling links between speculation and authorship for Trollope is that both suggest the possibility of exchange value that is not reducible to abstract labor (see Jaffe, "Detecting"). In *The Three Clerks*, the relationship between laborer and hire is brought to the government office to be weighed and measured. The origins of the Victorian Civil Service were in mercantile holdings, run like independent franchises of the main business of government: "Being paid by those who benefited from his services implied that [the bureaucrat] was in their service, not in that of an employer. His position was not very different from that of a merchant or a shopkeeper in relation to his customers" (Chester 15). An office was property (Chester 18), and the sense of "proprietary right" both to place and promotion, lingered well into the nineteenth century (Donajgrodzki 105–6). At the same time, attempts to impose a chain of command on government offices provided a conflicting model of administration, and eventually led to the abandonment of the proprietary model (Donajgrodzki 106–7). For example, clerks at the Home Office were originally paid out of the fee charged for each instrument they prepared. But this system gradually gave way to salaried labor. By 1849, Sir George Grey of the Home Office was insisting that "the whole time of the Clerks during Office hours with the exception of the holidays allowed them ought to be at the disposal of the Government in return for the regular salaries they receive" (Donajgrodzki 107).

At the same time, "the right to leisure and the authority to regulate the hours of work was becoming a major distinction between the gentleman and the worker" (Lansbury 9). As a clerk at the General Post Office, Trollope "resented the servitude of regular hours from ten to four and complained about them ... bitterly" (9). In *The Three Clerks* this "servitude" is indeed resented—but also depicted as an alternative to an alienation of identity which is akin to both slavery and stealing. The "servitude" ideal is critiqued when, though a parliamentary office-holder rather than a permanent civil servant, Undy Scott boasts of his devotion to the Service "during Office hours". He uses his faithful attendance as an excuse to exploit his position when out of the Office, and to convince Alaric that he will not be compromising his report by purchasing shares in the mine he is engaged in inspecting:

> "I am as fond of the Civil Service as any man," said Undy; "just as fond of it as Sir Gregory [Hardlines] himself. I have been in it, and may be in it again. If I do, I shall do my duty. But I have no idea of having my hands tied. My purse is my own, to do what I like with it. Whether I buy beef or mutton, or shares in Cornwall, is nothing to anyone. I give the Crown what it pays for, my five or six hours a day, and nothing more." (168)

Despite his servitude, no one, of course, could accuse Undy of a lack of gentility. Trollope pokes fun at his own resentment of regular hours through Alaric's wife Gertrude. When she expresses this class-consciousness, her defensive pride undermines her position. She bridles when Miss Neverbend gives her brother's reasons why Alaric ought not to run for Parliament and still retain his post at the Civil Service Commission:

> "I heard my brother say that as Mr. Tudor's office is not parliamentary but permanent, and as he has to attend from ten till four—"
> "Alaric has not to attend from ten till four," said Gertrude, who could not endure the idea that her husband should be ranked with common clerks, like Fidus Neverbend. (421)

Unbeknownst to Gertrude, Alaric, while a faithful worker at the Commission, is planning to use his parliamentary seat as a stock-jobbing tool. Trollope objects to civil servants' lack of political freedom in *An Autobiography*, but Alaric's professional autonomy can be put to the same corrupt uses as Undy's professional servitude.

Undy's assertion that a civil servant serves his country adequately if he only does his duty during office hours is obviously specious, but Sir Gregory's "beau ideal of a clerk in the Civil Service," expressed in his speech at Alaric's wedding, is still more dangerous: "'His heart,' said he, energetically, 'is at the Weights and Measures;' but Gertrude looked at him as though she did not believe a word of it" (178). The appropriation of domestic power by the public sphere invites, in this case, a rivalry between wife and office, and Gertrude is by no means as certain to win as she thinks. Conflicting occupational and sexual loyalties are also the theme in Charley's burlesque of office devotion in "Crinoline and Macassar," as his heroine uses Sir Gregory's very words when she sings

> with melancholy cadence . . . the now celebrated song . . . from the pen of Sir G—H—...:
>
> My heart's at my office, my heart is always there—
> My heart's at my office, docketing with care;
> Docketing the papers, and copying all day,
> My heart's at my office, though I be far away.
> (241)

It is not by exchanging pay for labor that the office threatens marital bliss, but by exchanging pay for identity—for being "always there." The result is a kind of slavery, which is actually more characteristic of the unspecified and thus unlimited hours of labor Alaric gives to crime than the specified hours he gives to the office: "At the Weights and Measures Alaric's hours of business had been from ten to five. In Undy's office they continued from one noon till the next, incessantly; even in his dreams he was working in the share market" (353).

When Gertrude complains of the civil servant's "thraldom," the fact that her husband has left it for Millbank prison provides ironic comment:

> "[A] government office in England is thraldom. If a man were to give his work only, it would be well. All men who have to live by labour must do that; but a man has to give himself as well as his work; to sacrifice his individuality; to become body and soul a part of a lumbering old machine."
>
> This hardly came well from Gertrude, seeing that Alaric at any rate had never been required to sacrifice any of his individuality. (513)

Indeed, the problem with selling one's "individuality" rather than one's labor is that one can so easily go back on the deal, as the slippery Undy once again demonstrates most forcefully. Undy begins his career by following Lord Gaberlunzie's "fatherly precept":

> "Ye maun be a puir chiel, gin ye'll be worth less than ten thoosand pound in the market o' marriage; and ten thoosand pound is a gawcey grand heritage!" . . .
>
> Undecimus, with filial piety, had taken his father exactly at his word, and swapped himself for £10,000. He had, however, found himself imbued with much too high an ambition to rest content with the income arising from his matrimonial speculation. He had first contrived to turn his real £10,000 into a fabulous £50,000, and had got himself returned to Parliament for the Tillietudlem district burghs on the credit of his great wealth; he then set himself studiously to work to make a second market by placing his vote at the disposal of the Government. (82–83)

Undy's sale of his genteel self to his wife is thus the basis of a series of increasingly unreal financial transactions in alienable identity, culminating in the theft (through Alaric) of another £10,000 from his brother's stepdaughter's fortune. In alienating one's name—and refusing to put it at the bottom of a check—one gives no guarantee that anything else will go with it, and such is certainly the case in Undy's deal with the Honorable Mrs. Scott:

> Undy was one of those men who, though married and the fathers of families, are always seen and known *'en garcon.'* No one had a larger circle of acquaintance than Undy Scott; no one, apparently, a smaller

> circle than Mrs. Undy Scott. So small, indeed, was it, that its *locale* was utterly unknown in the fashionable world. At the time of which we are now speaking Undy was the happy possessor of a bedroom in Waterloo Place, and rejoiced in all the comforts of a first-rate club. But the sacred spot, in which at few and happy intervals he received the caresses of the wife of his bosom and the children of his loins, is unknown to the author. (88)

Undy sells *only* his name; his time, attention, and effort—his labor—are not included in the bargain. And his conspicuous lack of feminine attachments underlines the danger he poses to Alaric when he replaces Norman as his closest friend. Harry's and Alaric's friendship is strongly triangulated by their common attachment to the ladies at Surbiton Cottage, to whom Harry introduces Alaric in the first place. Undy, by contrast, tempts Alaric away from spending time with wife and child to the all-male world of his club, the City, and shooting parties in Scotland. The implication is that Sir Gregory's demand for the hearts of his subordinates is not only unreasonable, not only likely to meet with the same response as Mrs. Scott's demand for more than her husband's name—it is even slightly obscene. The use of identity to represent, rather than produce, value is associated in the person of Undy Scott with an "unmanly" aristocratic ostentation.

Sir Gregory believes that the nation buys its civil servants outright, hearts and all, and can ascertain the value of its purchase by academic examination. But in fact, the novel argues, the exam system buys only that which cannot be transferred: the promise of ability signified, though certainly not guaranteed, by a high score. Like Longman's name without Longman's check, the examination is only a promise. Like Arnold's Revised Code, it is only masquerading as a transaction. This is why, despite the fact that he slips into the Weights and Measures Office without passing the exam, the opportunistic Alaric latches on to Sir Gregory and his Civil Service Commission, while the better-educated Harry Norman, whose entry into the Weights and Measures is actually determined by competitive examination, does not. Super tells us that "Trollope throughout his career firmly believed that promotion in the

Civil Service (at least through the ordinary ranks) should be based strictly on seniority; a person had a right to know what he could count on for the future" (15), and fought Rowland Hill's establishment of promotion by merit at the Post Office throughout Hill's career (Super 51). Trollope's valuing of seniority over merit may seem to retain the element of a right to one's place from the old fee system, but, more importantly, it attests to his belief that value accrues from the worker's actual hours of labor, and that it is only labor that can be exchanged for money—not inalienable, indefinable qualities like merit.[12]

Trollope's boss Hill writes in his journal on September 6, 1862 that "Trollope is suspected of neglecting his official duties to attend to his literary labours. . . . —In confirmation see in Athenaeum of this day letter from Trollope in which he speaks of earning 'his bread by writing'—as though literature were his 'profession' &c." (Super 58). But, if we are to believe *An Autobiography*, Hill misunderstands Trollope's statement. Writing might earn him his bread, but "[i]t is . . . absolutely true that during all those years I had thought very much more about the Post Office than I had of my literary work, and had given to it a more unflagging attention" (282). Unlike his famously mercenary description of his literary work, Trollope depicts his surveying duties as those of an "angel" and his Post Office work as a "passion" (89) that transcends monetary considerations: "But I was attached to the department, had imbued myself with a thorough love of letters,—I mean the letters which are carried by the post,—and was anxious for their welfare as though they were all my own" (278). While he scorns those who pretend not to write for money, he boasts proudly that "during the period of my service in the Post Office I did very much special work for which I never asked any remuneration,—and never received any, though payments for special services were common in the department at that time" (163).

J. Hillis Miller contrasts what he calls "the public and institutional side, so to speak, of Trollope's theory of the novel" in *An Autobiography* to a "counter-doctrine" that emphasizes the passionate progeneration of fictions (*Ethics* 90–91). And yet, as we have seen, Trollope's literal work at a public institution is figured in *An Autobiography* as much more like the latter. Like Arnold, Trollope seems to imagine a parental, domestic state. But while Arnold imagines the state-funded school as a cradle for working-class identity, Trollope adheres even here to his notion that identity cannot change hands, even from "parent" to "child." Instead of a self, his paternal state provides the working class with a job. Here is his enthusiastic depiction of the Post Office's London Telegraph Office in 1882:

> Eight hundred young women at work, all in one room, all looking comfortable, most of them looking pretty, earning fair wages at easy work,—work fit for women to do, work at which they can sit and rest and not be weary, with a kitchen at hand and a hot dinner in the middle of the day, with leave of absence without stoppage of pay every year, with a doctor for sickness, and a pension for old age and incompetence . . . and the chance of rising to be a superintendent open to each girl! Is not that the kind of institution that philanthropic friends of the weaker sex have been looking for and desiring for years? . . . And all this in a government office, under government surveillance, which, in this country, is of all surveillance the most tender. . . . The Civil Service in this country has been a rock of safety to very many men, a haven of refuge when no other haven could be reached. And it is so still, in spite of that great barrier at the mouth of the harbour which we call competitive examination. ("Telegraph" 1–2)

4. Schoolmasters' Schemes

Henceforth, the able and successful teacher takes the place of the parliamentary whipper-in, as the guide to government employment, and the only question now remaining to be solved is, how the great educational work before us is to be effectually accomplished.
   —Grammar School Headmaster E. R. Humphreys in 1856

Critics have speculated about the relationship between the two "parts" to *An Autobiography*: the dolefully intimate tale of humiliating years at

Harrow and Winchester doesn't seem to fit the briskly professional account of successful author and zealous civil servant (see, for example, Kincaid "Fictional" and Gilead). This insistence on a disjunction between education and labor systems echoes another aspect of Trollope's quarrel with Northcote–Trevelyan—a disagreement about the relationship between school and work. Public examinations and Victorian novels have this in common: they both advertise themselves as education by other means, education free of legislation and prescription, depending instead on the more natural laws of supply and demand. Novelists like Trollope counted on the distribution mechanisms of the press, booksellers, and circulating libraries to disseminate the gentle moral lessons of popular literature. The language of political economy and the language of pedagogy meet in the ideology of professional authorship. "[I]f my writings be popular, I shall have a very large class of pupils" (*Autobiography* 225), claims Trollope, reasoning from Horace's truism that "[t]he writer of stories must please, or he will be nothing. And he must teach whether he wish to teach or no" (222).

The supporters of Northcote–Trevelyan expected competitive examinations to fill a similar role. They counted on the interaction between the existing education system and the new labor market they envisioned to improve education levels for future civil servants of every class. "Feeding on inputs from the educational environment, reacting back on the educational system and becoming self-reproducing" (Gowan 16–17), the Civil Service imagined by Northcote and Trevelyan can replace other forms of government involvement in education. In fact, Gladstone first recommended civil service reform as an alternative to the extension of state-funded working-class schooling. "As a college tutor," Jowett celebrates the Report's "great importance to the University, supplying as it does, to well-educated young men a new opening for honourable distinction" and claims that even "the effect of it in giving a stimulus to the education of the lower classes can hardly be over-estimated" (Northcote–Trevelyan 31). For midcentury exam enthusiasts, as Osborne demonstrates, "the exam was not to be some kind of neutral, transparent technique for testing the presence of . . .

virtues in the candidate. Rather, there was to be a direct tie between the examination and the *cultivation* of virtue" (Osborne 306). Jowett maintains in his contribution to the Report:

> For the moral character of the candidates I should trust partly to the examination itself. University experience abundantly shows that in more than nineteen cases out of twenty, men of attainments are also men of character. The perseverance and self-discipline necessary for the acquirement of any considerable amount of knowledge are a great security that a young man has not led a dissolute life. (Northcote–Trevelyan 24)

He argues that the choice of subjects for higher-level civil service exams should depend in part on what actual schools and universities are teaching, but also on what the government wants them to teach (27). Like the novel, the examination allows the direct coercion of the schoolmaster to be mediated by economic exchange.

As Trollope suggests in his *Dublin University Magazine* review, the commentaries attached to the Report indicate a lack of support for exams on the part of civil servants, and support for them from educationalists. In 1856 Lord Robert Cecil declared that the introduction of civil service exams "was neither more nor less, from beginning to end, than a schoolmasters' scheme" (Hughes 227). At midcentury, "the ethos, mores and indeed the institutions of traditional education became the models increasingly accepted by the middle class and the new social forces now bidding for hegemony" (Simon 31). As Headmaster Humphreys suggests, one kind of political influence is giving way to another—the patronage exercised by the "parliamentary whipper-in" has passed to the "able and successful teacher." From the first few pages of *The Three Clerks*, schoolroom associations establish while mocking the social and intellectual signification of the various government offices in the novel. We hear, for example, that "the great body of clerks attached to other offices" regard the socially impeccable, relatively well paid, and hard-working clerks at the Weights and Measures "as prigs and pedants, and look on them much as a master's favourite is apt to be regarded by other boys at school" (3). Meanwhile the far less prestigious Internal Navigation Office is staffed by misbehaving class clowns, who tease their underbred supervisor Snape as if he were one of Dickens's hapless school ushers. When Charley begins rooming with Alaric and Norman, and accompanies them on a visit to the Woodwards in Hampton, we learn that "he began to appreciate the comfort of decency, and almost wished that he also had been brought up among the stern morals and hard work of the Weights and Measures" (118).

The discourse on midcentury civil service reform is, in fact, saturated with associations, even identifications, between competition and education, workers and students, workplace and school. These identifications range from the idealizing to the contemptuous, invoking the educational institution as the source of moral as well as intellectual power, but also invoking it as infantilizing and narrow. Jowett maintains that the civil service examiners "should be permanent officers, and, except for proved misconduct, irremovable.... Their irremovability, as in the case of the judges, is the best guarantee for their independence" (Northcote–Trevelyan 26), and it comes as no surprise that an Oxford don would liken the majesty of the invigilator to that of the law. But the test-giver may also be depicted, as in *The Three Clerks*, as a schoolmaster out of school, and thus out of place, as an invigilator on the loose, infiltrating the working world with the irrelevant values of the pedant.

When he discusses it seriously, Trollope is far from regarding the Civil Service as a school. In an essay included in the original version of *The Three Clerks*, he suggests the founding of a vocational school specifically to prepare for it (569–70). Such a college, of course, already existed in Haileybury, the college of the Indian Civil Service. But while working on the Report, Trevelyan was also working to close Haileybury, partly because it was "geared to training administrators in knowledge relevant to their work" (Gowan 15–16), entailing an administrative elite separate from the social-educational elite of Oxbridge: "Gladstone was quite explicit in linking together the issues of Oxford Reform, the abolition of Haileybury and the Northcote–Trevelyan report" (Gowan 28). Trollope opposes the Report on precisely this issue in his *Dublin University Magazine* article as well as in *The Three Clerks*. His is an apprentice model, where the needs of the workplace set the educational agenda: "[T]he education of a Government clerk ... should be insisted on, *and be provided for*.... We would recommend that they be previously taught those special branches of knowledge which certainly will be of use" ("Civil" 1855, 421).

For Jowett, Northcote, and Trevelyan, on the contrary, the values of the education system ought to set the agenda for the work of the state, influencing not only the appointment process, but the actual arrangement of office work as well. "[T]he proper maintenance of" a distinction between "intellectual" and "mechanical" labor forms a crucial part of the project of linking academic competition to gentility:

> It is ... very important, that when the first appointments are made by open competing examination, the line should be carefully drawn between the superior and inferior class of appointments. There should be two distinct classes of appointments to be contended for, and two distinct classes of candidates to contend for them. The subjects of examination should also be different. (Northcote–Trevelyan 421)

In special additions to the published version of their report on this topic, Northcote and Trevelyan both admit that this division of labor will involve a good deal of overlap in practice. Entry-level civil service clerks, of whatever class, spent the vast majority of their time copying and filing documents (Donajgrodzki 88–89). Even gentleman-clerks on the way to better things "ought to go through a certain amount of drudgery, on the principle on which a law student copies out with his own hand a number of common forms and precedents, and on which a young subaltern goes through the exercises of the drill sergeant" (Northcote–Trevelyan 423). Despite their appeals to efficiency, recruitment, and economy, the distinction between intellectual and mechanical work is far more important to Northcote and Trevelyan as a principle than as a practice, and it is to be made most concretely not in the office, but in the examination room. For example, Trevelyan writes that while the subjects in which lower-class clerks are to be examined can be specified, the appropriate subjects for higher-class clerks cannot:

> In respect to the higher class of appointments, the candidates should be examined in whatever branches of knowledge, constituting a liberal education, happen to have been cultivated by them. In respect to the lower class, quick and legible handwriting, facility of deciphering, familiarity with all the ordinary arithmetical processes, and knowledge of bookkeeping, should be the principle subjects of examination. (Northcote–Trevelyan 427–28)

Trevelyan wants "the appropriate motives . . . brought to bear upon the respective classes of persons employed" (426) and looks to the examination as a way of establishing these motives. The division between management trainee and clerical worker depends not on the kind of work they do—both copy letters—but on the tests they have passed in order to do so. Higher-level clerks will use their general facility with texts, as established in their academic exam, to learn from the documents they copy—their work is learning, not copying. Lower-level clerks, whose examination deals with "handwriting" and "deciphering," are working by copying, not learning. As Northcote puts it, the gentleman-clerk

> should take the mechanical work which he does take, not for its own sake, but for the sake of educating himself by means of it; and . . . the due performance of the mechanical work of the office should depend, not wholly or even principally, upon the highly-educated clerks, but upon the mechanical labourers. (423–24)

The exam-induced division between the classes of civil servants can be imagined as that between production and management, raw material and processing (and not, for example, servant and master, or businessman and private secretary) through the use of the powerful term "mechanical": Trevelyan divides the work of Civil Service offices into "purely mechanical work, and that which is employed in superintending the mechanical workmen, and in digesting and applying the result of their labour" (426). Like Northcote and Trevelyan, HMI Arnold returns over and over to this word. His repetition of it in this excerpt from his Report of 1867 (predictably enough, on the Revised Code) is a good example:

> In a country where every one is prone to rely too much on *mechanical* processes, and too little on intelligence, a change in the Education department's regulations, which by making two-thirds of the Government grant depend upon a *mechanical* examination, inevitably gives a *mechanical* turn to the school teaching, a *mechanical* turn to the inspection, is and must be trying to the intellectual life of a school. In the inspection, the *mechanical* examination of individual scholars in reading a short passage, writing a short passage, and working two or three sums, cannot but take the lion's share of room and importance. (*Reports* 1867, emphasis added)

For Arnold, "intelligence," always already established as the opposite of the mechanical, replaces it through the medium of the inspector, who unites through opposition both meanings of the word: he is vibrant, sensitive, flexible, human—and he is also, unlike mechanics or mechanical laborers, very definitely a gentleman. Northcote and Trevelyan also make generous use of the word's multivalence, drawing on its association with the working class as well as with the inhuman production of machines:

> [I]f, on the one hand, a mass of formal routine work be found to exist, requiring, perhaps, less real exercise of mind than bricklaying or carpentering, and on the other, responsible functions have to be performed which call for a high degree of vigilance and judgment, a proper division of labour ought to be established, always taking care that those who will be called to the performance of the higher class of duties obtain a sufficient acquaintance with the details of the machinery of the department. (425)

Oddly enough, the formality of red tape and routine are associated here not with the stultifying ceremonies of the courtier, as they are for so many satirists of the Civil Service (most notably Dickens in *Little Dorrit*), or even with the monotonous drudgery of the factory worker, but with the concrete tasks of the artisan—the bricklayer, the carpenter.

But Trollope has very different things at stake in his definition of the professional gentleman. Like many of its critics, Trollope in his 1855 essay points to the vagueness with which mechanical and intellectual labor are defined in Northcote–Trevelyan. He sees the difference between different kinds of clerks, when it can be established at all, as marked by simple class identity, not by exam (413). He goes on to suggest that Northcote–Trevelyan's interest in dividing them has its roots in a general societal prejudice against the mechanical and routine, and adulation of the original and striking:

> Latterly, also, another equally grave charge has been brought forward. Papers are too systematically docketed! The minds of public servants are given up to indexes and pigeon-holes; and clerks creep through their work in routine, instead of dashing out for themselves an original course, in which genius can be displayed and trammels overcome! (418)

The association of routine deskwork with artisanal labor like "bricklaying or carpentering" should, after all, hardly sound derogatory to readers of Trollope's *Autobiography*. "Mechanical" labor, the production of page after page of "copying," describes not only the activity of the junior civil service clerk, but also Trollope's own avowed method of writing fiction.[13] Like Northcote and Trevelyan, Trollope himself refers to artisanal labor to differentiate the working class from intellectual laborers. But he also uses it as the paradigm for all labor, that which assures us that work is work, for which one ought to be paid full value:

> I had long since convinced myself that in such work as mine the great secret consisted in acknowledging myself to be bound by rules of labour similar to those which an artisan or a mechanic is forced to obey. A shoemaker when he has finished one pair of shoes does not sit down and contemplate his work in idle satisfaction. "There is my pair of shoes finished at last! What a pair of shoes it is!"

> The shoemaker who so indulged himself would be without wages half his time. It is the same with a professional writer of books. (*Autobiography* 323)

Trollope scoffs in *The Three Clerks* at Jowett's extension of examinations to the working class by parodying it. Mr. Jobbles believes that "every man should . . . be made to pass through some 'go.' The greengrocer's boy should not carry out cabbages unless his fitness for cabbage-carrying had been ascertained, and till it had also been ascertained that no other boy, ambitious of the preferment, would carry them better" (125). But he also complains that Northcote and Trevelyan "would change the clerks about from office to office, and would, we presume, if they had the power, force the butcher to measure tape and the shoemaker to whip cream" ("Civil" 1855, 414). It is pointless for a grocer to be educated like a gentleman, but this does not mean that gentlemen do not work like grocers—or shoemakers or tailors—performing concrete, specialized tasks, differentiated by function, not by their degree of conformity or creativity.

In his notorious depiction of mechanical authorship in *An Autobiography*, Trollope reclaims the mechanical for the gentleman. The difference between working-class and professional labor slips by unnoticed when he insists that

> [the author's] language must come from him as music comes from the rapid touch of the great performer's fingers; as words come from the mouth of the indignant orator; as letters fly from the fingers of the trained compositor; as the syllables tinkled out by little bells form themselves to the ear of the telegraphist. A man who thinks much of his words when he writes them will generally leave behind him work that smells of oil. (177)

If the analogy had not been so close, he might have added "as words come from the clerk copying a letter in a public office."[14] Labor that is automatic rather than thoughtful is here depicted, paradoxically, as that which produces fresh and original work rather than "work that smells of oil"—here the oil of the scholar's lamp, not the mechanic's engine.

Trollope's work is often described as reproductive rather than creative —his fiction is likened to a mirror, a photograph, a faithful reproduction. Both nineteenth- and twentieth-century critics turn to this aspect of Trollope's realism as a way of explaining his terrifyingly vast output, associating it by turns with the natural, slightly obscene production of the childbearing woman as well as the automatic, mindless output of the machine. The author as machine or mother suggests production without agency to Trollope's readers, separating it from the workaday agency of the artisan. But this, of course, is not how Trollope sees it. In *An Autobiography*, he welcomes in order to transform the literary man's dangerous association with femininity and physical labor.

Trollope's productivity was an important factor in the decline of his reputation during his lifetime, and his smirking reference in *An Autobiography* to his fears of emulating "the fecundity of the herring" (110) suggests that he was perfectly aware of this. Nicola Thompson shows the gradual increase of feminization in reviews of his work over his lifetime: in order for him to scribble away so rapidly, his readers reason, he must find writing effortless, like the women writers for whom realism's domestic subject matter, its everyday-ness, its lack of "imagination," make it a natural genre (Thompson 161–64).[15] Henry James likens Trollope's work to that of women writers, when he claims that "[h]is great, his inestimable merit was a complete appreciation of the usual. This gift . . . would naturally be found in a walk of literature in which the feminine mind has laboured so fruitfully" (101). Almost excessively parental, Trollope's treatment of "the youthful feminine . . . is full of . . . fatherly indulgence, . . . almost motherly sympathy" (121). And there is inevitably something slightly obscene about this maternity; James finds "Trollope's fertility . . . gross, importunate" (98).

In *An Autobiography*, Trollope is explicit about the advantages to himself of literary labor's requiring no training and no capital—the very reasons women were supposed to have turned to it in such numbers during the nineteenth century. He even accepts the association of prolific authorship with fertile femininity, though distancing it from his own career by containing it in the figure of his mother, Frances.

Although (as Allen among others notes) his depiction of her maternal authorship is ultimately ambivalent, he welcomes rather than shuns the common nineteenth-century trope of woman-author-as-mother and her writing as an extension of literal motherhood when he describes her scribbling away while nursing her husband and children at Brussels:

> The doctor's vials and the ink-bottle held equal places in my mother's rooms. I have written many novels under many circumstances; but I doubt much whether I could write one when my whole heart was by the bedside of a dying son. *Her power* of dividing herself into two parts, and keeping her intellect by itself clear from the troubles of the world, and fit for *the duty it had to do*, I never saw equalled. I do not think that the writing of a novel is the most difficult *task* a man may be called upon to do; but it is a *task* that may be supposed to demand a spirit fairly at ease. *The work of doing it* with a troubled spirit killed Sir Walter Scott. My mother went through it unscathed in strength, though *she performed all the work of day-nurse and night-nurse* to a sick household. (29, emphasis added)

If Mrs. Trollope cares for her family by both writing and nursing, this care is depicted by her son as *work*, requiring the performance of tasks as different from each other as baking is from shoemaking, each demanding its own tools and talents, each demanding full-time effort and energy. Trollope may accept the feminization of prolific authorship, but only by insisting that feminine work involves feminine agency.

Miller notes, in Trollope's comparison of writing to telegraphy and typesetting, "[t]he emphasis on the efficiency of the transmission, through the novelist's conscience (and consciousness) back to his readers, of what they already know, in a closed circuit exchanging the same for the same.... In these figures the medium vanishes in its flawless working" (*Ethics* 89–90). And James paints a similar picture: "[T]he writing of novels had ended by becoming, with him, a perceptibly mechanical process" (97), and describes his writing as a version of photography: "This exact and on the whole becoming image, projected upon a surface without a strong intrinsic tone, constitutes mainly the entertainment that Trollope offered his readers. The striking thing to the critic was that his robust and patient mind had no particular bias, his imagination no light of its own" (101–2). James cedes Trollope the status of worker, but like the mother, the machine melts into the common, the animal, the obscene: "[T]here was always in him a certain infusion of the common. He abused his gift, overworked it, rode his horse too hard" (99).

In *An Autobiography*, however, Trollope restores heroic purposefulness to "mechanical" labor. He proudly cites Hawthorne's commendation of his fiction, replacing the machine with the mechanic:

> I have always desired "to hew out some lump of the earth," and to make men and women walk upon it just as they do walk here among us,—with not more of excellence, nor with exaggerated baseness,—so that my readers might recognise human beings like to themselves, and not feel themselves to be carried away among gods or demons. (145)

Just as he refuses to associate feminine fecundity with effortless production, so does he refuse to associate mechanical labor with the automatic, the effortless, or the mindless. Far from being a passive recording, or even birthing, realist fiction is compared to such effortful tasks as hewing and making. As Trollope continues, he masculinizes the reproductive image, while at the same time reserving to himself the maternal function of instituting proper gender roles:

> If I could do this, then I thought I might succeed in impregnating the mind of the novel-reader with a feeling that honesty is the best policy; that truth prevails while falsehood fails; that a girl will be loved as she is pure, and sweet, and unselfish; that a man will be honoured as he is true, and honest, and brave of heart. (145)

The Civil Service Commissioner may teach through the testing of an alienable identity, but the novelist-as-teacher performs his alternative pedagogy only insofar as he displays the massive product of his laborious toil.

5. "Working for Money"

> *All those I think who have lived as literary men,—working daily as literary labourers,—will agree with me that three hours a day will produce as much as a man ought to write. But then he should so have trained himself that he shall be able to work continuously during those three hours,—so have tutored his mind that it shall not be necessary for him to sit nibbling his pen, and gazing at the wall before him, till he shall have found the words with which he wants to express his ideas. It had at this time become my custom,—and it still is my custom, though of late I have become a little lenient to myself,—to write with my watch before me, and to require from myself 250 words every quarter of an hour. I have found the 250 words have been forthcoming as regularly as my watch went.*
> —*An Autobiography*

Whatever doubts he has about the examination as a representation of identity, or about the examiner's educative function, for Trollope, as for Arnold, the intellectual laborer must be a subject who is also the object of a spectacle. In *An Autobiography* he accounts for his writing in two ways: he quantifies it by reporting its monetary equivalent and he renders it inspectable through his unusual attention to the physical details of writing, whether the contrivances he employs for writing in pencil on the trips he takes for the Post Office, or the early-morning routine with "my watch before me." Trollope writes to his brother-in-law (and former superior at the Post Office) John Tilley that "a man who works for his bread is so much nobler than he who takes his bread for nothing.... You say of me:—that I would not choose to write novels unless I were paid. Most certainly I would;—much rather than not write them at all" (April 18, 1878, qtd. in Super 72–73). It is almost as if "working for money" is a value in and of itself that transcends payment.[16] The very public examinations that resolve the plots of *The Three Clerks* provide an antidote to the abstract and irrelevant academic tests of the Civil Service Commissioners: they not only punish their wicked or incompetent victims for *not* working, but also display, rather than enveloping in academic mystery, the solid brutality of the work of the examiner at his not-very-respectable job. The foiling of Undy

Scott and the collapse of the Internal Navigation Office are not narrative requirements merely; they are necessary for the showcasing of a particular kind of intellectual labor. Unlike all three clerks, the barrister Chaffanbrass and Alaric Tudor's fierce replacement at the Civil Service Commission have no mercy and no scruples. They are professional torturers, and proud of it.

"That horrid young lynx-eyed new commissioner, . . . a personification of conscious official zeal" who replaces the disgraced Alaric to inflict "barbaric tortures" (528) on the incompetent Mr. Oldeschole reverses the code of his own role model, Sir Gregory, when he asks Mr. Oldeschole to "define to us what is the . . . exact use of the Internal Navigation Office":

> What a question was this to ask of a man who had spent all his life in the Internal Navigation Office! O reader! should it chance that thou art a clergyman, imagine what it would be to thee, wert thou asked what is the exact use of the Church of England; and that, too, by some stubborn catechist whom thou wert bound to answer; or, if a lady, happy in a husband and family, say, what would be thy feelings if demanded to define the exact use of matrimony? Use! Is it not all in all to thee? (528–29)

Mr. Oldeschole's view of his job is actually closer to that of Sir Gregory Hardlines than he thinks—with the unquestioning, total belief in his office that Hardlines has in competitive examinations, and that Undy has in his own right to a living at the expense of the public. By introducing the criterion of "Use!" the new Commissioner puts an end to trafficking in identity with ruthless efficiency.

Far from the idealized Civil Service Commissioner of Northcote–Trevelyan, the unscrupulous lawyer Mr. Chaffanbrass has no intellectual credentials at all: "As a lawyer, in the broad and high sense of the word, it may be presumed that Mr. Chaffanbrass knows little or nothing. He has, indeed, no occasion for such knowledge" (469–70). But he is very good at his job: "His business is to perplex a witness and bamboozle a jury, and in doing that he is generally successful. . . . To apply the thumbscrew, the boot, and the rack to the victim before him was the work of Mr. Chaffanbrass's life.... He was as little averse to this toil as the cat is to that of catching mice" (469). Trollope's amoral lawyers are a well-known feature of his fiction. In *The Three Clerks*, as in his later appearance in *Orley Farm*, however, the ferocious Chaffanbrass provides a crucial service for the reader. We long to see Undy punished, though we know he has put himself beyond the reach of the law, just as we long to see Lady Mason escape the punishment we know she deserves, and it is only Chaffanbrass who can do this for us. Undy can only be conquered by someone even cheekier and less scrupulous than himself, but who, unlike Undy, is "little averse to the toil," willing and eager to "work for his bread," and to do so in front of everyone (484–88). Working for money, Chaffanbrass transcends the too malleable or too inflexible letter of the law to reach truly moral judgments, beating the speculator at his own game.[17]

When Trollope visits the London Telegraph Office, he expresses a deep interest in the sight it reveals of eight hundred women working in a single room, open to a single gaze. His interest seems to have nothing to do with Dickensian humanitarianism, nor is it (particularly) prurient. He explains his fascination:

> [I]t is not only the work which is done by any great mass of persons working together which is interesting, but all that which must necessarily be done beyond the work.... They who look only to what labourers can be made to produce are too apt to regard these living souls as though they were wound up by some key or windlass, or set in motion by the power of heat, and that they would so do a certain fixed task, and that then there would be an end of them.... To me, when I have seen a half-naked brawny puddler turning the iron, or a miner digging out the gold-containing rock, or the ploughman in his tucked-up frock striving to drive his furrows straight and deep, I have felt more interest in the man's willingness to serve, or in his mutiny, in his conversation, if I could hear what he was talking, or even in his silence, in the expenditure of his wages, in his bread-and-cheese and beer, in his hilarity or sadness as he sits during his allot-

ted minutes of idleness with his pipe in his mouth, than I have in the profit or loss accruing from his work. ("Telegraph")

Part of the thrill of mechanical work, Trollope suggests here, is that it is not performed by machines. The almost lascivious language Trollope bestows on the "half-naked brawny puddler" and the "ploughman ... plowing his furrows straight and deep" (though not, of course, on the "young lady telegraphists") demonstrates the pleasure to be derived from the elaborate display not only of work, but of life *at* work. As he goes on to a minute description of the physical arrangement of the Telegraph Office and the job's benefits package—"all that which must necessarily be done beyond the work"—Trollope insists that we watch not the work alone, nor the worker alone, but what competitive examination can never show us: the worker working for money, the subject of labor. Like the gentleman, and unlike the examination candidate, this figure is instantly recognizable—the line between working and not working, and indeed between different kinds of labor, is as patent as the difference between Tudor and Norman. This is not, however, the case in the text I turn to in my next chapter, Dickens's *Our Mutual Friend* (1865). There, an anxiety about identifying and valuing labor properly becomes one of the central concerns of the novel.

Chapter Four

"IN THE WAY OF SCHOOL": DICKENS'S 'OUR MUTUAL FRIEND'

1. "Why is a Raven like a Writing Desk?"

Arnold and Trollope use figurative examinations to combat real ones, but their uses go beyond this, and well beyond the problems facing literary men who are also civil servants. In the next two chapters, I will look at examinations designed to solve problems not only in the display of intellectual labor, but also in its definition and containment. HMI Arnold's ideal examiner is the heroic inspector, who renders ideology visible as labor by showing the work that goes into making humans human. For Trollope, the goal is the display of the subject of labor, revealed in the ruthless interrogation of an examiner working for money. In Dickens's last completed novel, *Our Mutual Friend*, figurative examinations feature a feminine student who evaluates and places the masculine intellectual worker by producing and containing a reified knowledge immune from the risks of exchange. If we trace the series of examinations that lead to the emergence of the novel's two normative intellectual workers—John Harmon and Eugene Wrayburn—we find that the debunking of domestic ideology plays a key role in legitimating intellectual labor's place in the Victorian economic system. In order to provide a model of professional expertise, as valuable yet invaluable as domestic power, yet freed from its fragility, the novel must appropriate and reinvent the examination for the world outside the Victorian state and its institutions.

Dickens was extremely active in writers' professional organizations, taking a famously aggressive position on the subject of international copyright, and Dickens's work has often been read in relation to the opportunities and contradictions generated by the professionalization of authorship in the nineteenth century (see Feltes; Welsh, *Copyright*; Poovey, *Uneven*; and Duncan). If, as many of these readers have argued, *David Copperfield* explores and problematizes nineteenth-century notions about the professional career, *Our Mutual Friend* represents a shift in Dickens's attention to notions about the classification and closure of occupational categories. How, for example, does one adequately classify the work performed by scavengers like Gaffer Hexam, Mr. Venus, and Jenny Wren? Throughout the novel, the reader is inundated with jokes about occupational names ("schoolmaster," "secretary," "literary man," etc.) and conventions (the fictitious "sweat," for example, dripping from Rogue Riderhood's brow), and with a constant stream of questions about what job a given character is doing, what job he or she ought to do, and how to determine the appropriate qualifications for and usefulness of this employment. A confusion over job qualifications fuels each of the novel's main plots: most of the major male characters enter *Our Mutual Friend* either refusing to do the work for which they are suited (Eugene Wrayburn, John Harmon) or placed in a position for which they are not suited (Noddy Boffin, Silas Wegg, Bradley Headstone). Toward the end of *Our Mutual Friend*, Silas Wegg's indignant cry, "And how can a man put a price upon his mind!" is summarily answered as he is dumped, mind and all, into a "scavenger's cart" (862). This receptacle for the novel's grotesque "literary man" will prove appropriate in more ways than one. But for most of the novel, the pricing of men's minds, or the proper valuation of masculine intellectual labor, is a much more difficult task. The re-placing of inappropriately employed characters within their proper occupational niches becomes one of the novel's main narrative problems, and Dickens's extra-institutional exams its main narrative solution.

When Mortimer Lightwood questions his friend Eugene about his intentions toward Lizzie after Bradley visits their chambers, Eugene complains that "'one would think the schoolteacher had left behind him a catechizing infection'" (348). This "infection" pervades *Our Mutual Friend*. There is scarcely a Dickens novel without a portrait of some kind of school, but not even in *Hard Times* is a preoccupation with the methods and effects of pedagogy so marked as in *Our Mutual Friend*.[1] Narrative progress depends on pedagogical progress, as we see when we compare the static presentation and thwarted projects of the "Social Chorus" characters to the novel's two main plots, packed with action by the struggle over who will teach Lizzie and by Boffin's famous testing of Bella. The novel's well-known obsession with reading and writing (see Baker) is filtered through a continual barrage of quizzes and qualifying examinations, often comic (Wegg's job interview, Bella's quizzing of her infantilized "schoolboy" father, Miss Peecher's self-interested questioning of her favorite pupil Mary Anne), but also chilling (Rogue Riderhood's "inspection" of Bradley's class, Gaffer's scholarly display of his "Body Found" posters), thought-provoking (Jenny's questioning of Lizzie about her feelings for Eugene, John's "cross-examin[ation]" (433) during his first proposal to Bella), and melodramatic (the final testing of Bella's loyalty by the near-arrest of her husband, Jenny's discovery of Eugene's sickbed desire to marry Lizzie). If, as J. Hillis Miller claims, "the true mode of existence in *Our Mutual Friend* is intersubjectivity" (*Dickens* 288), the true mode of intersubjectivity in the novel mimics the examination.

Like twentieth-century theorists of the role of intellectual labor in capitalism (see Chapter 1), *Our Mutual Friend* demonstrates the failure of categorizations based on class, mode of production, and the division between the economic and the extraeconomic to classify that labor. In fact, the novel seems to suggest that by using these terms we are asking the wrong questions, questions that place professional authority in incompetent hands. As the lawyers Eugene and Mortimer, the schoolteacher Bradley Headstone, the secretary John Rokesmith/Harmon, and the "literary man" Silas Wegg are introduced, their lack of conformity to crucial Victorian social categories is highlighted by a series of comic contradictions. The novel's jokes at the expense of intellectual labor at once invite us to assume and to question that some objects and services are exchangeable and some are not, and that there exists a historically appropriate mode of exchange for those that are. There would be nothing to laugh at if the novel did not take the binarisms labor/capital, feudalism/capitalism, and public/private for granted. At the same time, the novel insists that they are inadequate for the classification of intellectual labor. Repeatedly, *Our Mutual Friend* calls attention to the seriousness of the challenge this classification poses for Victorian systems of meaning.

Nicodemus Boffin is often the vehicle for jokes about the confusion between subject and object demanded by professionalization. The comic satisfaction of the consumer who has got a deal surfaces in Boffin's characterization of the greedy villain Silas Wegg as "a literary man —*with* a wooden leg" (143). He further confuses professional and commodity in his assumption that his would-be secretary Rokesmith is offering his services as "a piece of furniture, mostly of mahogany, lined with green baize or leather, with a lot of little drawers in it" (227).[2] In one of the first scenes of *Our Mutual Friend*, Boffin interviews Silas Wegg for the job of "literary man" (89), and in the process reveals his uncertainty about what sort of work literature entails, and what system of exchange can procure it:

> "Now, it's too late for me to begin shovelling and sifting at alphabeds and grammar-books. . . . But I want some reading—some fine bold reading, some splendid book in a gorging Lord-Mayor's-Show of wollumes" (probably meaning gorgeous, but misled by association of ideas); "as'll reach right down to your pint of view, and take time to go by you. How can I get that reading, Wegg? By . . . paying a man truly qualified to do it, so much an hour (say twopence) to come and do it." (94)

Boffin begins by depicting learning to read as a version of his former job as a dustman ("shovelling and sifting") and ends by assuming that, like that job, reading itself fits neatly into a conventional capitalist/worker relationship. The "profit" he expects from this relationship, however, cannot be characterized as the capitalist's surplus value. Part of a realm of luxury and leisure, intellectual labor may not be labor at all. Sandwiched between his market-based analogy, Boffin's "Lord Mayor's Show" hints not so much at the power of a Victorian consumer as at the anachronistic glamour of Renaissance display, implying that intellectual attainments might not be something that nineteenth-century money can buy. Wegg's view of his own role matches Boffin's confusion. While his view of his relations with the mythical denizens of "Our House" is sentimentally feudal ("he had...settled it with himself...that he...was one of the house's retainers and owed vassalage to it and was bound to leal and loyal interest in it" [88]) and his view of his peddling unsentimentally entrepreneurial, in his first approach to Boffin he mixes these qualities, figuring a feudal gesture of servitude as money capital: "'Come!'" he suggests to himself, "'I'll speculate! I'll invest a bow in you'" (90). At the same time, the narrator's knowingly literate parenthetical comment on Boffin's use of "gorging" suggests an authentic realm of professional authority that, inaccessible to characters like Bradley and Wegg, hovers over these confusions. However complex the valuing of intellectual labor may prove, it has value nevertheless.

As the narrator introduces Bradley Headstone, he remarks that there is "a want of adaptation between him" and his "decent" schoolmaster's dress, "recalling some mechanics in their holiday clothes" (266). As the passage continues, however, Bradley's unclear class placement extends from his unfortunate person to his occupation itself. Like Arnold and the authors of Northcote–Trevelyan, Dickens makes use of the slipperiness of the term "mechanical," seeming to suggest that it is the "mechanical" training of the schoolteacher (rather than, say, his working-class background or low pay) that threatens to proletarianize him into a mechanic. Here again the joke is based on a defamiliarizing commodification—this time of the professional's expertise, if not of the professional himself:

> He had acquired mechanically a great store of teacher's knowledge. He could do mental arithmetic mechanically, sing at sight mechanically, blow various wind instruments mechanically, even play the

great church organ mechanically. From his early childhood up, his mind had been a place of mechanical stowage. The arrangement of his wholesale warehouse, so that it might be always ready to meet the demands of retail dealers—history here, geography there, astronomy to the right, political economy to the left... —this care had imparted to his countenance a look of care. (266–67)

If knowledge is like goods in a warehouse, then it must take the same variety of specialized functions to process it. Bradley's "look of care" seems to come from the extra work of filling two very different occupational niches at once. He must exert not only the physical dexterity of the working-class mechanic in "acquiring" his knowledge, but also the skill of the bourgeois wholesaler in "arranging" it. The lack of clear class-placement for schoolteachers was a widely acknowledged problem in this period—one anxious well-wisher suggested that they combine their positions with that of the local tax collector (Digby and Searby 191–92). The tensions associated with Bradley's unstable class placement lead him to murder and suicide. The novel's many jokes about the classification of intellectual work, then, have serious consequences; they result in Bradley's fatal "look of care" and Boffin's incautious hiring of the incompetent Wegg and the sinister Rokesmith. All joking aside, intellectual labor's refusal to fit within Victorian economic categories thus poses a serious problem that the novel must solve.

In fact, the first few paragraphs of *Our Mutual Friend* set the reader a problem in job classification (though the job in question can hardly be called intellectual labor): how does Gaffer Hexam get his living? The sinister mystery with which Gaffer is introduced is, of course, appropriate to his macabre employment, but here, this mystery takes the form of a riddle for the reader, as we are asked to guess where among an array of suggested occupations his task fits in:

> [T]he man, with the rudder-lines slack in his hands, and his hands loose in his waistband, kept an eager look out. He had no net, hook, or line, and he could not be a fisherman; his boat had no cushion for a sitter, no paint, no inscription, no appliance beyond a rusty boathook and a coil of rope, and he could not be a waterman;

his boat was too crazy and too small to take in cargo for delivery, and he could not be a lighterman or river-carrier; there was no clue to what he looked for, but he looked for something. (43)[3]

Our fascination with Gaffer's mysterious activity is deepened by the assurance that, whatever it is, it is his regular job: "Half savage as the man showed... still there was business-like usage in his steady gaze" (44). The suspense is more thrilling because its solution promises to illuminate a dark corner of contemporary (or, for us, Victorian) economic life. By representing it as "business-like," Dickens raises the activity of picking drowned men's pockets from the merely criminal to the excitingly esoteric. This excitement makes visible certain assumptions about what it means to be working. Labor signifies in three ways within capitalist production. Actual labor may or may not *produce* value, depending on whether or not it is expended in the creation of a commodity. Labor also *has* value—it can be exchanged just as any other commodity can. But it is only in the form of abstract "labor power" that labor *is* value—that element "congealed" (*Capital* 76) in an object which brings that object within the system of capitalist exchange. The critique of capitalism as well as its support requires this reifying abstraction—"labor power"—in order to demystify the exchange of commodities. Our conception of Gaffer's activity at the opening of *Our Mutual Friend* is shaped in two ways by this abstraction. First of all, just as in Marx's famous example, so many yards of linen are somehow equivalent to a coat, so many hours of weaving linen are somehow equivalent to so many hours of sewing the coat. And, of course, so many hours of scavenging corpses from the Thames are equivalent to so many hours of any other kind of work. If Gaffer is not merely stealing, but working, then his labor can be translated into ours. Secondly, the idea of "homogenous human labor" not only makes all kinds of labor equivalent, but establishes a crucial binarism between labor and all other human activities. If Gaffer is not merely working, but stealing from corpses, his activity destabilizes this opposition. His savage business raises the question of where valuable "business" ends and extra-economic "savagery" begins.[4]

Our initial inability to determine which trade Gaffer follows thus leads not only to a satisfyingly chilling discovery, but also to a less easily resolved confusion about the nature of labor itself. The passage's wondering progression through the possible legitimate trades Gaffer might (but does not) ply pushes him beyond the boundaries of work even as we are assured that he is working. Unlike fishermen, watermen, and lightermen, "no name dispels the mystery of Gaffer Hexam's occupation" (Ermarth 212). The name we *are* eventually supplied with, "bird of prey," is fully appropriate to Gaffer's contradictory position: it both is and is not a job classification and points beyond the human in the same way that his occupation points beyond the market.

Many readers have agreed with J. Hillis Miller in noting that *Our Mutual Friend* is saturated with the imagery of capitalist exchange. Much of the criticism on the novel focuses on the problem of whether or not—and how—the novel presents an alternative to this marketable world.[5] Are there or are there not, as Mr. Boffin claims, "some things that I never found among the dust" (136)? At first, corpse-pickpocketing seems to cross this boundary merely because it is illegal and macabre. But Gaffer's very attempt to legitimate his work hints at a further anomaly: the element in his labor that makes it most "savage" is also that which, for Gaffer, brings it within the pale of licit economic dealings. Gaffer seems fully aware of the importance of distinguishing between stealing and working. While he condemns Rogue Riderhood for "robbing a live man," he insists that taking money from a corpse is not criminal: "'What world does a dead man belong to? 'Tother world. What world does money belong to? This world. How can money be a corpse's?... Don't try to go confounding the rights and wrongs of things in that way'" (47). According to Gaffer, his "living" comes not from the exchange of labor-as-commodity for other commodities, but from the very impossibility of exchange with the extraeconomic realm of the dead. This legitimating argument places a firm boundary between the economic ("this world") and the extraeconomic ("'Tother world"). But Gaffer's job, in which dead men's money becomes the raw material which he transforms into a valuable commodity through his labor, erases that boundary. Gaffer's death, towed in his own line like one of his "bits of luck," suggests that the erasure of the boundary between the economic and the extraeconomic paves the way for the erasure of the boundary (for Gaffer) between "this world" and "'tother." Indeed, the novel insists over and over on a crossable boundary between the economic and the extraeconomic, but such a crossing brings us not only to Jenny Wren's transcendental cry—"[C]ome up and be dead!" (335)—but to the exploitation of "'tother world" through the savagery of Gaffer's occupation.

The work of female scavengers associates this blurring of the boundary between the market and the extraeconomic with the blurring of class and gender categories. Like Lizzie Hexam's gentlewomanly "look of dread or horror" at her father's and her own occupation (44), Jenny Wren's gentlewomanly work at "pincushions" and "pen-wipers" is not an occupation for a gentlewoman's leisure, but part of her job. Jenny turns the "waste" she buys from Pubsey and Co. into dolls' clothing, and, like Gaffer and Venus, makes her first appearance in the novel through a series of questions about her occupation. She turns the pedagogical tables on the schoolteachers Bradley Headstone and Charley Hexam as, once again, job classification is presented in the form of a riddle:

> "You can't tell me the name of my trade, I'll be bound," she said. . . .
> "You make pincushions," said Charley.
> "What else do I make?"
> "Pen-wipers," said Bradley Headstone.
> "Ha! Ha! What else do I make? You're a schoolmaster, but you can't tell me."
> "You do something . . . with straw; but I don't know what. . . ."
> (272)

Jenny's coyness about her job, while soon dissipated, reminds us of the paradoxes it continues to raise. While she differs from Gaffer in the perfect respectability of her trade, by doing as work what other children do as play she too provides an esoteric thrill for both nineteenth- and twentieth-century middle-class readers because she produces value through an activity our culture is reluctant to recognize as work. Pincushions and penwipers seem more like the leisure-time productions of genteel young ladies than the commodities produced by a working-class laborer, and dressing dolls seems more like a young girl's training for motherhood than a business. As Pam Morris notes, there is a further association suggested by Jenny's job. In the 1860s the word "doll" could also have the connotation "prostitute," and Jenny's "flaunting dolls" link her to that occupation which, for the Victorians, symbolized most profoundly the disturbance of the division between economic and personal life. Like the narrator's name for Gaffer, Jenny's choice of pseudonym points to her blending of these categories: she abandons the surname "Cleaver" (that symbol of human work, a tool) for "Wren" (a being, like the "bird of prey," for whom the human distinction between work and leisure is meaningless). If the borderline nature of Gaffer's occupation eventually leads to his death, with her rooftop cry Jenny too claims citizenship in the country beyond the borders of the value-able—transcendent and illicit death.

Charley's and Bradley's confusion about Jenny's occupation is echoed by the novel's refusal to clarify anything it tells us about her. She is introduced as "a child—a dwarf—a girl—a something" (271), and the uncertainties about her age and deformity are never fully resolved. Most disturbing of all, perhaps, is her reversal of her relationship with her father, whom she calls "my child," and whom she helps to support by dressing dolls. When Eugene first hears Jenny's topsy-turvy reference to her father, he guesses that she is referring to "'a doll?'" (291)—one, presumably, that she mothers as play rather than dressing as work. When he later introduces Mr. Cleaver to Mortimer, he solidifies this connection between Jenny's anomalous occupation and her anomalous domesticity: "'This interesting gentleman,' said Eugene, 'is the son . . . of a lady of my acquaintance. My dear Mortimer —Mr. Dolls.' Eugene had no idea what his name was, . . . but presented him with easy confidence under the first appellation that his associations suggested" (600). If, like Gaffer's savagery, Jenny's play is work, it is scarcely surprising, the novel suggests, that her biological father is her economic child. It is as if the inhabitants of the borderland between the economic and the extraeconomic cannot keep any of Victorian culture's crucial organizational categories straight.

The schoolmasters' initial failure to guess Jenny's employment suggests that the difficulty of categorizing and controlling work performed at the borders of the marketplace lies ultimately with the intellectual worker, whose responsibility it is to construct these categories. We are first introduced to Jenny's job through the eyes of schoolmasters, and to Venus's through the eyes of the "literary man," Silas Wegg. If Gaffer's task pushes "business" dangerously close to "savagery," in reading about him we push extraeconomic readerly pleasure toward the newly professionalized task of job classification. And we too find what we are looking for when Gaffer finds the dead body of the supposed John Harmon, revealing the nature of his activity. Elizabeth Ermarth cites the opening descriptions of both Gaffer and Venus, as well as "Eugene's struggle for the word that will save him . . . 'wife'" as instances "giving importance to the power of grasping the right clue, the key that gives name and form" (212). In all three instances the "right clue" designates an occupational category whose place in the division between public and private is problematized by the novel, and the "power of grasping" that clue is associated with the responsibilities of the professional observer. In Henry Mayhew's *London Labour and the London Poor*, on which Dickens drew heavily while writing *Our Mutual Friend*, such an observer emphasizes the ease with which he can classify river scavengers. The scavenger and his

> boat may be immediately distinguished from all others; there is nothing similar to them on the river. The sharp cutwater fore and aft, and short rounded appearance of the vessel, marks it out at once from the skiff or wherry of the waterman. (qtd. in Cotsell 17)

In the passage that introduces us to Gaffer, however, the same information links us with Gaffer's hesitating search rather than distancing us from it. From the first pages of *Our Mutual Friend*, intellectual labor is brought to bear on scavenger's work, and the result is an uneasy association between these tasks.

When Gaffer and Jenny are introduced to us, then, intellectual labor's hesitation in the classification of scavenger's work not only provides itself with a job to do, but also disturbs the division between market-oriented labor and extraeconomic activities and begins to threaten the entire meaning-making fabric of Victorian social divisions. In fact, the novel's famous crowd of scavengers—dustmen, "birds of prey," articulators of bones, dolls' dressmakers, bond brokers, and so on—illustrate the dangers of the border zone between the economic and the extraeconomic for those who also cannot avoid inhabiting it: the novel's equally numerous intellectual laborers—lawyers, secretaries, "literary men," and schoolteachers. *Our Mutual Friend* thus provides an answer to the riddle the Mad Hatter asks Alice in Wonderland: a raven is like a writing desk because ravens are scavengers, which, like writing desks, are associated (and even sometimes confused) with intellectual labor.

This linking of scavengers' and professionals' work is illustrated most vividly when Rogue Riderhood announces to Eugene and Mortimer his plans to "earn from five to ten thousand pounds by the sweat of my brow" by having his fictional account of Gaffer's confession "took down" (196). As Riderhood takes advantage of the confusion between stealing and work that Gaffer creates at the novel's opening, this confusion passes from macabre to comic. But Riderhood's expanded definition of labor is supported by the presence of the reluctant professionals Eugene and Mortimer, whose proper work—writing down people's statements, for example—is equally unlikely to produce sweating brows. Scavengers and intellectual laborers are similar, *Our Mutual Friend* seems to argue, because both obtain access to traditional capital by untraditional methods, methods that problematize the division between the economic and the extraeconomic. Gaffer himself is caught and assessed by the reader as he catches and assesses his prey, and the real John Harmon is soon engaged in the same task as Gaffer—catching and assessing what he can of the Harmon fortune, albeit by very different means and for very different purposes. As Boffin's secretary John Rokesmith, he seeks "the power of knowledge, the power derivable from a perfect comprehension of his business" (241). The economic realm is thus vulnerable to invasion not only by scavenging savages, but by the possessors of intellectual capital. The most sustained uneasiness in *Our Mutual Friend* about the value of particular forms of labor in a market economy thus finds its expression in the classificatory problems raised by intellectual workers.[6]

2. "That Necessity of Dropping It"

For the Victorians, the distinction between the economic and the extraeconomic is inevitably tied to the gendered division of labor. *Our Mutual Friend* begins to loosen this link when Noddy Boffin interviews Silas Wegg for the job of reader. As Boffin and Wegg complete their agreement, they emphasize a division between the public, masculine genre of history (in the suitably impressive form of Gibbon's *Decline and Fall of the Roman Empire*) and the intimate, feminine genre of "poetry" (in the less-canonical form of Wegg's stock of penny ballads, most of which feature domestic settings):

> "Was you thinking at all of poetry?" Mr. Wegg inquired, musing. . . .
> "To tell you the truth Wegg," said Boffin, "I wasn't thinking of poetry, except in so far as this:—if you was to happen now and then to feel yourself in the mind to tip me and Mrs. Boffin one of your ballads, why then we should drop into poetry."
> "I follow you, sir," said Wegg. "But not being a regular musical professional, I should be loath to engage myself for that; and therefore when I dropped into poetry, I should ask to be considered so fur, in the light of a friend." (95)

In other words, Wegg and Boffin agree to classify intellectual work as both production and consumption, capitalist and precapitalist, valuable and invaluable, by invoking the doctrine of separate spheres: one masculine, public, market-dominated (the historical reading Wegg does for Boffin at an hourly wage), one feminine, domestic, devoted to leisure (Wegg "dropping into poetry" for "me and Mrs. Boffin," not as an employee, but as a friend). Together, these separate spheres make a whole which fixes the relation between the money value produced in the marketplace and the moral values produced at home. The implication is that intellectual labor, rather than challenging this relation, reproduces it within itself.

But the problems posed by intellectual labor's relation to capitalist market relations cannot here be solved by recourse to the doctrine of separate spheres. Wegg, after all, possesses no genuine intellectual authority; he is a humorous grotesque whose legitimating use of the domestic sphere continually exposes his incompetence and greed. Although the "poetry" Wegg frequently drops into usually depicts domestic scenes of a sentimentally imagined past, he uses it, with often-ludicrous results, to express his own thoroughly prosaic, market-dominated concerns. For example, Wegg expresses his satisfaction at receiving the caretakership of the Bower rather than being merely pensioned off in a parody of Moore's Irish Ballad "Eveleen's Bower":

> Now, I no longer
> Weep for the hour,
> When to Boffinses bower,
> The Lord of the valley with offers came;
> Neither does the moon hide her light
> From the heavens tonight,
> And weep behind her clouds o'er any individual in the present Company's shame ...
> (236)

Stephen Gill's notes in the 1971 Penguin edition of *Our Mutual Friend* quote the original lines:

> Oh, weep for the hour
> When to Eveleen's bow'r
> The Lord of the valley with false vows came;
> The moon hid her light

From the heavens that night
And wept behind the clouds o'er the maiden's shame
(901)

Wegg uses the ballad to make an analogy between Eveleen's shame at succumbing to the Lord's "false vows" and his own at accepting money without "working" for it. The powerful analogy between class and gender relations, invoked by such different thinkers as Mary Wollstonecraft and (as we shall see) John Ruskin, is reduced here to yet another example of Wegg's shameless greed and hypocrisy and made to seem cheap and ludicrous—Wegg is far more like the exploiting "Lord" than the exploited Eveleen. The Victorian writer's feminized authority may place him above the dangers of the marketplace, but Wegg's parody of such authority, as Frances Armstrong notes (140–41), makes even the marketplace look good.

When he first arrives at Boffin's Bower, Wegg provides a textbook example of professional authority's simultaneous reliance on and exclusion of the private sphere when he corrects his employer's mistitling of *The Decline and Fall*:

> "I think you said Rooshan Empire, sir?"
> "It is Rooshan, ain't it, Wegg?"
> "No sir. Roman. Roman."
> "What's the difference, Wegg?"
> "The difference, sir?" Mr. Wegg was faltering and in danger of breaking down when a bright thought flashed upon him. "The difference, sir? There you place me in a difficulty, Mr. Boffin. Suffice it to observe, that the difference is best postponed to some other occasion when Mrs. Boffin does not honour us with her company. In Mrs. Boffin's presence, sir, we had better drop it." (103)

To save his status as "literary man," Wegg marks out history as an area from which proper ladies must be excluded. At the same time, he transforms a joke about Britain's imperial competitor into a lesson in the proper way of conducting middle-class gender relations.[7] Boffin, newly risen from the working class, takes the lesson to heart, feeling that "he had committed himself in a very painful manner" (103). But as Wegg begins to read, the Boffins' interpretations of the public and political activities of the Roman Empire challenge his reliance on the complementarity of public and private by taking unintentional advantage of his incompetence: "Then Mr. Wegg...entered on his task... stumbling at Polybius (pronounced Polly Beeious, and supposed by Mr. Boffin to be a Roman virgin and by Mrs. Boffin to be responsible for that necessity of dropping it)" (103). The combined work of Wegg, Mr. Boffin, and Mrs. Boffin transforms the ancient historian (one of Gibbon's sources for the *Decline and Fall*) and progenitor of cultural capital into a woman whose offspring we can only imagine as literal and illegitimate. In the figure of Silas Wegg, we see the androgynous intellectual's "manly delicacy" (103) subverting the very task it sets out to accomplish.

It is not only Wegg's incompetence that allows this subversion. The very Bower he invades does so as well. In his lecture "Of Queens' Gardens," John Ruskin describes the beneficent power of womanly influence: "And wherever a true wife comes, this home is always round her...and for a noble woman it stretches far round her, better than ceiled with cedar, or painted with vermilion, shedding its quiet light far, for those who else were homeless" (*Sesame* 122–23). This "stretching" shelter almost seems to be parodied in Mrs. Boffin's spreading and retreating carpet in Boffin's Bower. Explaining the division of the Bower's sitting room into ostentatious bourgeois parlor and homey working-class pub, Boffin tells Wegg:

> If I get by degrees to be a higher-flyer at Fashion, then Mrs. Boffin will by degrees come for'arder. If Mrs. Boffin should ever be less of a dab at Fashion than she is at the present time, then Mrs. Boffin's carpet would go back'arder. (100)

For Ruskin, the domestic woman provides men with both comfort and fashion, without needing any equipment to do so. In Dickens's version, however, our attention is drawn not to the interdependence of masculinity and femininity, but to a comparison of their accoutrements. It is significant that, as the novel begins to abandon its early jokes at the Boffins' expense, they also abandon the divided Bower for the undivided "fashion" of their West End house—and Wegg's "manly delicacy" for the sounder advice of the secretary Rokesmith.

In fact, the doctrine of separate spheres, parodied by the Boffins' first inept social pretensions and the last resort of intellectual pretenders like Silas Wegg, receives a sustained attack in *Our Mutual Friend*. When Eugene Wrayburn and Mortimer Lightwood set up house together, Eugene has one room "very completely and neatly fitted as a kitchen," joking that its "'moral influence ... in forming the domestic virtues, may have an immense influence upon me'" (337). Despite the disapproval we are expected to feel toward Eugene at this stage, this literalizing parody of the benefits of domestic influence would seem to be echoed by the novel itself. Its well-known condemnation of capitalist exchange is not balanced by a celebration of the home as an enclave shielded from market forces; instead, the domestic woman's special influence is depicted over and over again as illusory or futile. Indeed, in Dickens's fiction in general the family cannot be trusted to provide an automatic solution to the problems posed by the public sphere; that solution must be artificially constructed from extrafamilial elements. Dickens often depicts the bourgeois nuclear family as the site of disorder, lovelessness, and conflict, and domestic femininity as more likely to prohibit than promote domestic bliss (think, for example, of the instrument-maker's shop versus the Dombey home in *Dombey and Son*, the circus versus the Gradgrind home in *Hard Times*, and Wemmick's castle versus the Pockets' household in *Great Expectations*). Alexander Welsh notes that "the Dickensian celebration of hearth and home is so familiar that it requires little documentation in itself," but goes on to remind us that Dickens's famous snug interiors are most often created by additions to or variations on "the conjugal family" (*City* 142). Patricia Ingham writes of "a pervasive disturbance of family relationships" in Dickens's fiction, "overwritten by new and more highly valued bonds" (118). In *Our Mutual Friend* this disturbance extends from the family itself to the very idea of domestic femininity. Bella Wilfer and Lizzie Hexam do provide their eventual husbands with certification as the novel's normative voices—but *not* by embodying domestic power. In fact, the counterfeit secretary John Rokesmith/Harmon and the reluctant barrister Eugene Wrayburn—the men who will turn out to be "truly qualified" at novel's end—gain their qualifications through the demystification of domestic power and its replacement by pedagogic authority.[8]

Although Bella Wilfer charmed many of her contemporaries (see Collins, *Critical Heritage* 453–76), twentieth-century readers tend to be disappointed by the transformation of the independent and intelligent girl into a paragon of bourgeois domesticity at Blackheath, immersed in cookery books and living in true wifely ignorance of her husband's City job. Ruth Yeazell, for example, complains that "Bella begins as one of Dickens' more complex female characters, but on her way to becoming a redeemed and redeeming heroine, Dickensian sentiment overtakes her" (348–49). But this process is also one in which bourgeois domesticity itself is first parodied, then shown to be artificially constructed, and finally rendered irrelevant. When Mr. Inspector arrives at the cottage to arrest Bella's husband, he plays on the distinction between "matters of business" and those "of a strictly domestic character" in order to avoid arresting him in front of her:

> "[L]adies are apt to take alarm at matters of business—being of that fragile sex that they're not accustomed to them when not of a strictly domestic character—and I do generally make it a rule to propose retirement from the presence of ladies, before entering upon business topics." (830–31)

The inspector's intervention, of course, will result in no rough masculine business from which Bella must be shielded. Rather, it will reveal that Bella's contented isolation at Blackheath is not the novel's happy ending, but merely a test of her loyalty and lack of avarice, the passing of which will lead her out of that isolation. In fact, the novel's actual happy ending demands the dissolution of the division between matters of "business" and those of "a strictly domestic character": once Bella is installed in her West End mansion, she will be too rich to need her housewifely expertise, and her husband's City job will be exposed as a mere fiction. Bella accomplishes her husband's triumph not by adopting domesticity, but through the placement of that domesticity in a pedagogical framework, not by *becoming* a good bourgeois wife, but by *passing a test* as a good bourgeois wife.

The rewriting of domesticity as examination entails the replacement of domestic power with invigilatory power. Entering the Wilfer household as a substitute for Mrs. Wilfer's ill-fated "ladies' academy" (76), John Rokesmith/Harmon is much better at testing Bella than Mrs. Wilfer would have been at teaching the "young ladies" recommended by the milkman. Even before the famous ruse begins, their mutual attraction casts Bella as student and John as moral inspector. He is able to elicit in her a new sense of responsibility toward her family merely by remarking that "'You never charge me, Miss Wilfer, ... with commissions for home. I shall always be happy to execute any commands you may have in that direction'" (363). By the end of their "little interview," Bella finds "that he unquestionably left her with a penitent air upon her, and a penitent feeling in her heart," and realizes "that she had not had an intention or a thought of going home, until she had announced it to him as a settled design" (364).

Once the ruse does begin, Bella is always accompanied by John's "semi-omniscient" invigilation (Jaffe, *Vanishing* 14–15). When she and John leave Betty Higdon's funeral, narrator, reader, and even the train they take are asked to share in John's eroticized view of her:

> O boofer lady, fascinating boofer lady! If I were but legally executor of Johnny's will [where he leaves "a kiss for the boofer lady"]! If I had but the right to pay your legacy and take your receipt!— Something to this purpose surely mingled with the blast of the train as it cleared the stations, all knowingly shutting up their green eyes and opening their red ones when they prepared to let the boofer lady pass. (594)

In other words, although we do not see him, as the ruse progresses John's perspective melts into that of a suddenly arch and personified narrator, always present to supervise and judge Bella's progress in her scholarly attempts at domesticity:

> [A]bove all such severe study! For Mrs. J. R., who had never been wont to do too much at home as Miss B. W., was under the constant necessity of referring for advice and support to a sage volume entitled The Complete British Family Housewife, which she would sit consulting, with her elbows on the table and her temples on her hands. (749)

The growing reliance of British housewives on manuals like Mrs. Beeton's 1861 *Book of Household Management* formed part of the professionalization of women's domestic roles at midcentury, denaturalizing women's natural aptitude for household chores (Burstyn 38). The archness of this description reminds us that the professionalization of housework does not necessarily guarantee its importation into the public sphere. Bella and John demonstrate that traditional gender roles require no gendered division between professional life and domestic life; it can be replaced, indeed improved upon, by the division between teacher and student.

When we first meet that most domestically angelic of heroines, Lizzie Hexam, she plans a future with her father, "keeping him as straight as I can, watching for more influence than I have" (73). But as she seems to guess, Lizzie exudes womanly influence to singularly little effect. Not only does she fail to reform Gaffer, but the brother she raises with such perfect womanly self-sacrifice grows up selfish and cruel. Her would-be seducer, Eugene, changes his ways not because of her virtuous pleading but because of a schoolteacher's more masculine chastisement. When Lizzie does wield domestic power effectively, she does so against her own will, and destructively. Bradley claims that Lizzie "could draw me to any good," but this seems an afterthought to his main point, which is that "'you could draw me to any exposure and disgrace. This, and the confusion of my thoughts, so that I am fit for nothing, is what I mean by your being the ruin of me'" (455). When he discovers her hiding place, Eugene makes use of the concept of womanly influence to suggest that Lizzie's power be blamed for her own potential ruin as well: "'I don't complain that you design to keep me here. But you do it, you do it'" (759).⁹

Eugene's pursuit of Lizzie is nevertheless synonymous, as Sedgwick shows in *Between Men*, with his transformation from aristocratic to professional gentleman. Lizzie makes Eugene into a good lawyer—not, however, as an angelic influence, but as the contested site of pedagogic action. Coaxing her to accept his gift of lessons, he claims that

> "Your false pride does wrong to yourself and does wrong to your dead father."
>
> "How to my father, Mr. Wrayburn?" she asked, with an anxious face.
>
> "How to your father? Can you ask! By perpetuating the consequences of his ignorant and blind obstinacy. By resolving not to set right the wrong he did you. By determining that the deprivation to which he condemned you, and which he forced upon you, shall always rest upon his head."
>
> It chanced to be a subtle string to sound, in her who had so spoken to her brother within the hour. It sounded more forcibly because of the change in the speaker for the moment; the passing appearance of earnestness, complete conviction, injured resentment of suspicion, generous and unselfish interest. (286)

His claim to be the "idlest and least of lawyers" (287) is hardly convincing: expert at arguing a shaky case, and at convincing the jury of his belief in his client's innocence, Eugene demonstrates in his pursuit of Lizzie-as-pupil the makings of an excellent barrister.

The novel's replacement of the domestic angel with the schoolgirl raises two questions. First, why *school*? Why does the novel turn from the domestic haven to the figurative classroom as a site for the legitimation of professional authority? Second, why *girl*? How can masculine intellectual labor make use of a femininity robbed of domestic authority? Bourdieu and Passeron show how what they call "Pedagogic Action (PA)" assists a given class or group in enforcing boundaries between acceptable and unacceptable categories of knowledge. It would seem that the examination is particularly suited to this goal, but at the opening of *Our Mutual Friend* examinations quite ostentatiously fail to achieve it. By novel's end, however, tests administered by Noddy Boffin and Bradley Headstone successfully sort people and information into their proper places. In the rest of this chapter, I will show how the Dust-Heap and River plots of *Our Mutual Friend* are also plots about the perfecting of pedagogical mechanisms, making the novel itself into a vast examination room.

3. The Angel in the State

In *Our Mutual Friend* Dickens follows Arnold and Trollope in depicting the state as embued with the virtues of domesticity. If the novel's homes fail to provide an effective setting for domestic power, professional power is comfortably at home in the novel's state institutions. Whatever the problems faced by professional expertise in private or commercial life, the authority of such figures as the doctors in the Children's Hospital, the police inspector, and the schoolmistresslike Abbey Potterson goes unchallenged within institutional walls. When the inspector orders "'You *must* come up. I mean to have you,'" even Gaffer's hidden corpse responds, becoming untangled from the rope in which it is caught: "There was so much virtue in this distinctly and decidedly meaning to have it, that it yielded a little, even while the line was played" (220–21). An "inveterate visitor of institutions" (Collins, *Education* 27), Dickens was also a famously inveterate critic of schools, prisons, courts, workhouses, and government offices. In *Our Mutual Friend*, however, while Betty Higdon's story condemns the Victorian workhouse, it is hinted that keeping little Johnny in her charming cottage leads to his death. At the Children's Hospital where he goes to die, the doctor comments, "'This should have been days ago. Too late!'" (383). Once arrived at the hospital, however, the former rather sulky infant becomes "one of a little family, all in little quiet beds," guarded by "a coloured picture ... representing as it were another Johnny seated on the knee of some Angel surely who loved little children" (384). Throughout the novel, government institutions are havens of peace, order, nourishment, and tenderness (F. Armstrong 148). The violence and disorder of the riverside neighborhood are excluded when Mortimer and Eugene go to view Gaffer Hexam's find at "the wicket-gate and bright light of a Police Station; where they found the Night-Inspector, with a pen and ink, and ruler, posting up his books in a whitewashed office, as studiously as if he were in a monastery on top of a mountain" (66). Positive depictions of private businesses in the novel depend on their mimicking, not families, but public institutions: Miss Abbey Potterson, landlady of the Six Jolly Fellowship Porters (one of Dickens's most inviting pubs), has "more of the air of a schoolmistress than mistress of" a pub, and Riderhood approaches her "as if he were one of her pupils in disgrace" (107). At the paper mill that provides a haven for Lizzie Hexam when she flees from Eugene's seductions and Bradley's threats, the kindly Jewish proprietors protect her in the same way the Factory Laws were supposed to protect her real-life contemporaries, easing her workload and enabling her to remain a virtuous woman: "Indeed they do much more than their duty to us, for they are wonderfully mindful of us in many ways" (579).[10]

Our Mutual Friend is sometimes called Dickens's "modernist" novel, questioning the Victorian certainties of his earlier works. Jonathan Arac argues that the lack of a typical Dickensian overview in the novel is related to contemporary advances in centralization and institutionalization (181–82). Certainly, in resolving the contradictions of nineteenth-century intellectual labor, the novel gives the state-run institution a new role. The "public" institutions in the novel provide the only extraeconomic shelter available from the painful and disorderly "private" world of economic and domestic relations. In marked contrast to his earlier fiction, in *Our Mutual Friend* Dickens shares Arnold's belief that the familial havens provided by institutions can remake working-class culture in bourgeois culture's image. If, in Arnold's *Reports*, working-class domesticity is impossible to imagine, in *Our Mutual Friend* the working-class domestic realm is depicted as one of danger and corruption.

Working-class angels like Lizzie must be replaced by professionals—doctors, teachers, inspectors—angels in the state-run "house." But unlike the bureaucrats Arnold and Trollope, they cannot rest in this haven. Given the view of domesticity provided in *Our Mutual Friend*, this figuring of institutionalized professional power suggests that it might share the isolation and fragility of feminine influence.

Arac argues that institutionalization influenced *Our Mutual Friend* by taking the novelist's job: "What had once been the novelist's prophetic task [overview] is now safely in the hands of the constituted authorities.... [T]he novelist steps away from complicity with the establishment by abandoning the position of overview" (183). By 1865, centralized institutions provided the glue of Victorian society, so the novelist could abandon centralizing omniscience. But the actual institutions depicted in *Our Mutual Friend* represent its least-connected entities. Enclaves of comfort and order, they are nevertheless threatened enclaves, tiny, fragile, and, like Lizzie's womanly influence, ultimately ineffectual. Despite the power of professional expertise within their borders, it cannot transcend them. Like the novel's other institutions, the rather sterile schools run by Bradley Headstone and Miss Peecher are placed by their opening description in the realm of fantasy, fairytales, and childhood:

> The schools were newly built, and there were so many like them all over the country, that one might have thought the whole were but one restless edifice with the locomotive gift of Aladdin's palace. They were in a neighbourhood which looked like a toy neighbourhood taken in blocks out of a box by a child of a particularly incoherent mind. (267–68)

This placement, however, emphasizes the extent to which this realm is also one of dissociation and powerlessness, where the institution's very ubiquity suggests not plenitude, but a "restless" scarcity. Little Johnny can be comforted by the cleanliness and company at the hospital, but he dies nonetheless. The inspector proceeds with his monklike task only by ignoring the "howling fury of a drunken woman... banging herself against a cell-door in the back-yard at his elbow" (66), and he never does apprehend George Radfoot's murderer.

In *Reproduction in Education, Society, and Culture*, Pierre Bourdieu and Jean-Claude Passeron provide a valuable sketch of the actual mechanisms by which Althusser's School Ideological State Apparatus reproduces the subjects of capitalism, demonstrating how institutionalized education can dispense with the mystification that guards the inexplicit education provided by the family. The school

> would lay itself open to the question of its right to set up a relation of pedagogic communication and to delimit what deserves to be inculcated—were it not that the very fact of institutionalization gives it the specific means of annihilating the possibility of this question. (62)

Institutionalization allows the task of what Bourdieu and Passeron call the "Educational System"—the reproduction of relations of production—to become explicit without becoming demystified. Because of the tardy, gradual, piecemeal process of its institutionalization in Britain, however, the disinterestedness of the Educational System could never be taken for granted in the nineteenth century. The result of this "uneven development" is that the school became the focus of conflicts over the relationship between capitalism and the state. In *Our Mutual Friend*, Dickens takes advantage of this moment of ambivalence, creating figurative versions of the classroom examination that, like Arnold's inspections, authenticate an intellectual authority that transcends market value. At the same time, he insists with Trollope on the incapacity of the school—inextricable from a capitalist economy of "restless" exchange—to do so.

4. "A Little Free Trade"

Examinations do not at first glance seem to solidify social categories in *Our Mutual Friend*. Instead, the novel shows how the examination can blur these distinctions, as it does in Miss Peecher's quizzing of Mary Anne:

"And where," pursued Miss Peecher, complacent in her little transparent fiction of conducting the examination in a semi-official manner for Mary Anne's benefit, not her own, "where does this young woman, who is called but not named Lizzie, live? Think, now, before answering."

"In Church Street, Smith Square, by Mill Bank, ma'am."

"In Church Street, Smith Square, by Mill Bank," repeated Miss Peecher, as if possessed beforehand of the book in which it was written. "Exactly so." (394–95)

Her perversion of her professional role to gain information about her rival in Bradley Headstone's affections demonstrates the utter lack of separation between public and private in Miss Peecher's self-conception: "If Mr. Bradley Headstone had addressed a written proposal of marriage to her, she would probably have replied in a complete little essay on the theme exactly a slate long, but would certainly have replied Yes" (268). Rather than helping to keep occupational categories intact, for most of the novel educational testing merely demonstrates their lack of fixity. As examination follows examination, the novel's never-ending series of questions begins to point to an insufficiency of answers.

The indiscriminate testing in *Our Mutual Friend* calls into question one of the examination's most important functions: discrimination. The novel's "catechisms" vary widely in their aims and effectiveness, and the question soon becomes how to test the tests. If, as I have argued, the novel's scavengers and intellectual workers play analogous roles, one would expect that the examination would perform the same task for knowledge as the novel's scavengers do for rubbish: sorting it, sifting it, carrying it away, and refitting it into the grid of social and economic relations. But professional intellectual workers have no monopoly on the display of intellectual labor here, and there is no guarantee of examinations' ability to assign value. While Miss Peecher does get the right answers out of Mary Anne, the information does nothing toward helping her fulfill her desire for Bradley. Like so many of the novel's examinations, Miss Peecher's test fails to carry out its disciplinary function—it differentiates neither individuals nor cultural categories; it empowers neither the imparters nor the recipients of information. What qualifications ought testers and test-takers to possess? What ought an exam to demonstrate or change? How can it be made to work as both a certifying and an educational mechanism? These questions must be answered if the novel is to right its occupational displacements and thus its dangerously unfixed social hierarchy.

As we move from the Veneerings' lavish dining table to Gaffer's decrepit shack in the novel's second chapter, we are shown an obsolete class system of knowledge which cannot help exam givers and takers. As Mortimer Lightwood begins the story of "The Man from Somewhere," he proves himself a gentleman (and thus pays for his dinner) by displaying no professional or even scholastic knowledge, but instead showing off his ease of allusion to popular texts such as ballads, fairytales, and three-volume novels. When the working-class social climber Charley Hexam enters with his note about his father's find, he continues the story—but in the register of schoolroom learning, flashing an ostentatious wealth of biblical allusion:

> "Pharaoh's multitudes that were drowned in the Red Sea, ain't more beyond restoring to life. If Lazarus was only half as far gone, that was the greatest of all the miracles."
> "Halloa!" cried Mortimer, turning round with his hat upon his head, "you seem to be at home in the Red Sea, my young friend?"
> "Read of it with teacher at the school," said the boy. (61)

The hierarchy is made brutally clear; while Charley demonstrates his power over the printed word with his gaze at the books in the Veneering library ("he glanced at the backs of the books, with an awakened curiosity that went below the bindings" [60–61]), Eugene neutralizes this power by gazing at Charley's face:

> "You seem to have a good sister."
> "She ain't half bad," said the boy; "but if she knows her letters it's the most she does—and them I learned her."
> The gloomy Eugene, with his hands in his pockets, had strolled

in and assisted at the latter part of the dialogue; when the boy spoke these words slightingly of his sister, he took him roughly enough by the chin, and turned up his face to look at it.

"Well, I'm sure, sir!" said the boy, resisting; "I hope you'll know me again." (61)

This moment provides the starting point for the chain of triangulated relationships, "a chain reaching from the lowest class up to the professional class" (Sedgwick 105), which Eve Sedgwick powerfully demonstrates as eventually leading Eugene from homosocial bonds associated with an obsolete, aristocratic gentility to professional-class gentility and heterosexuality. Eugene's scrutiny also provides the starting point for a chain of examinations, through which the novel organizes the necessary institutional structures to support this new kind of gentleman. At the beginning of his journey, Eugene, who is quick to proclaim that "'I hate my profession'" (62), is placed in opposition to the values of intellectual labor. The intellectual worker's traditional weapon—the interpretive gaze—is here used against the intellectual worker-in-training Charley by an aristocrat and a working-class woman who read people and events, not books. Eugene's contemptuous gaze at Charley's scorn for Lizzie's lack of scholastic knowledge creates an alliance between his aristocratic authority and Lizzie's domestic authority, vindicating Lizzie's fortune-telling gaze at the fire and denigrating scholastic knowledge—the tool of the male middle class.

But this antischolastic alliance is extended to breaking point when Eugene and Mortimer arrive at the Hexams' in search of John Harmon's dead body. They are treated there to Gaffer's display of his collection of "Body Found" posters:

"I can't read, nor I don't want to it, for I know 'em by their places on the wall. This one was a sailor, with two anchors and a flag and G. F. T. on his arm. Look and see if he warn't."

"Quite right."

"This one was the young woman in grey boots, and her linen marked with a cross. Look and see if she warn't."

"Quite right."

"... They pretty well papers the room, you see; but I know 'em all. I'm scholar enough!" (64–65)

Gaffer invokes the authority that an examination wields in order to challenge the authority that gives examinations. With his perfect score on this test, he insists on an alternative definition of literacy, with its own texts (appropriately enough, those that attest to his unconventional expertise at finding bodies) and its own methods of interpreting them. Eugene and Mortimer are unable to challenge this alternative literacy because the power for that challenge can only come from within the pedagogical system itself. Without pedagogical authority, they can only deem Gaffer "'Quite right.'" Eugene's and Mortimer's aristocratic resistance to scholastic knowledge finds itself in alliance not only with Lizzie's fire-gazing but with Gaffer's working-class expertise. We are left with an array of knowledges, and no mechanism for hierarchizing them.

While Eugene and Mortimer lack the investment in scholarly knowledge necessary to differentiate themselves from Gaffer's illiteracy, the instructors at the church-run Ragged School where Charley Hexam gets his start lack the aristocrat's and woman's power to see things other than texts clearly, and the result is that

> Young women old in the vices of the commonest and worst life, were expected to profess themselves enthralled by the good child's book, the Adventures of Little Margery.... [U]nwieldy young dredgers and hulking mudlarks were referred to the experiences of Thomas Twopence.... An exceedingly and confoundingly perplexing jumble of a school, in fact, where black spirits and grey, red spirits and white, jumbled jumbled jumbled jumbled, jumbled every night. (263–64)[11]

The interaction of classes here certainly does not result in the takeover of working-class modes of knowledge by middle-class modes of knowledge. In order to perform his function of "reorganiz[ing] and reshap[ing] working-class life" (Ehrenreich and Ehrenreich 16), the professional must somehow combine the intellectual capital of the Ragged

School instructors with the extra-institutional gaze associated with aristocratic and domestic power.

Like the River plot, the Dust Heap plot also opens with a test that needs testing:

> "Did you ever hear of the name of Boffin?"
>
> "No," said Mr. Wegg, who was growing restive under this examination. "I never did hear of the name of Boffin."
>
> "Do you like it?"
>
> "Why, no," retorted Mr. Wegg, again approaching desperation; "I can't say I do."
>
> "Why don't you like it?"
>
> "I don't know why I don't," retorted Mr. Wegg, approaching frenzy, "but I don't at all."
>
> "Now, I'll tell you something that'll make you sorry for that," said the stranger, smiling. "My name's Boffin."
>
> "I can't help it!" returned Mr. Wegg. Implying in his manner the offensive addition, "and if I could, I wouldn't." (91)

Having decided to "invest a bow" (88) in Boffin, Wegg submits to "examination," but with as bad a grace as possible. And no wonder: it is hard to tell what Boffin hopes to determine about Wegg in this nonsensical quiz and the reader is given no hint to his interpretation of Wegg's responses. While possessed of the monetary power to purchase Wegg's literacy, Mr. Boffin lacks the criteria with which to judge it. Like Eugene and Mortimer's reluctant examination of Gaffer, Boffin's cross-questioning of Wegg produces no results because all three lack the pedagogic authority granted by an allegiance to the professional class's interests. Sensing this vacancy, Wegg is quick to fill it with spurious pedagogic authority of his own. He begins to word his answers to Boffin's quiz in smoothly (if ungrammatically) authoritative language that advertises his (nonexistent) erudition:

> "But there's another chance for you," said Mr. Boffin, smiling still, "Do you like the name of Nicodemus? Think it over. Nick, or Noddy."

"It is not, sir," Mr. Wegg rejoined as he sat down on his stool, with an air of gentle resignation, combined with melancholy candour; "it is not a name as I could wish any one that I had a respect for, to call *me* by; but there may be persons that would not view it with the same objections." (91)[12]

Boffin's and Wegg's transaction concludes with Boffin's helpless acceptance of Wegg's extortionate terms, as he confesses that "'You know better what it ought to be than I do, Wegg'" (96). But while both Gaffer's and Wegg's performances suggest the temporary success of illicit modes of knowledge, neither is able to instate their mode of knowledge as legitimate. If, at the beginning of their stories, Mr. Boffin and Eugene lack the pedagogic authority required in an examiner, Gaffer and Wegg have no standard to set up once they are in fact faced with genuine, certified intellectual labor. Only death saves Gaffer from being falsely accused in Riderhood's ostentatiously written "Alfred David" (195), and even Wegg is finally outfoxed with the help of Boffin's secretary, the ostentatiously literate Harmon/Rokesmith. As the River and Dust Heap plots develop, *Our Mutual Friend* begins to set up examinations that do grant pedagogic authority to examiners and the rewards of cultural capital to test-takers.

Of course, there is cultural capital and cultural capital, as dramatized most vividly in the career of the self-made schoolteacher-turned-homicidal maniac, Bradley Headstone. Bradley's education is firmly associated with the market economy so savagely critiqued throughout the novel (David 57). The contents of his "wholesale warehouse" of a brain, arranged "so that it might be always ready to meet the demands of retail dealers," seem almost a comic literalization of the term "cultural capital" itself. Under the Revised Code, the Education Department's institution of "a little free trade" in the state-funded classroom, each school was granted a specific amount for each passing grade awarded, and schoolteachers' jobs thus depended on their students' answers. With payment by results, "if child labour and irregular school attendance was a matter of essential hard cash for poor parents, the same was true, in reverse, for poor teachers" (P. Miller 141). G. W. Kekewich, later Secretary to the Board of Education, comments: "[I]magine the feelings of the unfortunate teacher when he looked over the inspector's shoulder and saw the failures being recorded wholesale, and knew that his annual salary was being reduced by 2 and eightpence for each failure" (Edmonds 81). During the yearly inspection of the Tysoe village school in Warwickshire, M. K. Ashby reports,

> The master hovered round, calling children out as they were needed. The children could see him start with vexation as a good pupil stuck at a word in the reading-book he had been using all the year.... The master's anxiety was deep, for his earnings depended on the children's work. One year the atmosphere of anxiety so affected the lower standards that, one after another as they were brought to the Inspector, the boys howled and the girls whimpered. (qtd. in Digby and Searby 9)

The instructor's dependence on the answers of his students in payment-by-results examinations, and the way in which the inspections undermined his authority by causing him to display his anxiety are taken one step further in *Our Mutual Friend*. The classrooms of Dickens are often places of violence or repression: one only has to think of Salem House, Mr. Squeers's and Doctor Blimber's academies, or Mr. Gradgrind's model school. But in these schools students are for the most part pitted against teachers, whether as thrashed, forced, or deadened victims or spoiled and misguided aggressors. In *Our Mutual Friend*, however, the classroom is a place of danger for the teacher, not because his students are bullies, but because they are docile. When Bradley heads grimly toward his final confrontation with Riderhood, he thinks of his school as "the place where the children with pointing arms had seemed to devote him to the demons in crying out his name" (868) during Riderhood's blackmailing inspection, "in the way of school," after the attack on Eugene:

> "Master, might I, afore I go, ask a question of these here young lambs of yourn?"

"If it is in the way of school," said Bradley, always sustaining his dark look at the other, and speaking in his suppressed voice, "you may."

"Oh! It's in the way of school!" cried Riderhood. "I'll pound it, Master, to be in the way of school. Wot's the diwisions of water, my lambs? Wot sorts of water is there on the land?"

Shrill chorus: "Seas, rivers, lakes, and ponds."

"Seas, rivers, lakes, and ponds," said Riderhood. "They've got all the lot, Master! Blowed if I shouldn't have left out lakes, never having clapped eyes upon one, to my knowledge. Seas, rivers, lakes, and ponds. Wot is it, lambs, as they ketches in seas, rivers, lakes, and ponds?"

Shrill chorus (with some contempt for the ease of the question): "Fish!"

"Good a-gin!" said Riderhood. "But wot else is it, my lambs, as they sometimes ketches in rivers?"

Chorus at a loss. One shrill voice: "Weed!"

"Good agin!" cried Riderhood. "But it ain't weed neither. You'll never guess, my dears. Wot is it, besides fish, as they sometimes ketches in rivers? Well! I'll tell you. It's suits o' clothes."

Bradley's face changed.

"Leastwise, lambs," said Riderhood, observing him out of the corner of his eyes, "that's wot I my own self sometimes ketches in rivers. For strike me blind, my lambs, if I didn't ketch in a river the wery bundle under my arm!"

The class looked at the master, as if appealing from the irregular entrapment of this mode of examination. The master looked at the examiner, as if he would have torn him to pieces. (866–67)

Although payment-by-results examinations were conducted child by child, this passage nevertheless bears a striking resemblance to the description of the Tysoe school inspection and others like it. As Altick comments, Riderhood takes on "the role of an illiterate Matthew Arnold, becomes H.M. Inspector of schools in Headstone's classroom" (246). His blackmailing threat fits with startling ease into the inspection scenario—whether Arnold's or the Revised Code's.

Riderhood's examination translates knowledge into money even more directly than actual payment-by-results inspections, as he threatens to clear out Bradley's literal, as well as his scholastic, bank account:

> "You can't get blood out of a stone, Riderhood."
> "I can get money out of a schoolmaster though." (871)

It would seem that the institution's fragility in *Our Mutual Friend* stems, paradoxically, from its not being institutional enough: to return to Bourdieu and Passeron's terms, when the "cultural arbitrary" inculcated by "pedagogic action" is insufficiently backed by the culture, it becomes merely—and all too visibly—arbitrary. Riderhood's exam raises the possibility that "free trade" renders "pedagogic authority" a little *too* free. Because of its emphasis on authorized versions, the Revised Code exam would seem to be the perfect way to distinguish legitimate from illegitimate knowledge. Indeed, Riderhood establishes his right to question Bradley's students with his pedagogically phrased question about "diwisions of water." By the time his lesson becomes less conventional, it is too late. Although the class notes and objects to the unorthodoxy of the answer "suits o' clothes," their only appeal is to the already conquered Bradley. Despite its constant policing of the boundaries of knowledge, free-trade education lets them slip here with fatal ease: the classification of bodies of water slides into the discovery of the clue to an attempted murder, failing to mark the distinction between the things children should know and the things they should be shielded from. Riderhood can cause this slippage, replacing the "highly certified" (265) Bradley and destroying the latter's authority over his students merely by "pounding" his threat "to be in the way of school."

Part of the horror in Riderhood's examination is that, while vanquishing Bradley, he also serves as his double—dramatizing (and demonizing) the class displacement Bradley himself represents. Like many Victorian advocates of increased state support for education, Dickens saw the education of the working class as a deterrent to crime (Collins, *Education* 6). In Riderhood's inspection of Bradley's class, however, the ability of education to replace crime seems to be figured in a nightmare reversal: the ability of crime to replace education, and of educational methods to represent the crime of blackmail. In fact, the novel draws many comparisons between Bradley's market-determined methods of learning and his methods of committing murder. He uses the same strategies of production and exchange when he attempts to implicate Riderhood by copying his clothing ("he must have committed [Riderhood's clothing] to memory, and slowly got it by heart" [697]) as he has used to fill his warehouse-brain with knowledge. There is even a hint that Bradley is an ineffective murderer for the same reasons that he is an ineffective teacher: "Riderhood occupied a very different place [in his thoughts], from the place of pursuer; and Bradley had been at the pains of devising so many means of fitting that place to him, and of wedging him into it, that his mind could not compass the possibility of his occupying any other" (776). He is incapable of realizing that Riderhood can betray him because he has placed him "mechanically" on a certain shelf of his mental warehouse. As teacher and as murderer, he is a slow, plodding, inflexible thinker.

Our Mutual Friend thus enacts a profound uneasiness about institutionalized free-trade education and the ease with which it can be perverted to private—indeed to criminal—ends. Bradley's market-classroom provides no protection against unauthorized systems of knowledge, whether aristocratic, working-class, feminine, or criminal, because it is unable to "resolve by its very existence the questions raised by its existence" (Bourdieu and Passeron 62). As fragile as the novel's other institutional enclaves, the school fails because it is too easily identified as imposing a cultural arbitrary. The novel instead asks us to invigilate at a series of examinations that take place outside the literal classroom, and that thus authorize legitimate agents of pedagogic action without displaying the arbitrariness of their authority.

5. The Critical Pedagogy of *Our Mutual Friend*

These examinations involve a pedagogical economy that continues to inform debates on gender and teaching. In recent years, critical pedagogy has argued for methods that develop, rather than displace, what already exists: students' identities, capabilities, and histories are to be fostered rather than formed (see, for example, Freire; Giroux and McLaren; and Ellsworth). In an early and indeed reductive version of this theoretical position, the 1986 *Women's Ways of Knowing* uses Paulo Freire's description of the "banking concept" of education in order to develop a gendered contrast between "objectivist" and "subjectivist" (Stone, "Toward" 122–23) models of education: "Midwife-teachers are the opposite of banker-teachers. While the bankers deposit knowledge in the learner's head, the midwives draw it out. They assist the students in giving birth to their own ideas, in making their own tacit knowledge explicit and elaborating it" (Belenky et al. 217). Later feminist theorists of pedagogy have been rightly suspicious of the banker/midwife couple. For example, Lynda Stone critiques versions of both the banking and the midwife models. While "objectivist" approaches to education figure knowledge as material to be absorbed by the pupil, "subjectivist" approaches entail the learning not so much of facts as of one's own approach to facts (122–23). Stone argues that both objectivist and subjectivist educational theories are "harmful because they have been theorized within the traditional epistemological dichotomy" of subject and object (125). Rather than deconstructing the gender-biased subject/object split, they merely replicate it. Like the better-known heterosexual couples subject/object, public/private, and production/consumption, the banker/midwife couple mystifies the mutually constitutive class and gender relations that structure both nineteenth- and twentieth-century Western culture. By placing it in a competitive relationship with the "masculine" banking model, the proponents of the midwife model allow us to forget where babies come from. Bourdieu and Passeron critique

> the spontaneist Utopia which accords the individual the power to find within himself the principle of his own "fulfillment.". . . The idea of a "culturally free" [teaching method] . . . presupposes a misrecognition of the . . . objective truth of a violence whose specificity lies in the fact that it generates the illusion that it is not violence. (16–17)

All pedagogic action inculcates a cultural arbitrary. But some pedagogies may hide this fact better than others, and thus prove more effective.

In *Our Mutual Friend*, as in *Women's Ways of Knowing*, the bringing forth of preexisting ideas in feminine pupils is strongly valued over the depositing of information in masculine heads: while the latter is associated with the illicit climb to professional status of working-class men like Bradley, Wegg, and Charley Hexam, the former is associated with the happy rise to haute-bourgeois wifehood of Bella Wilfer and Lizzie Hexam. Invigilating the novel's male and female test-takers, we can catch the banking-teacher's promiscuous transmission of knowledge being countered by a midwife-pedagogy where no transmission of knowledge takes place. Bourdieu and Passeron point out that the power relations maintained by pedagogic communication can remain intact "even when the information transmitted tends towards zero" (21). In *Our Mutual Friend*, the maintenance of these relations actually depends on the transmission of zero information; education escapes the fragility of institutional enclaves only when it does not involve the transference of knowledge from one person to another.

In the early nineteenth century, education was beginning to be seen as a tool for controlling the working class, but not until midcentury were middle-class voices representing it as a tool for social mobility. Here, the uneasy fit between education system and labor market meant that "education as such did not hold out much promise for economic and social mobility for the working classes," an issue not fully recognized by those higher on the class ladder who built the education system (Smelser 273–74). As a pupil-teacher, Charley Hexam takes the only direct path available from scholastic achievement to social success (Smelser 275). Joan Burstyn argues that while "individual betterment" structured most middle-class men's education, for working-class men and all women "social control was the predominant theme" (11). In *Our Mutual Friend*, however, self-betterment through education is closely associated with working-class men—and with the banking model. It is to improve their class standing and, as Lizzie puts it, "lead better lives" (70), that Bradley and Charley have embarked on their careers as bankers of cultural capital. It is with the expectation that "'a literary man—*with* a wooden leg ... will begin to lead me a new life!'" (97) that Boffin pays Wegg to start "shoveling and sifting" Gibbon's *Decline and Fall*. Conversely, the midwife-model is associated with women in order to fulfil the goal of social-control education, keeping characters in (or returning them to) their "socially-determined place" (Burstyn 11). *Our Mutual Friend* enables us to see the connection between the gendered opposition of social control and individual betterment and that between the midwife teacher and the banking teacher.

As feminist narrative theory demonstrates, bourgeois narratives of female education are traditionally paradoxical. Subject at once to the demands of the *bildung* and the retention of a marriageable inexperience, girls must become self-conscious producers of unconscious naturalness and accomplished scholars in ignorance. Ruth Yeazell suggests that the Podsnappian prevention of "a blush to the cheek of the [female] young person" in the English novel tradition poses a threat "to the essence of storytelling itself; without experience of some sort, there can be no narrative" (340). Narratives of female development are perforce paradoxical; their simultaneous insistence on innocence and experience leads to an insoluble paradox: "Podsnap's idea of his young person is that of a creature who cannot in fact exist" (343). Barbara Johnson develops a model of pedagogical paradox in "Teaching Ignorance: *L'ecole des Femmes*." The "teaching of ignorance," where feminine innocence must be both innate and learned, is coded as at once complementary to and competitive with masculine knowledge. Yeazell argues that Georgiana Podsnap's truncated story in *Our Mutual Friend* represents Dickens's recognition of the cultural contradiction generated by the relationship between feminine innocence and novelistic plot, while Bella and Lizzie, successfully negotiating the "vast interval" between maiden consciousness and secure middle-class marriage, suggest his retreat from that recognition. The important role played by the "teaching of ignorance" in their stories, however, implies that the distinction may be one of degree rather than kind. Bella and Lizzie pass their tests because their self-contradictory plots enable them to resist development.[13]

For example, Lizzie's virtue seems inseparable from her unconscious resistance to the most innocent transferred knowledge. As she and Jenny pursue their studies in Riah's rooftop garden, "they both pored over one book; both with attentive faces; Jenny with the sharper; Lizzie with the more perplexed" (331). Despite her conscious desire for book learning, Lizzie has no real need of it. She is already amply supplied with her own form of untransferable expertise. As Bradley comments to Charley Hexam,

> "[Y]our sister—scarcely looks or speaks like an ignorant person."
> "Lizzie has as much thought as the best, Mr. Headstone. Too much, perhaps, without teaching. I used to call the fire at home, her books, for she was always full of fancies—sometimes quite wise fancies, considering—when she sat looking at it."
> "I don't like that," said Bradley Headstone. (281)

Many observers besides Bradley have noticed that, indeed, Lizzie "scarcely... speaks like an ignorant person" (P. Morris 130). But here the novel calls attention to her middle-class diction not as the result of class bound classroom training but as an inherent virtue. It comes as no surprise that Bradley, exemplar of free-trade education, should have objections to such a relation to knowledge. Lizzie will not provide her more successful suitor Eugene with a return on an investment of transferable knowledge (sexual favors for the lessons he pays for), but with the gift of her intrinsic worth.

This gift is put to the test as she literally catches a middle-class husband by showing how little her subsequent education has affected her original skill as a waterwoman. Lizzie's reactions to Bradley's attack on Eugene function as a display of her expertise as she rushes to rescue the as yet unidentified victim:

> A sure touch of her old practised hand, a sure step of her old practiced foot, a sure light balance of her body, and she was in the boat. A quick glance of her practiced eye showed her, even through the deep dark shadow, the sculls in a rack against the red-brick garden-

wall. Another moment, and she had cast off (taking the line with her), and the boat had shot out into the moonlight, and she was rowing down the stream as never other woman rowed on English water. (768)

The final phrases, with their echo of the nationalistic language of a sporting commentary, suggest a competition if not an exam. Over and over again, this description dwells on the idea of Lizzie as well-trained —despite the fact that the only time we see Lizzie sharing the boat with her father is at the novel's opening. The most explicit message here, of course, is that Lizzie has done well not to forget the "old bold life" (767) with her father. In fact, she transcends it: finding Eugene's near-dead body, Lizzie accomplishes here what Gaffer has tried unsuccessfully to do in *his* "Body Found" examination—establish a genuine alternative to traditional bourgeois conceptions of what it means to be educated.

Bradley's initial view of the education of Lizzie is, like his rival Eugene's, perfectly in line with the banking model. Both hope to earn a sexual relationship with Lizzie through investing an education in her. Bradley, wants to do so, of course, so that she may become an appropriate wife for him:

> "Some man who had worked his way might come to admire— your sister—and might even in time bring himself to think of marrying—your sister—and it would be a sad drawback and a heavy penalty upon him, if, overcoming in his mind other inequalities of condition and other considerations against it, this inequality [of education] and this consideration remained in full force." (282)

Bradley does indeed help to bring Lizzie a respectable, hardworking, professional husband. But he does so not, of course, in his role as schoolmaster, but in his role as murderer when he attacks Eugene. In contrast, Lizzie's brother Charley, "a master now, in another school" (777), makes a special trip back to his old teacher in order to demonstrate the efficacy of Bradley's teaching:

> "I am going to be plain with you, Mr. Headstone," said young Hexam, shaking his head in a half-threatening manner, "because this is no time for affecting not to know things that I do know—except certain things at which it might not be very safe for you, to hint again. What I mean is this: if you were a good master, I was a good pupil. I have done you plenty of credit, and in improving my own reputation I have improved yours quite as much." (779)

In declaring himself "on equal terms," (779), owing nothing to his old teacher, Charley asserts his possession of payment-by-results knowledge here just as Lizzie asserts her rejection of it by saving Eugene.

Despite the difference in morality between the Hexam siblings, Charley and Lizzie end up with the same rewards: middle-class lives and middle-class marriages. The difference in their educations makes a very great difference, however, to their teachers. Charley's adherence to the banking model causes the final blow to Bradley's sanity. But Lizzie's undevelopmental development transforms Eugene from ambiguously attractive idle gentleman to professional hero.

Eugene's gentlemanly refusal to let Bradley teach him anything is one of his greatest weapons when the latter comes to challenge him in his chambers: "'You have my name very correctly,'" Eugene tells Bradley,

> "Pray what is yours?"
> "It cannot concern you much to know, but—"
> "True," interposed Eugene, striking sharply and cutting him short at his mistake, "it does not concern me at all to know. I can say Schoolmaster, which is a most respectable title. You are right, Schoolmaster."
> It was not the dullest of this goad in its galling of Bradley Headstone, that he had made it himself in a moment of incautious anger. (341)

In part, this meeting merely repeats Eugene's first meeting with Charley: the hardworking intellectual laborer's command of knowledge rendered futile by the aristocrat's ignorant and contemptuous gaze. It is clear that, here and throughout this scene, everything that

Bradley knows (Eugene's name, that Eugene has scored a point against him) hurts him. But Eugene calls Bradley "Schoolmaster" here not only to identify him as an intellectual laborer, but to make a distinction between different kinds of intellectual labor. After Bradley leaves, Eugene jokes with Mortimer that "'I fear my unexpected visitors have been troublesome. If as a set-off (excuse the legal phrase from a barrister-at-law) you would like to ask Tippins to tea, I pledge myself to make love to her'" (347). For in his battle with Bradley over Lizzie's education, Eugene's gentlemanly indifference is joined by a barrister's hectoring use of words as weapons.

Like Lizzie, Bella passes her test by deflecting, rather than absorbing, knowledge. Before her test in disinterested loyalty, Bella frequently proclaims her greediness for money, but most often as a joke in the quasi-flirtation the "lovely woman" carries on with her father; as Barbara Hardy argues, "she is always shown as partly affecting her mercenariness" (Hardy 49). Rather than learning goodness, the novel suggests, Bella simply needs to unlearn the surface knowledge that interferes with what she already knows. The final test she is set is whether or not she will allow new information (the identification of her husband with the sinister Julius Handford) to replace her unquestioning trust in John. She passes this final examination by being completely unable to draw any conclusions from this new information. Whirled down to the Fellowship Porters for the identification and vindication of her husband, she is "perfectly unable to account for her being there, perfectly unable to forecast what would happen next, or whither she was going, or why; certain of nothing in the immediate present, but that she confided in John, and that John seemed somehow to be getting more triumphant. But what a certainty was that!" (833). The narrowing of her awareness to this single certainty is what finally convinces John to reveal the ruse and present Bella with her reward. As Mrs. Boffin tells the story,

> "Then he says he'll only wait to triumph beyond what we ever thought possible, and to show her to us better than even we ever supposed; and he says, 'She shall see me under suspicion of having

murdered myself, and *you* shall see how trusting and how true she'll be.' Well Noddy and me agreed to that, and he was right, and here you are, and the horses is in, and the story is done, and God bless you my Beauty, and God bless us all!" (844–45)

John's triumph depends on Bella's unquestioning trust, and so does the happy conclusion to the Boffin/Harmon ruse.

The same process that Boffin and Harmon use to bring out Bella's innate trust and loyalty and which preserves Boffin's own innate generosity also brings out Silas Wegg's innate greed and treachery, providing a set of criteria for distinguishing between the recipients of Boffin's bounty. Both Bella and Wegg are tempted into acting independently of their benefactor, but while Bella is eventually welcomed back to "Our House," Wegg is, quite literally, thrown out. If Bella passes the test by being incapable of understanding new information, Wegg fails by understanding all too well the new books of Misers' Lives that Boffin provides for him to read. As Wegg reads Boffin the story of Daniel Dancer, he starts to pay attention for the first time to the subject matter he reads his employer:

> "'The house, or rather the heap of ruins, in which Mr. Dancer lived, ... was a most miserable, decayed building, for it had not been repaired for more than half a century.'"
>
> (Here Mr. Wegg eyed his comrade [Venus] and the room in which they sat; which had not been repaired for a long time.)
>
> "'But though poor in external structure, the ruinous fabric was very rich in the interior.... Captain Holmes found it a very agreeable task to dive into the miser's secret hoards.'"
>
> (Here Mr. Wegg repeated "secret hoards," and pegged his comrade again.) (544)

After the first session of miserly reading, "avarice, and the evening's legends of avarice, and the inflammatory effect of what he had seen, ... wrought Silas Wegg to ... a pitch of insatiable appetite." (552).

Just as Bella's success is a specifically gendered one, relying on the self-contradictory nature of her education, so Wegg's downfall, it is suggested, is related to his masculinity. Throughout the novel, Wegg's wooden leg functions as a comic phallic symbol, a parody of the more subtle forms of masculine authority he is incapable of wielding. Its intrusion into the midwife-style exam Boffin sets him signals his failure, as he swoons in a "pecuniary" orgasm during the reading session about Dancer's hidden treasures:

> Mr. Wegg's wooden leg had gradually elevated itself more and more, and he had nudged Mr. Venus with his opposite elbow deeper and deeper, until at length . . . he . . . dropped over sideways upon that gentleman, squeezing him against the settle's edge. Nor did either of the two, for some few seconds, make any effort to recover himself; both remaining in a kind of pecuniary swoon. (544–45)

Wegg's wooden leg calls our attention to the drawbacks for professional labor of the unification of the male subject. When we are introduced to him, it seems to threaten to extend to his entire body:

> Sooth to say, he was so wooden a man that he seemed to have taken his wooden leg naturally, and rather suggested to the fanciful observer, that he might be expected—if his development received no untimely check—to be completely set up with a pair of wooden legs in about six months. (89)

By late in the novel, it is at any rate getting continuously stuck in mounds of dust, and preventing Wegg from making a full search of the Bower. For Wegg's objectified masculinity causes him to fail not only as a test-taker, but as an invigilator as well. At the opening of the novel, when Wegg passes Boffin's initial test, we are told that "Mr. Wegg was an observant person, or, as he himself said, 'took a powerful sight of notice'" (89). Under Boffin's more effective midwife-model testing later in the novel, however, he is incapable of performing the role of surveilleur. Although he plans to keep Mr. Boffin "under inspection" once he has been informed of the "Friendly Move," and orders him to "ask me to dinner. Give me the run of your 'ouse" (727), he is "baulked in that amiable design of frequently dining with him, by the machinations of the sleepless dustman" (851)—or Sloppy in disguise, who has been keeping a watch on *him*. Despite Wegg's ability to manipulate gender roles when he appropriates the domestic sphere, when he is subjected to a gendered pedagogy his power is rendered ineffectual.

In contrast to Arnold's fears that a pedagogical economy based on the market will reduce educators to the status of gossiping shopkeepers and their feminine customers, Dickens's representative of the market-classroom shares Wegg's excessive masculinity as well as his failures as a watcher. Bradley is introduced with a typically Dickensian characteristic gesture: "'Look here, Hexam,' Mr. Bradley Headstone, highly certified stipendiary schoolmaster, drew his right forefinger through one of the buttonholes of the boy's coat, and looked at it attentively.... Bradley Headstone looked at his finger again, took it out of the buttonhole and looked at it closer, bit the side of it and looked at it again" (265). Like Wegg's simultaneously rising leg and poking elbow, Bradley's forefinger, with which he emphasizes the useless advice he gives Charley, becomes a symbol of inadequate intellectual labor. But even this symbol quickly becomes unnecessary, and it is abandoned. Indeed, Bradley's macho rage does away with any need for the narrator to insist upon bodily props, and the ineptitude with which Bradley stalks Eugene amply testifies to his disqualification from invigilation:

> Looking like the hunted and not the hunter, baffled, worn, with the exhaustion of deferred hope and consuming hate and anger in his face, white-lipped, wild-eyed, draggle-haired, seamed with jealousy and anger, and torturing himself with the conviction that he showed it all and they exulted in it, he went by them in the dark, like a haggard head suspended in the air: so completely did the force of his expression cancel his figure. (608)

Of the competing intellectual laborers in *Our Mutual Friend*, only Eugene and Mortimer are left plying their trades (or at any rate, promising to) at the end of the novel: John Rokesmith the secretary disappears into John Harmon the wealthy benefactor, Wegg disappears into a scavenger's cart, and Bradley into the Thames. The novel's curtain falls on Mortimer wandering with Twemlow through the streets of London, and Eugene remains one of the least securely placed characters in the finale's well-organized social hierarchy. We see the last of him and his wife on a "visit" (883) to the Harmons—recipients of their bounty, but hardly feudal retainers. Eugene's hardly won professional authority does establish, as Wegg's cheap imitation could not, proper gender relations. As Mr. Twemlow pronounces: "'[I]f such feelings on the part of this gentleman, induced this gentleman to marry this lady, I think he is the greater gentleman for the action, and makes her the greater lady'" (891).

Mr. Boffin expresses his faith in Bella's innate unselfishness and love for John: "She may be a leetle spoilt, and nat'rally spoilt . . . by circumstances, but that's only the surface, and I lay my life, . . . that she's the true golden gold at heart" (843). If Bella is not really mercenary, at least on a metaphorical level her examiners would seem to be. The "Golden Dustman's" choice of metaphor here draws attention to the central contradiction of Bella's education. Bella *is* the "true golden gold," rather than wishing to possess the Golden Dustman's—with which she will be rewarded for her preciousness (Barbour 65–66). Boffin and Harmon wish (like Gaffer Hexam as he turns corpses' pockets inside out, like Wegg and Venus as they explore the dust heaps, like Fascination Fledgby buying up junk bonds) to displace the spoiled "surface" and uncover the "true golden gold." Bella's "certainty" is thus assigned a value, but one that—like a scavenger's find—cannot easily be subjected to a valuation based on the labor theory of value. Whereas Bradley's knowledge is currency to be passed from hand to hand, Bella's "certainty" is a treasure buried within the heart. The novel's gendered opposition of pedagogies achieves what recourse to the doctrine of separate spheres cannot: the paradoxical figuring of a reified knowledge that nevertheless escapes commodification.[14] If, as we have seen, intellectual labor must balance on the line between the market and transcendence, then a pedagogical economy that blurs that division may be more valuable than transcendence itself. The testing of Bella and Lizzie provides such an economy for John and Eugene, one that supplements the exchange of commodities with the finding and keeping of treasure. It is thus fully appropriate that the novel's most brilliant examiner, Noddy Boffin, is also its "Golden Dustman."

For Ruskin as well as for Dickens, women's stories make a difference for masculine structures of knowledge, granting them access to freedom from cause and effect. In their work we can trace links between self-contradictory plots of female development and the establishment of a flexible, self-consciously self-contradictory, masculine professional authority. In *The Speculum of the Other Woman*, one of the founding texts of contemporary feminist thought, Luce Irigaray identifies subjecthood, for the Western philosophical tradition, as masculine, and as dependent for its coherence on an incoherent female object. As Yeazell argues, the class and gender privilege of "Podsnappery very much depends upon the existence of a daughter" (339). My own argument will show, however, that it is the incoherent formation of a female *subjectivity* that empowers a specifically nineteenth-century construction of masculinity through identification rather than differentiation. In the next chapter I will suggest that Ruskin goes one step further than Dickens: his pedagogical economy allows him to imagine femininity as a commodity that *does* circulate, but whose value cannot be fixed.

Chapter Five

"Preached to Death By a Mad Governess": Ruskin's Anti-Exam

> L. (*perceiving various arrangements being made of footstool, cushion, screen, and the like*). Yes, yes, it's all very fine! and I am to sit here to be asked questions till supper-time, am I?
>
> Dora. I don't think you can have any supper to-night:— we've got so much to ask.
>
> Lily. Oh, Miss Dora! We can fetch it him here, you know, so nicely!
>
> L. Yes, Lily, that will be pleasant, with competitive examination going on over one's plate; the competition being among the examiners. Really, now that I know what teasing things girls are, I don't so much wonder that people used to put up patiently with the dragons who took *them* for supper.
>
> —The Ethics of the Dust

> [E]very true pedagogue is in effect an anti-pedagogue, not just because every pedagogy has historically emerged as a critique of pedagogy..., but because, in one way or another, every pedagogy stems from its confrontation with the impossibility of teaching.
>
> —Shoshana Felman, "Psychoanalysis and Education"

1. Anti-Exam and Anti-Examiner

In each of the pedagogical economies I have sketched so far, the Victorian literary man maintains the cultural authority of his intellectual labor by appropriating and rewriting some aspect of the nineteenth-century examination. For Arnold, Trollope, and Dickens, the examination solves a problem related to intellectual work by allowing it to be displayed, categorized, investigated, or embodied. For John Ruskin, such a move is impossible. Labor is only real for Ruskin when it *cannot* be displayed, categorized, or investigated—and need not be embodied, because it is already. Work is impossible to impersonate—essential, instinctual. He insists in his lecture "The Mystery of Life" that "[c]ompetitive examination" can only be "wholesome" when it "will be daily, and calm, and in practice" (*Sesame* 184), without any of the theatricality so central to the examinations of his fellow literary men:

> All good work is essentially done ... without hesitation, without difficulty, without boasting; and in the doers of the best, there is an inner and involuntary power which approximates literally to the instinct of an animal— ... an instinct as much more divine than that of the lower animals as the human body is more beautiful than theirs. (*Sesame* 167)

In Dickens's ideal exam, knowledge is resisted instead of absorbed, and certification is granted to examiner rather than test-taker. Like *Our Mutual Friend*, Ruskin's writing on girls' education during the 1860s bases a pedagogical economy on an ironic relationship between femininity and knowledge. In Dickens's novel, this relationship transforms the meaning of the exam, while retaining its structure. In Ruskin's work, however, moments of testing and certification are not reinvented; they are deliberately and ostentatiously erased by pedagogical rituals that transform the relation between the subject and object of knowledge and blur the lines between observer and spectacle, teacher and student.

Written for as well as about the education of middle-class girls,[1] the lecture "Of Queens' Gardens" (1865) enacts a narrative with a missing link where an exam should be. In this narrative, girls learn and girls teach, but the logical bridge between these two actions is absent: girls never know. As I will argue, for Ruskin's queenly students, learning *is* teaching, and questions and answers can be traded without establishing the ownership of a body of knowledge. His bizarre mineralogical dialogue for children, *The Ethics of the Dust* (1865), places this "anti-exam" in its ideal setting, the girls' school. An introduction to crystal formations delivered in a series of interrupted lectures, the dialogue crosses gender, genre, and disciplinary boundaries, and, as Carlyle observed, "twists symbolically in the strangest way all its geology into morality, theology, Egyptian mythology, with fiery cuts at political economy" (Burd 479). *The Ethics* features an "Old Lecturer" whose half-flirtatious, half-bullying interactions with his pupils, based on Ruskin's real-life students at Winnington Hall School, suggest an almost pathological anxiety about pedagogical exchange. As I will argue, the connections the Old Lecturer draws between girls and rocks spatialize the narrative of history and locate it irretrievably within the many-faceted and impenetrable "little mind" of the schoolgirl. The physical and psychic economies of the school allow these girls to represent history without having a history, and to represent, indeed epitomize, labor—through play.

Ruskin's anti-examinations, then, do not put intellectual labor on display—instead, they use processes of identification and personification to contain and control it. Play, not work, is made visible in these interchanges, a constant digital play of identity and difference. As an exchange between the "Old Lecturer" of *Ethics* and one of his pupils illustrates, this play is inextricable from the invocation of a typically Ruskinian pathos:

> FLORRIE. Now you're just playing, you know.
> L. So are you, you know.
> FLORRIE. Yes, but you mustn't play.
> L. That's very hard, Florrie; why mustn't I, if you may?
> FLORRIE. Oh, I may, because I'm little, but you mustn't, because you're—(*hesitates for a delicate expression of magnitude*).
> L. (*rudely taking the first that comes*). Because I'm big? No; that's not the way of it at all, Florrie. Because you're little, you should have very little play; and because I'm big, I should have a great deal. (*Ethics* 211)

As the above passage suggests, Ruskin's paradigmatic anti-examinee is the middle-class schoolgirl. For the Victorians, as for us, the child wields a special kind of representational power: at once the ultimate other, and the other for whom time inevitably dissolves the difference between otherness and identity, metaphor and metonymy. The child opens up an "other" space, to which all adults have access (through memory and the unconscious), but from which all adults are utterly divided. As Carolyn Steedman points out, one of the most potent aspects of the image of the child for the Victorians was its ability to personify, even encapsulate, an ontogeny that recapitulates phylogeny (84). Nineteenth-century biology, she argues, found the past in the child: "A child psychology was partly constructed in the expectation that cultural and historical evidence enclosed within the child's body and mind could be retrieved and used" (85). The Victorian child's body may narrativize identity, but it also spatializes the temporal and dehistoricizes history, paving the way for Freud's discovery of the unconscious —the timeless space of childhood within us all.[2]

For Ruskin, the child's paradoxically static personification of change is at once tragic and deeply attractive in its inevitability: "Children are as bad as clouds at sunrise—golden change—but change always," he complains in a letter to the Winnington Hall girls on May 6, 1861.[3] Mid-Victorian science's fascination with the inevitable and inexplicable process of development, maturity, and decline grew alongside an equally strong fascination with the figure of a girl-child (Carroll's Alice, Dickens's Little Nell and Amy Dorrit, Brontë's elfin Jane Eyre) who somehow transcends these processes. Ruskin's participation in this fascination is well known.[4] The tone in which he addresses the girls of "Queens' Gardens" and *Ethics of the Dust* is at once erotic, aestheticizing, hostile, paternal, and sisterly. But Ruskin's girls are not all (or even mostly) prepubescent; the *Ethics* auditors range in age from nine to twenty and Rose La Touche was sixteen when Ruskin wrote "Queens' Gardens" for her. It is thus not simply girls' physical immaturity that attracts Ruskin. It is also, as I will argue, their placement inside a specific educational system, perpetually solidifying and compacting subject-object relations in the anti-exam.

As Diana Fuss suggests in *Identity Papers*, the line between desire and identification is permeable, and draws our attention to "moments of contamination, in which the desire/identification binary becomes confused and undecidable" (Fuss 45–46). In Ruskin's writing on girls' education in the 1860s, we can trace the pedagogical economy entangled in "confused and undecidable" moments between Ruskin's desire for and identification with feminine childhood. Recent work by Sheila Emerson, Dinah Birch, and Sharon Weltman shows how Ruskin repeatedly links his own authorial power with childishness and femininity.[5] In the 1882 preface to *Sesame and Lilies*, Ruskin digresses immediately after asserting that "the best strength of a man is shown in his intellectual work, as that of a woman in her daily deed and character," to admit that "only the other day one of my friends put me in no small pet by saying that he thought my own influence was much more in being amiable and obliging than in writing books." Ruskin calls his very irritation at this accusation by the girlish name of "pet" and goes on to dismiss the "intellectual work" of his ineffectual response: "[T]he influence of my books was distinctly on the increase, and I hoped—etc., etc.,—it is no matter what more I said, or intimated" (*Sesame* 49–50). Nothing could provide a greater contrast to Arnold's, Trollope's, or Dickens's ideal examiners. An exclusively masculine (though not, as we have seen, *too* masculine) power is absolutely necessary to the omniscient Noddy Boffin and John Harmon, to Arnold's subtle Inspector, and to Trollope's wily Chaffanbrass. The anti-exam requires an anti-examiner, and Ruskin, in his role of "mad governess," is happy to oblige.[6] Birch writes that in the mid-sixties (just after his father's death) "one of the first things Ruskin did was . . . to change his profession. He had been a writer; he became a lecturer." This shift toward "an authority of personality" (Birch, "*Ethics*" 148)—oedipally motivated or not—is a shift that links the specifically pedagogical power of the lecturer to an ineffectual girlishness.

Writing of his "manner of work" in *Praeterita*, Ruskin differentiates his experience of composition from "the kind of pain of which Carlyle so wildly complains," asserting that

> My own literary work, on the contrary, was always done as quietly and methodically as a piece of tapestry. I knew exactly what I had got to say, put the words firmly in their place like so many stitches, hemmed the edges of chapters round with what seemed to me grace-

ful flourishes, touched them finally with my cunningest points of colour, and read the work to papa and mamma at breakfast next morning, as a girl shows her sampler. (336)

The well-worn analogy between writing and sewing is gradually stretched to breaking point here, as sewing's gender associations become more apparent and more outrageous. The passage enacts yet another of *Praeterita*'s "firm beginning[s]" (*Sesame* 129) that end in a retreat to childhood.[7] It slowly tinges Ruskin's writing with femininity, moving from an assertion of control and power with words like "methodically" and "firmly" through the more gender-specific "graceful flourishes" to the self-infantilizing drag of "cunningest points of colour" and "papa and mamma." Like many drag artists, Ruskin is girlishly coy here about his own ultimate lack of girlishness. The pathos, as well as the humor, of this and many other passages in Ruskin depends on his status as an adult male, for whom childhood and femininity are impossible dreams. A half-angry, half-mournful insistence on his difference from precisely the girls he identifies with as often as not closes Ruskin's excursions across gender lines. I will argue that part of what Ruskin seeks in identifying with girls is the impossibility of that identification. But before I return at the end of this chapter to the significance of this failure, I will first trace the route Ruskin takes to get there, following him through the mazes of the anti-exam, exploring its setting, its economic logic, its self-contradictory plot, and the results it produces.

In her discussion of Freud's theory of identification, Fuss suggests that

> The analytic scene ... does not reproduce a universal or inherent psychological structure but rather produces the prototype for it. ... Freud's theory of identification is a *projection* of the struggle for power and the process of negotiation that organizes every professional relation between doctor and patient. (Fuss 50)

Institutional relationships—between analyst and patient, and also teacher and student—underwrite psychic mechanisms such as identification and desire. Recent readings of Ruskin tend to trace Ruskin's objections to competitive exams, as well as his embracing of femininity, to sources in his psychosexual biography (see, for example, Emerson 199). While these readings are surely correct, I would like to follow Fuss's lead by taking them one step further, reading the economic and institutional implications of Ruskin's pedagogy rather than its psychoanalytic origins. A reading of Ruskin's *Sesame and Lilies* and *Ethics of the Dust* will make these implications "crystal" clear.

2. The Pedagogical Economy of Winnington Hall

> *Listening returns me the vanity of my own speech, its price, for, whether I like it or not, I am placed in a circuit of exchange.*
> —Roland Barthes, "The Lecture" 203

> *The place is really very lovely in its perfect green, and the girls look very pretty glancing in and out among the park trees. They have all kinds of active games now that they can be out of doors all day—and except that the hours are always regular, what it is called a "school" for I can't think—except that if Miss Bell called it a "Playhouse" it might be mistaken for a theatre.*
> —Letter to John Ruskin, Sr., 8 August 1863

So Ruskin describes Winnington Hall, the private girls' school near Manchester that he patronized and visited periodically from 1858 to 1869. At Winnington, work is so far from being displayed that it is not even visible in this passage, and even the "Play" is *not* open to the public. It is the ideal Ruskinian school: a beautiful, fairytale spot, an institutionalized Wonderland, safe from the ravages of time, and yet up-to-the-minute in its methods. Ruskin wrote portions of *Sesame and Lilies* and delivered the mineralogy lectures that became *The Ethics of the Dust* while staying at Winnington Hall, as well as cricketing, boating, and dancing with the children and giving them lessons in art and religion. He donated more than his pedagogical services to the school, contributing (and persuading his unenthusiastic father to contribute) money for running costs, tuition for needy pupils, books, pictures, casts, and mineralogical specimens (Burd 98). Under the dynamic leadership of owner-headmistress Margaret Bell, Winnington combined the style of the "old-fashioned seminary... commonly run by... fear and espionage" (Avery 12–13) with an ambitious and progressive curriculum. Bell's pedagogy was in step with the most advanced theories of female education in her day, anticipating later reformers in rejecting the Victorian version of "banking-concept education" (Freire 53) and advocating "problem-posing education" (Freire 61). She would have enthusiastically agreed with the educational reformer Dorothea Beale in "aiming to give as little help as possible, but to lead [the students] on to find out for themselves; under no circumstances to let them learn by heart, and to induce them to do without explanation as far as they can, so as to call out their own powers" (Walford 58). Like Bell, Ruskin advocated "teaching by question rather than assertion," and emphasized observation rather than explanation or hypothesis (Gully 164).

Bell also evidenced "a remarkable concern for the physical welfare of her students," demonstrated by her encouragement of all kinds of sports: cricket as well as the more ladylike croquet, boating and running as well as singing and dancing (Burd 37). She was thus also in the vanguard of educators changing the role of physical education in the middle-class girl's curriculum. During the 1870s and 1880s, innovators were to claim that games-playing "would improve health and reproductive potential and counteract mental overstrain" (Walford 37). In fact, Victorian girls' schools came up with "scientific" physical education programs, including medical inspection and elaborate organized games, before boys' schools did (Walford 41). Athletics could form a link between girls' bodies and the medical profession, providing an opportunity for them to be watched, examined, and defined as vessels being prepared to carry the next generation of Britons. But the trend was also toward games involving competition, that "would impart valuable moral qualities, such as loyalty, discipline, determination, and resourcefulness, that had previously been identified exclusively with males" (Walford 37). As well as making the female body into an object of examination, physical education would make the middle-class schoolgirl into the subject of competitive testing.

As a child and at Oxford, Ruskin hated organized games (A.

Bradley 757), and his view of girls at play rejects both medicalization and competition. The Winnington games as he describes them are as far as possible from the playing fields of Eton, or even Cheltenham. For Ruskin (as the quotation with which I begin this section suggests) they are permeable spectacles of innocence, productive of aesthetic pleasure, yet always welcoming the observer's inclusion in a romp of ungendered childhood joy. And as I will suggest, Ruskin's version of progressive pedagogy is as out of step with its mainstream forms as is his version of girls' physical education.

The many similarities between Miss Bell's and Ruskin's theories are no accident. On Ruskin's first visit to the school in 1859 he writes to his father that

> the little six-year-old ones . . . I find know me by the fairy tale [*The King of the Golden River*] as the others do by my large books—so I am quite at home.
>
> They have my portrait in the library with three others—Maurice, the Bp of Oxford, & Archdeacon Hare . . . —so that I can't but stay with them over the Sunday. (to John Ruskin, Sr., 11 March 1859)

No sooner has he arrived at Winnington, than he finds himself already there, installed as an authority—and thus already involved in a transaction with those who have so installed him. Not only the idyllic setting, but his own presence at the school, seems to escape (thanks to his fame) ordinary cause and effect, ordinary temporal processes. As Ruskin joins his "portrait in the library," so does his "amiable and obliging" femininity join the masculine power of his "intellectual work." He can safely enjoy the absolute authority promised by the portrait, with none but the purely social responsibilities of a guest. Throughout his correspondence with the Winnington girls and teachers, Ruskin insists upon the voluntary, accidental nature of their exchanges. He worries that his pupils will consider as compulsory his sternly authoritative "Sunday Letters," consisting of etymological lessons on key words in the Bible, with texts for them to find and copy: "And now, I think, when I've come to giving you what we used to call 'Impositions'—it's time for me to stop!! But I do think you will find this interesting if you take it gently" (to the students at Winnington Hall, 3 April 1859). And when, in 1862, he commiserates with Miss Bell over their common loss of faith in the wake of Bishop Colenso's *The Pentateuch and Book of Joshua Critically Examined*, he depends on his amateur status in order to excuse himself from writing the "Sunday Letters," while urging Miss Bell to continue to teach what she no longer believes. Ruskin needs Winnington at least in part because his power there is doubly safe: pedagogical and extra-institutional, situational and essential.

Ruskin wrote what would eventually become the third lecture of *Sesame and Lilies*, "The Mystery of Life and Its Arts," when he was staying at Winnington in 1868. The lecture reflects his need for an ideal school, a place of unfallen nature where everyone has nevertheless already read his books. As in most of his work of the 1860s, Ruskin is concerned in this lecture with rewriting classical political economy (see Helsinger; Austin *Practical*) and he indulges here in one of its most well-worn clichés: a parable about the origins of politics and commerce. Ruskin's own note to the published version of the lecture, confessing that "I have sometimes been asked what this [parable] means" (*Sesame* 164), suggests that his hearers were confused about its application. And no wonder: he sets it not in the traditional desert island or savage community, but at a "child's May-day party, in which every means of entertainment had been provided for them, by a wise and kind host. It was in a stately house, with beautiful gardens attached to it" (163). While he does not call it a school, Ruskin's description of the house and its amenities sounds remarkably like his descriptions of the "Playhouse" at Winnington:

> [T]he children had been set free in the rooms and gardens, with no care whatever but how to pass their afternoon rejoicingly. They did not, indeed, know much about what was to happen next day; and some of them, I thought, were a little frightened, because there was a chance of their being sent to a new school where there were examinations; but they kept the thoughts of that out of their heads as well as they could, and resolved to enjoy themselves. (*Sesame* 163–64)

Instead of preparing for the examinations of Hereafter, and in spite of their enjoyment of the good things provided for them, the children proceed to invent war in the garden (reducing it, of course, to rubble), and commerce in the house, ignoring its numerous attractions to compete for "the brass-headed nails that studded the chairs" (165).

In this version of the political-economic cliché, Ruskin dispenses with one of its central elements: in his parable, the state of nature is not depicted as prior to or outside culture; it is a thoroughly civilized paradise. The children playing in the house, for example, are provided with

> every kind of indoor pleasure: there was music for them to dance to; and the library was open, with all manner of amusing books; and there was a museum full of the most curious shells, and animals, and birds; and there was a workshop, with lathes and carpenter's tools, for the ingenious boys; and there were pretty fantastic dresses, for the girls to dress in; and there were microscopes, and kaleidoscopes; and whatever toys a child could fancy; and a table, in the dining-room, loaded with everything nice to eat. (164)

The gendered division of labor and categories of arts and industry, like Ruskin's intellectual authority at Winnington, are timeless givens, predating the pointlessly destructive introduction of political and economic laws. It is in fact the introduction of war and private property that introduces temporality, and leads to the inevitable future of "examinations" at the new school. The children playing in the garden, for example, enjoy an initial happiness without incident, but when war makes history begin, it does so with an abundance of chronological markers. The children

> were happy for *a little while*, but *presently* they separated themselves into parties; and *then* each party declared it would have a piece of the garden for its own.... *Next*, they quarreled violently which pieces they would have; and *at last* the boys took up the thing, as boys should do, "practically," and fought in the flower-beds *till* there was hardly a flower left standing. (164, emphasis added)

The school is a place where normal distinctions between nature and culture break down—and where new ones can be invented.

Not only can school represent a state of nature, but "nature" can also be used to represent a state of school. Like the "stately house" of "The Mystery of Life and Its Arts," the "Gardens" of "Queens' Gardens"—Britain's precious countryside—are associated with the kind of school Ruskin found at Winnington, where "the children having room to run wild, are as active as hares; and run—or dance—or ballplay me out of breath all day long" (to Sir John Naesmyth, 5 April 1861). He uses nearly the same language when he cautions his listeners in "Of Queens' Gardens" that "the whole country is but a little garden, not more than enough for your children to run on the lawns of" (*Sesame* 134). Ruskin calls on middle-class girls to create such gardens out of the wilderness of the world:

> Far among the moorlands and the rocks,—far in the darkness of the terrible streets,—these feeble florets are lying, with all their fresh leaves torn, and their stems broken: will you never go down to them, nor set them in order in their little fragrant beds, nor fence them in their trembling, from the fierce wind? (*Sesame* 142–43)

This wilderness, which includes "terrible streets" as well as moorlands and rocks, is not the natural realm Ruskin celebrates in association with middle-class femininity. Rather, it provides a contrast to a feminized literal wilderness, "the pleasant places, which God made at once for... schoolroom and... play-ground" for England's "daughters" (135). This essentializing of bourgeois space paradoxically revises the distinction between nature and culture as a competition between the separate spheres of home and industry, where the latter becomes a pitilessly wild invasion of property and the former a naturally civilized "play-ground."

Explicitly modeled on Winnington Hall, the spaces of *The Ethics of the Dust* prove the school to be the ideal domestic, as well as the ideal natural, space. Moving between lectures for all the pupils in "the large Schoolroom, to which everybody has been summoned by ringing of the great bell," and less formal talks for the Old Lecturer's favorites by "the sunniest window" or in "the comfortablest corner" of a cozy drawing room, Ruskin's very un-Dickensian representation of the school provides that most characteristically Dickensian bliss: a domestic haven *from* family. Playground and schoolroom are here inhabited only by schoolgirls and spinsters, requiring the explicitly masculine presence of the Old Lecturer to bring the girls "by the fireside," making the school a home. As I will demonstrate, however, like the children's party of "The Mystery of Life," the natural domesticity Ruskin finds at Winnington Hall also becomes the setting of a figurative market of pedagogical and erotic exchange, allied metaphorically to politics and commerce, but nevertheless prior to them and just barely escaping their association with temporal change.

Ruskin's "continual concern with the financial condition of" Winnington eventually led to money disputes with Miss Bell, contributing to his eventual break with the school in the late 1860s (Burd 98, 590). In his letters to and from Winnington, Ruskin self-consciously participates in a literal set of economic transactions in and about the school, in which he figures as writer, wealthy donor, celebrity, and teacher, and in which the school figures as an economic enterprise. Miss Bell was certainly interested in the publicity value of Ruskin's celebrity status, and it is not long before Ruskin too appreciates it. When, as he brags to his father, "the school is fuller than I ever knew it—as full as it can hold," he takes partial credit, and the timeless authority symbolized by his portrait does its bit in the economic as well as the pedagogical life of the school, nullifying the debt he owes to their adulation: in "the library, ... there are portraits of all sorts of nice people, myself among them ... and it is pleasant to think that one has saved the place, and got it all into this perfect state again" (to John Ruskin, Sr., 8 August 1863). As he is careful to let his father know, he insists on a return for both his cash and cachet. He writes defensively that

> I wished, *at whatever moderate loss, to maintain that school a year or two longer, partly because I did not like its failing as soon as* I had been known to take an interest in it; *partly because I thought if it broke up, it would split into seven or*

eight cases of minor & separate distress, which would cause me more vexation, than at that time: I was able to bear without risk to health, and probably cost me at last, as much money as would keep the thing afloat for some time longer. (to John Ruskin, Sr., 25 September 1861; Ruskin's emphasis)

He is eager to assure his father that his pleasure in the school is not excessive. Since it is merely his money's worth, it is being paid for and will leave no residue. And so the charisma of its viewer and preserver assigns an unspecified market value to the pre-economic, prehistorical school-made-tableau-vivant:

I do wish you could, for once, see the whole school in the evening, when I've anything to read or say to them.... [T]he long tables with the bright faces above them are so like Paul Veronese's great picture in the Louvre ["The Marriage at Cana"]—the mere picturesqueness of the thing is worth a great deal. (to John Ruskin, Sr., 2 December 1863)

Gifts from a doting celebrity both are and are not reducible to other currencies. Ruskin's entire oeuvre teems with objects—mountains, trees, clouds, and carpets as well as buildings, sculptures, and paintings. The pedagogical objects with which his letters to and from Winnington teem are specifically objects of exchange. Kisses, questions, answers, lessons, crystals, money, books, drawings, and influence, among other things, are all depicted as exchange- as well as use-values. Whenever Ruskin expresses an anxiety about his relationship with the Winnington girls, he does so in the language of exchange and equivalencies:

I would never reject any person's or any child's affection and would always value it at its full value—only I can't pay for it; and in a quite just and true measure of its full value, the person who gives it nearly always wants its price or at least *some* price. If you do not give them a like or somewhat like, regard in return they very naturally think themselves cheated—the general feeling is that they *must* somehow be answered—that it is impossible but that, when they care so truly for you, you also should care for them and I've precious gifts given me, of affection continually, by strong hearts as well as weak ones—but I'm bankrupt long ago—and can pay you nothing—or only some paltry farthings fraction for your pound. (to Julia Mary Cooke, 1 August 1866)

Ruskin flirts anxiously with the scandalous possibility of assigning an exchange value to a child's affections—which are valuable only insofar as their value cannot be fixed. In his extraeconomic exchange system, Ruskin *almost* prices what Viviana Zelizer calls the "priceless child."[8] The risk is particularly scary because it is not so much cupboard love as child prostitution that lurks beneath the almost-economic language. He writes to a former pupil: "Give Lanty my love, and some kisses—only I've no right to give your kisses—which are so much better—for mine—One of yours will be worth 'some' of mine—and two—ever so many, so you may give her two for me, and I'll write to her soon" (to Lily Armstrong, 27 June 1865).

Whether dealing in the authority of the Victorian Sage, aesthetic pleasure, or childish affection, Ruskin insists on the stern necessities of quid pro quo while leaving specific exchange values unfixed. No accounting system can keep track of this wild mix of currencies, a set of equivalencies which spiral out of control, piling up an excessive variety of excesses, and evading a final tally. After all, how can one calculate the cost of "fall[ing] in love with thirty-five young ladies at once"? Paradise Lost becomes paradise found, as architectural sights are exchanged for musical sounds, enchantment for celebrity, drawings for letters, and posted unletters ask questions that only receive answers in unposted letters:

[I]t is really a hard fate—of which so far as I know—the description is unattempted yet in prose or rhyme—to fall in love with thirty-five young ladies at once. I have lost Southwell Minster—& Peterborough cathedral—and arrived here only at 12 o'clock at night—but I consider that by these losses & penalties I have cheaply purchased the Mozart "gloria"—& the "Padre eterno" [performed by the girls]—and the leaves of the silver tree—and the wave of hands in the morning from the bow-window.

> I... must write one, or even two—rather long letters; which of the—"children"—shall I write to?—I mean that as three or four have scraps of drawing, perhaps some one who has not a drawing would like to have the letter—(see how naively & sincerely I accept their valuing of these—& rejoice in it—only don't put me to shame by showing this to anybody but the "children")—....
>
> It would be a great pleasure to me if they all would get into the habit—when anything comes into their heads that they would like to ask me about drawing or anything else—of just putting it on a scrap of paper—without any ceremony or superscriptioning, post the same. I don't say I should—became I could not—always answer—but if I did not, they might always trust that it was because inevitableness hindered me—not from disregard of their question—and that it would always give me pleasure to have the little sign of recollection—and still greater pleasure—to be able sometimes still to serve—or please them. (to Margaret Bell, 17 March 1859)

Perhaps forgetting that many of them are the daughters of Manchester manufacturers, Ruskin figures himself as introducing the Winnington natives to the dangerous yet pleasurable practice of exchange—always risking, yet never quite achieving, the accompanying fall into temporality and loss.

3. The Productive Consumption of *Unto This Last*

In a division spelled out most explicitly in "Queens' Gardens," Ruskin's ideal masculine workers make things, while his ideal feminine workers manage their use. In his best-known work on political economy, *Unto This Last* (1860), it is not only "the farmer who cuts his hay at the right time; the shipwright who drives his bolts well home in sound wood; the builder who lays good bricks in well-tempered mortar" but also "the housewife who takes care of her furniture in the parlour, and guards against all waste in her kitchen; and the singer who rightly disciplines and never overstrains her voice" who "are all political economists in the true and final sense: adding continually to the riches and well-being of the nation to which they belong" (181). Here,

Ruskin begins to dissolve the traditional gendered distinction between consumption and production, leaving in its place a gendered distinction between the production of goods and the production of consumption. Christina Crosby claims that the distinction between "decorative" and "profane" accumulation becomes gendered in Gothic Revival discourse, pitting masculine art critics and interior designers against feminine shoppers: "[I]n reforming 'taste,' revivalism forms 'women,' associates the feminine ... with the corruption of pure consumption, with unredeemed commodification" (112). In works of the 1860s, however, Ruskin figures feminine consumption not as "unredeemed," but as itself redemptive.

If feminine management—whether of a voice, or the resources of a household—is as much productive labor as the masculine creation of goods, it is not so surprising that "the most directly negative labour [is] murder, and the most directly positive the bearing and rearing of children" (*Unto This Last* 217). Ruskin even adds a footnote that associates feminine management, rather than masculine making, with creation:

> Observe, I say, "rearing," not "begetting." ... It is strange that men always praise enthusiastically any person who, by a momentary exertion, saves a life; but praise very hesitatingly a person who, by exertion and self-denial prolonged through years, creates one. (217n)

Ruskin deliberately blurs the distinction between economic production and social and biological *re*production.[9] He insists that "the true veins of wealth are purple—and not in Rock, but in Flesh," and indeed considers it "open ... to serious question, ... whether, among national manufactures, that of Souls of a good quality may not at last turn out a quite leadingly lucrative one" (189). This means that use-value inheres in the process of production as well as in consumption, and that production itself is not over once the goods leave the factory: "[T]he agreeableness or exchange value of every offered commodity depends on production, not merely of the commodity, but of buyers of it" (207n). The importance Ruskin places on the production of buyers moves the most valuable work of production into the sphere of "wise consumption":

> [P]ossession... is not an absolute, but a graduated power; and consists not only in the quantity or nature of the thing possessed, but also (and in a greater degree) in its suitableness to the person possessing it and in his vital power to use it.... Wealth, therefore, is "THE POSSESSION OF THE VALUABLE BY THE VALIANT." (210–11)

Consumption, in other words, through its gendered link to reproduction, *is* production in its most precious form. *Unto This Last* depicts subject-formation as part of a gendered economic system, thus making possible the recognition of gender ideology's economic base. But it also endows categories like consumption and production with the power, flexibility, and naturalness of Victorian gender categories. The granting of productive power to feminine consumption transforms the complementary relationship between the creation of goods and their use into a competitive—and gendered—relationship between more and less valuable goods. The most valuable of these goods is, of course, consumption itself.[10]

And yet Ruskin is as far from collapsing these categories as he is from conflating the gardens of domesticity with the streets of the urban wilderness. A productive realm of consumption remains distinct from, and in noble competition with, the destructive realm of industry. Delineating the "separate characters" of men and women in "Of Queens' Gardens," Ruskin defines "woman's power" as that of a skillful shopper: "[H]er intellect is... for sweet ordering, arrangement, and decision. She sees the qualities of things, their claims, and their places. Her great function is Praise; she enters into no contest, but infallibly judges the crown of contest" (*Sesame* 122). Consumption's conceptual separation from production is here so complete that it requires no commodities: Ruskin's women choose, praise, beautify, and "use nobly," but they never buy:

> And wherever a true wife comes, this home is always round her. The stars only may be over her head; the glowworm in the night-cold

grass may be the only fire at her foot: but home is yet wherever she is; and for a noble woman it stretches far round her, better than ceiled with cedar, or painted with vermilion, shedding its quiet light far, for those who else were homeless. (*Sesame* 122–23)

Within the semiotic system of consumption, says Baudrillard, "a need is not a need for a particular object as much as it is a 'need' for difference (*the desire for social meaning*)" (33). Ruskin literalizes the distinction between specific objects of consumption and "social meaning" by suggesting here that objects are not necessary for the generative power of Woman the Consumer.

Sesame and Lilies literalizes the association of women with consumption and of men with work in complementary images of masculine and feminine education, exploiting education's flexible relation to economic categories. As Noddy Boffin's confusion about the labor of reading makes clear (see Chapter 4), reading can be figured simultaneously as consuming words and as producing meaning, as a leisure activity and as work. In "Of Kings' Treasuries," Ruskin tells male readers: "When you come to a good book, you must ask yourself, 'Am I inclined to work as an Australian miner would? Are my pickaxes and shovels in good order, and am I in good trim myself...?'" (*Sesame* 64). In "Queens' Gardens," however, girls are depicted as literally consuming books: "Let her loose in the library, I say, as you do a fawn in a field. It knows the bad weeds... and will eat some bitter and prickly ones, good for it" (*Sesame* 131). But, as in *Unto This Last*, consumption is far from being a passive absorption of the products of an active industrial sphere. Capable of transforming wasteland into drawing room and existing independently of its purchases, it is a process which rivals production in its creative powers. In Ruskin's gendered model of education men work when they read, while women merely consume, but the former process merely interprets, the latter transforms. Reading well, as Ruskin tells his Winnington pupils, is simply obedience to language, and the difference between masculine and feminine reading follows from the difference between girls' and boys' relation to obedience. In "Kings' Treasuries," Ruskin exhorts male readers to "enter into [authors'] thoughts... enter into theirs, observe; not to find your own expressed by them" (63). In "Queens' Gardens," however, a girl should be taught

> to enter with her whole personality into the history she reads; to picture the passages of it vitally in her own bright imagination; to apprehend, with her fine instincts, the pathetic circumstances and dramatic relations, which the historian too often only eclipses by his reasoning, and disconnects by his arrangement: it is for her to trace the hidden equities of divine reward, and catch sight, through the darkness, of the fateful threads of woven fire that connect error with retribution. (126)

The girl's consuming of a text is figured as an act of creation: as she repairs the historian's tattered cloth of history, she transforms it into the more effective garment of moral exemplum.

Although he teaches girls literary history and crystallography in *Sesame and Lilies* and *Ethics*, Ruskin limits the tasks for which their education is to prepare them to three: dancing, dressing, and cooking—or rather, entertaining, clothing, and feeding the world. As he puts it in *Ethics*,

> L. ... [A]lways ... dress yourselves beautifully—not finely, unless on occasion; but then very finely and beautifully too. Also you are to dress as many other people as you can; and to teach them how to dress, if they don't know; and to consider every ill-dressed woman or child whom you see anywhere, as a personal disgrace; and to get at them, somehow, until everybody is as beautifully dressed as birds.
>
> (*Silence; the children drawing their breaths hard, as if they had come from under a shower bath.*)
>
> L. (*seeing objections begin to express themselves in the eyes*). Now you needn't say you can't; for you can: and it's what you were meant to do, always. (297–98)

Brushing aside the distinction between adorning oneself and producing clothing for the entire world, Ruskin insists—over the silent objections of his audience—that their creative consumption is limitlessly productive. In girlhood, then, we have production without capital, power without agency, limitless production capabilities without the means of production. This paradoxical economy makes the anti-exam possible.

4. Plotting the Anti-Exam

> *For the Psalms are written for all men & for all times.... Consequently you know they can't be all written for Birds [Ruskin's collective nickname for the Winnington girls], particularly for young Birds... —society not being wholly or eternally constituted of young Birds....*
>
> *[M]ind there is no harm in singing them for others' sake. It is very good & right of you to sing them as you would a war-song to a soldier or a sleep song to a child. But mind & know what you are about. What you clearly understand & can yourselves say, sing for yourselves—what you cannot, sing knowingly & with clear rejection not for yourselves.*
>
> —Letter to the students at Winnington Hall, 11 March 1860

Describing Miss Bell's pedagogical methods at Winnington, Burd cites Frederick Maurice, whose portrait hung with Ruskin's in the school's library: "The schoolroom should be freed from frivolous employment on the one hand and dull routine, rote learning, and the drudgery of compulsory assignments on the other" (35). A larger compulsion, of course, underlies this freedom at Winnington: while their brothers are frantically cramming for exams in order to make careers for themselves, these girls are not to make careers for *themselves* at all. In "Queens' Gardens," when Ruskin's "fawn in the field" is let loose in the library, she transforms what she learns "for others' sake": "All such knowledge should be given her as may enable her to understand, and even to aid, the work of men: and yet it should be given, not as knowledge,—not as if it were, or could be, for her an object to know; but only to feel, and to judge" (*Sesame* 125). The language of this passage seems to trip over itself in its hurry to erase the possibility of a girl's possession of knowledge. The shift in grammatical direction here hints at the disruption of cause and effect; it advertises a gap in the place where we ought to find the answer to a question—where we should be shown what knowledge *should* be "given as," if not "as knowledge." In order to be interpellated as the bourgeois subject of knowledge, a girl must learn, but as the future agent of this interpellation in her role as wife and mother, she must learn not to know, but to teach. Despite Ruskin's instructions to the Winnington girls to "sing for yourselves" of "what you clearly understand and can for yourselves say," here there can be no display of an interiorized expertise. In "Queens' Gardens," girls are only to "sing knowingly & with clear rejection not for yourselves."

While a man's education "should be foundational and progressive," Ruskin argues a woman's should be "general and accomplished for daily and helpful use" (*Sesame* 128). A narrative is prescribed here for men's education; women's education has "daily usefulness" rather than a plot. But Ruskin's language hints at the paradoxical nature of this plotless education: he envisions it both as "a firm beginning" and as complete (in opposition to knowledge a girl "half-knows or misknows")—both start and finish (129). A similar suspension of temporal logic characterizes Ruskin's gloss on two lines from Wordsworth's "She Was A Phantom of Delight":

> "A countenance in which did meet
> Sweet records, promises as sweet."

> The perfect loveliness of a woman's countenance can only consist in that majestic peace, which is founded in the memory of happy and useful years,—full of sweet records; and from the joining of this with that yet more majestic childishness, which is still full of change and promise;—opening always—modest at once, and bright, with hope of better things to be won, and to be bestowed. There is no old age where there is still that promise. (*Sesame* 125)

A "perfect" woman should be both younger and older than she really is. Dwelling only in the "records" of the past and the "promises" of the future, her subjectivity has no present. Narrative is disrupted—teleology's promise is revoked—because this story has a gap where the examination should be. The resulting temporal confusion frees a girl from developmental logic: her education enables her to become a vessel capable of carrying the past into the future.

The central conceit of "Queens' Gardens"—because of her ability to create by consuming, every middle-class woman is a potential queen—plays on and develops the idea of a portable past contained and carried by feminine education. The Victorian Gothic Revival in general can be read as reifying and incorporating a residual feudalism through the commodification of its artifacts.[11] Dwight Culler remarks that "Victorian medievalism," unlike other forms of nineteenth-century historicism, "was peculiarly static. The Middle ages seem not to have been related by their admirers to the present by any process of historic change but are simply set over against the present as an ideal or paradigm" (160). In the 1882 preface, Ruskin insists that *Sesame and Lilies* "is wholly of the old school, . . . it . . . assumes for perennial some old-fashioned conditions and existences which the philosophy of to-day imagines to be extinct with the Mammoth and the Dodo" (*Sesame* 51). Although an actual queen sat on the throne of England as Ruskin delivered "Of Queens' Gardens," he insists at once on the obsolescence of this Victorian ghost of feudalism—it is "old-fashioned"—and on its freedom from temporality—it is "perennial." Without losing its status as history, then, feudalism is depicted as a contemporary alternative to capitalism. The relation of past to present is metaphorical rather than metonymic, appropriative rather than supersessive: spatial rather than temporal.

Edward Fitzgerald's *Euphranor* (1903) recalls one of Victorian Gothic's greatest moments of conspicuous consumption, the ill-fated Eglinton Tournament[12]: "There was the Queen of Beauty on her throne —Lady Seymour—who alone of all the whole affair was *not* a sham— . . . the rain began, and the Knights threw down their lances, and put up their umbrellas" (Girouard 103). Here, the masculine relation to history is expressed as a narrative: men throw down the lances of chivalry to pick up the umbrellas of commerce. Women, however, are connected to the feudal past in an honest, unforced way that makes such a narrative unnecessary: as long as they remain beauties, women remain queens. For

Ruskin as well as Fitzgerald, the plotless life of the good woman allies her with the reified category of the historical. The history of gender relations in "Queens' Gardens" takes the objectified form of a collection of books. In his unchronological survey, he finds the same queen of beauty on her throne in Shakespeare, Scott, "the great Italians and Greeks," and Coventry Patmore. He quotes the following lines from the early Italian poet Pannuccio dal Bagno, in which a lover's obedience is given at the command of his all-powerful mistress:

> For lo! thy law is passed
> That this my love should manifestly be
>   To serve and honour thee:
> And so I do; and my delight is full,
> Accepted for the servant of thy rule.
>   (117)

In Patmore's *Angel in the House*, quoted a few pages later, that obedience is given in exchange for a woman's "sweet self":

> Ah, wasteful woman! she who may
>   On her sweet self set her own price,
> Knowing he cannot choose but pay,
>   How has she cheapen'd Paradise;
> How given for nought her priceless gift,
>   How spoiled the bread and spill'd the wine,
> Which, spent with due, respective thrift,
>   Had made brutes men, and men divine!
>   (120)

Ruskin's quotation of these lines just a few pages after dal Bagno's silently tells the story of the replacement of "lances" with "umbrellas" while at the same time denying that it *is* a story. Dal Bagno's figuring of women's rule as the paradigmatic relation of feudalism, or the lord's power over his vassal, is replaced by Patmore's version, where it is figured as the paradigmatic relationship of commodity exchange, that between commodity and consumer. Nevertheless, Ruskin refuses to depict this relationship as temporal: in "Queens' Gardens," dal Bagno and Patmore are expressing the same "eternal truth" (120).

Marx's *Eighteenth Brumaire* draws a distinction between such truly revolutionary appropriations as the French Revolution's use of the "names, battle cries, and costumes" of the Roman republic, and the merely "parodic" appropriation of Napoleon I by his nephew:

> Thus the awakening of the dead in [the former] revolutions served the purpose of glorifying the new struggles, not of parodying the old [as the latter does]; of magnifying the given task in imagination, not of fleeing from its solution in reality; of finding once more the spirit of revolution, not of making its ghost walk about again. (17)

The distinction is between the laudable, because necessary, accomplishment of something new temporarily disguised as something old, and the despicable, because reactionary, reactivation of something old as a parody or ghost of itself. In "Queens' Gardens" Ruskin "awakens" the feudal past not only as a means of urging the transformation of the present, but also as a ghost emptied of its historical content, and thus rewriteable as a phantom solution to the contradictions of high capitalism.[13]

This ghost of history—caught in the temporal gap created by the anti-exam—refigures the categories of the present as well. Ruskin's reification of the past as a present alternative risks making it into just one among other alternatives, merely a commodity which can be transformed into other commodities and whose value cannot be determined without them. But Patmore's woman-as-commodity hints at an imaginary solution to this dilemma: ". . . she . . . may / On her sweet self set her own price." As in the Winnington letters, in "Queens' Gardens" Ruskin leaves value unthumbed; unpriced, intact. The self-pricing commodity—like a self-grading student—suggests a value so contingent it is absolute. It opens for the anti-examiner the possibility of a category of objects that are exempt from the ceaseless evaluative exchange of a commodity culture.

In the 1872 preface to *Sesame and Lilies* Ruskin makes use of this category when he suggests a scheme for his girl readers that embeds the domestic production of the feudal household in bourgeois consumer values:

> [L]et a certain part of your day ... be set apart for making strong and pretty dresses for the poor. Learn the sound qualities of all useful stuffs, and make everything of the best you can get, whatever its price.... [B]e sure you get everything as good as can be: and if, in the villainous state of modern trade, you cannot get it good at any price, buy its raw material, and set some of the poor women about you to spin and weave, till you have got stuff that can be trusted. (39–40)

Ruskin's pedagogical economy here is essentially the pre-industrial capitalist's putting-out system, but his self-consciously archaic description of this process ("set some of the poor women about you to spin and weave") suggests the relationship, unmediated by monetary exchange, between the lady of the manor and her dependants. This feudal entrepreneurship is envisioned, moreover, as merely a part of the middle-class girl's training in effective consumption. The queen in-training of "Queens' Gardens" contains a feminized history within the feminized, domestic sphere of consumption.

She is thus a genuine queen: both the embodiment of and the power behind Ruskin's ideal state. In his anti-exam, Ruskin collapses the examination's mediating structure of exchange not only between pupil and teacher, but also between the state and the subject. While both the lectures which originally made up *Sesame and Lilies* depend on a central royal metaphor, Ruskin's celebration of royal *power* for both sexes is largely confined to "Queens' Gardens," while in "Kings' Treasuries" he focuses on the difficulties of obtaining royal *rank*. Indeed, Ruskin opens "Kings' Treasuries" by maintaining that the climbing of male professional ladders, whether nautical, clerical, or political, is motivated, not by the desire for power he describes as "God-given" in "Queens' Gardens," but by "our thirst for applause" and "love of praise": "[A] prince does not usually desire to enlarge, or a subject to gain, a kingdom, because he believes that no one else can as well serve the State, upon its throne; but, briefly, because he wishes to be addressed as 'Your Majesty,' by as many lips as may be brought to such utterance" (*Sesame* 56). Ruskin points to the status, rather than the power, inherent in such titles as "captain," "My Lord," and "Your Majesty." The exercising of beneficent power—in "Queens' Gardens," woman's special task—in the ruling of ship, diocese, or state is relegated to second place in the list of motives for men's "advancement in Life" (*Sesame* 55). Feminine power, however, is so important that, when delivering "Queens' Gardens" as a lecture, Ruskin makes women responsible for "thousands of Circassians ... being driven from their country, with dreadful loss of life from suffering and exhaustion. This, he said, was all the fault of English men and women, but chiefly English ladies. If they cared about it and wept over it, it could not be" (qtd. from the *Manchester Examiner*, *Sesame* 127).

Ruskin announces his shift in focus from the royal status he discusses in "Kings' Treasuries" to the royal power he advocates for women in "Queens' Gardens" by suggesting in the second lecture's first few pages that the "old-fashioned" political relations he wishes to revive in the present are better conceptualized as an objet d'art than as a narrative:

> Observe that word "State";.... It means literally the standing and stability of a thing; and you have the full force of it in the derived word "statue"—"the immovable thing." A king's majesty or "state," then, ... depends on the movelessness of both:—without tremor, without quiver of balance; established and enthroned upon a foundation of eternal law which nothing can alter nor overthrow. (110)

Despite the gender of the monarch here, the notion of royal power is quite clearly that which "Queens' Gardens" assigns to women, rather than the royal rank assigned to men in "King's Treasuries." For Arnold, the Voluntary school pupil can be made to display the beneficent working of an active state power embodied in the figure of the Inspector. For Ruskin, however, the players and the goal are both different: a "moveless" ghost of feudalism and a powerfully "moveless" state are preserved and contained in the body of the middle-class schoolgirl.

5. Like A Rock: Girls Become Crystals in
The Ethics of the Dust

> *When . . . is [Darwin] going to write . . . the "Retrogression" of Species—or the Origin of Nothing? I am far down on my way into [becoming] a flint-sponge.*
> —Letter to Charles Eliot Norton, 1868
>
> ISABEL. *Oh, no, no! we won't be diamonds, please.*
> L. *Yes, you shall, Isabel; they are very pretty things, if the jewelers, and the kings and queens, would only let them alone. You shall make diamonds of yourselves and rubies of yourselves, and emeralds.*
> —*The Ethics of the Dust*

In his preface to *The Ethics of the Dust*, Ruskin remarks that the book's format, "fragmentary answers to questions," derives from lessons he gave at Winnington (201), and certainly it echoes the Winnington letters' obsession with exchange. *The Ethics* is Ruskin's one foray into Socratic dialogue, and its initial lack of success left him defensive about the work. On the surface, a pedagogical dialogue sounds just like an examination—a series of questions and answers between a teacher and his pupils. But in fact, a very different kind of "play" is being performed.[14] The Lecturer, like any good teacher, wants his pupils to work in earnest and create their own wisdom through independent thought. But the decentering of this classroom does not have exactly the effect we might expect. The girls want clear answers to clear questions, value for money, a genuine transaction: they want an exam. The clash between their "banking model" of education and the Lecturer's critical pedagogy gives rise to constant bickering and teasing. Over and over, the Lecturer insists on his position, and then stops short, refusing to justify himself or answer questions, sending the girls off to "think," and excluding these thoughts from the text. They, in turn, seem to feel not so much as if they are being forced to think, as that they are being forced to do without answers: "DORA *(biting her lip)*.

Well, then, tell us what we ought to mean. As if you didn't teach it all to us, and mean it yourself, at this moment, more than we do, if you wouldn't be tiresome!" (*Ethics* 286). The Lecturer's frequent spats with his pupils are never resolved; they often leave him looking pointlessly brutal, as when he makes the pious Violet cry and the outspoken Dora exclaim "(*scarlet*). It's too bad—it's a shame:—poor Violet!" (290).[15]

The anxiety about the exchange of use-values between teacher and students raised by this battle takes the form in *Ethics* of a constant fretting about questions. The Lecturer and his pupils are intensely interested in the value and ownership of their questions and answers, and struggle constantly over the rules governing their exchanges: What rights belong to questioners and answerers? What are their duties? Who ought or ought not to ask what kinds of questions? Under what circumstances? Can—and how can—they be exchanged for answers? The unresolvable contradiction between students preparing for an exam and a teacher trying to hold a dialogue is dramatized by the bad fit between question and answer at several points in *The Ethics*. Sometimes the Lecturer impatiently supplies the students' side of the interchange himself: "I hope you feel inclined to interrupt me, and say, 'But we know our places; how do the atoms know theirs?'" (222). And the children are properly cowed when he exclaims:

> L. What a boundless capacity for sleep, and for serene stupidity, there is in the human mind! Fancy reflective beings, who cut and polish stones for three thousand years, for the sake of the pretty stains upon them . . . —and never a curious soul of them, all that while, asks, "What painted the rocks?"
> (*The audience look dejected, and ashamed of themselves.*) (331–32)

One of the Lecturer's sauciest pupils, Dora, demands equal question-asking between teacher and students: "I'm sure you ask us questions enough! How can you have the heart, when you dislike so to be asked them yourself?" The Lecturer responds by refusing to institute a rate of exchange between student-questions and teacher-questions: "My dear child, if people do not answer questions, it does not matter how many they are asked, because they've no trouble with them. Now, when I ask you questions, I never expect to be answered; but when you ask me, you always do; and it's not fair."

In *The Ethics*, interrogative excess is associated—always jokingly—with sexual as well as economic reproduction. The irrepressible Dora, for example, is associated with both, through a joke about marrying for money that scandalized the real Winnington Hall girls. Even when the mild and sensible Mary promises that "There's one question more; then I've done," the Lecturer queries her:

> L. Only one?
> MARY. Only one.
> L. But if it is answered, won't it turn into two?

But the Lecturer need not fear—as Mary responds, "No; I think it will remain single, and be comfortable" (239). Despite the Lecturer's constant destabilizing of equivalencies, this pedagogical economy is ultimately one of zero-sum gain. By the end of *The Ethics*, the proliferation of currencies we find in the Winnington letters has been somehow halted and questions, like crystals, have come together in perfect order. As Mary tells Dora, "I think all the questions come into one, at last, nearly" (340). The uncertainties of pedagogical exchange are suspended in the dialogue's central metaphor.

The Lecturer opens *The Ethics* with what at first seems like an examination for his youngest students. Isabel and Florrie are playing a game based on the Valley of the Diamonds episode in *Sinbad*, and he joins in by transforming the Valley into an elaborate allegory on corrupting riches, obviously inviting decoding. And the girls obediently set to work to provide a translation, only to be met with the Lecturer's refusal to provide an answer sheet:

> SIBYL. ... Isabel ... wanted so much to ask about the Valley of Diamonds again, and she has worked so hard at it, and made it nearly all out by herself.... Won't you tell us what it means?
> L. Now, Sibyl, I am sure you, who never explained yourself, should be the last to expect others to do so. I hate explaining myself.

SIBYL. And yet how often you complain of other people for not saying what they meant. How I have heard you growl over the three stone steps to purgatory, for instance!

L. Yes; because Dante's meaning is worth getting at; but mine matters nothing: at least, if ever I think it is of any consequence, I speak it as clearly as may be. But you may make anything you like of the serpent forests. I could have helped you to find out what they were, by giving a little more detail, but it would have been tiresome.

SIBYL. It is much more tiresome not to find out. Tell us, please, as Isabel says, because we feel so stupid....

ISABEL (*who has crept up to her side without any one's seeing*). Oh, Sibyl, please ask him about the fire-flies!

L. What, you there, mousie! No; I won't tell either Sibyl or you about the fire-flies; nor a word more about anything else. You ought to be little fire-flies yourselves, and find your way in twilight by your own wits.... Away with you, children. You have thought enough for to-day. (*Ethics* 366–68, n. 6 to p. 355)

Placed at the end of the volume, this final interchange drips with pathos, which merely thickens in the letter he appends in a further footnote showing the "real" girls continuing to translate the allegory against his refusals—and the "real" Lecturer capitulating by finally explaining that the fireflies stand for vanity.[16] In the body of the text, however, the Lecturer abandons the allegory abruptly in the first lecture, shifting with no transition from allegorical elaboration to a literal analysis of his allegory's vehicle: "Meantime, Florrie, though all that I have been telling you is very true, yet you must not think the sort of diamonds that people wear in rings and necklaces are found lying about on the grass. Would you like to see how they really are found?" (216). Ruskin first ostentatiously places jewels in their figurative role as commodities, to be exchanged not only for money but for "right" answers to the allegorical exam. He then wrests them from this setting, placing them in a completely different figurative universe. Diamonds are abruptly removed from their allegorical meaning (corrupting wealth), and placed in the schoolroom for study as crystals—

which, we discover, are themselves personified as schoolgirls. If Florrie and Isabel begin *The Ethics* by playing at looking for diamonds, they are merely sidetracked by looking for their meaning outside themselves. By the end of *The Ethics of the Dust*, they *are* diamonds.[17]

Like the queens of "Queens' Gardens," the Old Lecturer's pupils are exhorted to wield the power of productive consumption through sympathy, love, and praise:

> L. ... Do not think you will ever get harm by striving to enter into the faith of others, and to sympathise, in imagination, with the guiding principles of their lives. So only can you justly love them, or pity them, or praise. By the gracious effort you will double, treble— aye, indefinitely multiply, at once the pleasure, the reverence, and the intelligence with which you read ... and, believe me, it is wiser and holier, by the fire of your own faith to kindle the ashes of expired religions, than to let your soul shiver and stumble among their graves. (356)

Identification with, rather than desire for, the object of knowledge is clearly the motive power in this mode of production. In *The Ethics*, Ruskin's pedagogy combines the progressive insistence that pupils draw their own conclusions with a contradictory emphasis on the object lesson, copying, and practicing—learning through repetition and identification. When that object, as it is in *The Ethics*, is rock crystal, an important corollary to the anti-exam becomes apparent. As Fuss suggests, "To be open to an identification is to be open to a death encounter, open to the very possibility of communing with the dead" (Fuss 1). In the process of productive consumption, girls are indeed "preached to death"—or at least to the deathlike solidity of rock.

In *Praeterita*, Ruskin refers with rueful pride to "the habit which has remained with me during life, of ... looking exclusively at the thing before my eyes till I could see it" (202), lending an air of pathos to the classic position of masculine subjectivity: "My entire delight was in observing without being myself observed" (156). Despite his expertise as an observer, however, and the power he cedes to the act of observing, for Ruskin this power is as much that of the object as the subject—and so there is no direct or simple connection between seeing and possessing, or seeing and assessing. As Peltason notes, as an observer, Ruskin cultivates "a passivity that blurs the distinction between spectatorship and creation" ("Ruskin's" 676). To trace—repeat, imitate—is to see, and to see is to create, to acquire an object without possessing it. The object gains new meaning, associated not with passivity but agency. Indeed, the constant slippage from agency to passivity in the Lecturer's description of crystalline power in *The Ethics* renders the distinction almost meaningless:

> There seem to be in some crystals, from the beginning, an unconquerable purity of vital power, and strength of crystal spirit. Whatever dead substance, unacceptant of this energy, comes in their way, is either rejected, or forced to take some beautiful subordinate form; the purity of the crystal remains unsullied, and every atom of it bright with coherent energy. (263)

Everywhere in *The Ethics* Ruskin courts the blurring of lines between teacher and student as well as between subject and object, agent and patient. In fact, the conflating of the identification with his pupils and a distancing power over them forms an inevitable part of this revision of the relation between subject and object, dramatizing a number of contradictions in pedagogical relationships. Ruskin's pedagogy at once foreshadows and parodies Pablo Freire's utopian blending of the roles of teacher and student:

> Through dialogue, the teacher-of-the-students and the students-of-the-teacher cease to exist and a new term emerges: teacher-student with students-teachers. The teacher . . . is himself taught in dialogue with the students, who in turn while being taught also teach. They become jointly responsible for a process in which all grow. In this process, . . . authority must be *on the side of* freedom, not *against* it. Here, no one teaches another, nor is anyone self-taught. People teach each other. (Freire 61)[18]

Ruskin's insistence on identification between teacher/subject and student/object causes this vision of reciprocity to collapse on itself, as he dashes to and fro, straining to occupy both ends of the pedagogical exchange at once. In a number of letters to his Winnington students, Ruskin phrases his pedagogical imperatives in these dizzying terms: "I don't mean to help you:—Rather to puzzle you—If I can (I'm partly puzzled myself)" (ltr., April 1859), he claims, and ends one assignment by apologizing that "that looks like a formidable letter—now its done —but I don't think it's so tiring as the others. At least it has not tired *me* so much" (ltr., 4–5 December 1859). When Dora objects to the Lecturer's claim that "[g]irls ought to like to be seen" (294), the already-vitiated division between subject and object is further eroded by the blending of the masculine gaze with the professor's invigilation:

> L. ... I don't think Jessie and Lily will agree to that. You like me to see you dancing, don't you, Lily?
> LILY. Yes, certainly,—when we do it rightly. (294)

Burd tells us that "Ruskin apparently intended that the [Winnington] children should copy his Sunday letters and add the text of his Biblical references at the foot of each page" (198). Their learning through copying did not stop here. Ruskin's cousin Joan Agnew, visiting Winnington with him, writes that "last night I went into a room and to my amusement and delight I found about seven nice intelligent girls busy writing out all they could remember of a little talk he had been giving them" (Joan Agnew to Mrs. Ruskin, 11 May 1868). Whether advising the copying of drawings or of texts, what seems to matter to Ruskin is the physical contact with the object of knowledge, and an identification with its creator that is nevertheless synonymous with obedience. Freedom equals imitation equals "obedience by *action*":

> I shall leave the search to you:—only I want you to notice one (or *two*; rather,) main points in the way they are scattered.
> ... you will find and feel the full stress laid in both on obedience by *action*. Read in this view—Matt. 5th.19, 20, 48. Matt 6th.19–33. and 7th.21.24: or better than reading, write them out neatly altogether. (to the students at Winnington Hall, 27–28 March 1859)

Despite—or, perhaps, because of—Ruskin's celebration of the infinite possibilities of productive consumption, we can sense in *Ethics* a constant anxiety about containment. Ruskin wants his students to stop thinking when their ideas are no longer clear, contained, and separate. "It seems to me," says the Lecturer near the end of *Ethics*, "that you have got quite as many new ideas as are good for any of you at present: and I should not like to burden you with more; but I must see that those you have are clear, if I can make them so" (339). He may mix up mythology, mineralogy, ethics, domestic science, and religion in *Ethics*, but he is also clearly attracted by the neat and definite compartmentalization of school life: "Here, for instance, you children are at school, and have to learn French, and arithmetic, and music, and several other such things. That is your 'right' for the present; the 'right' for us, your teachers, is to see that you learn as much as you can, without spoiling your dinner, your sleep, or your play; and that what you do learn, you learn well" (266). Like forming crystals, girls are in danger not so much of erupting as of losing their shape and oozing out, if insufficient pressure (or the wrong kind of pressure) is applied. Like the crystals, they need to be packed tight:

> L. ... Here, for instance, is a good garnet, living with good mica; ... the mica leaves exactly room for the garnet to crystallise comfortably in; and the garnet lives happily in its little white house fitted to it, like a pholas in its cell. But here are wicked garnets living with wicked mica. See what ruin they make of each other! You cannot tell which is which; the garnets look like dull red stains on the crumbling stone. (267)

Throughout *Ethics*, while explicitly encouraging the formation of ideas inside his listeners' "little heads," he even more explicitly discourages their irruption outside:

> MARY. Oh, if we could but understand the meaning of it all!
> L. We can understand all that is good for us. It is just as true for us, as for the crystal, that the nobleness of life depends on its consistency,—clearness of purpose,—quiet and ceaseless energy. All

doubt, and repenting, and botching, and retouching, and wondering what it will be best to do next, are vice, as well as misery. (264)

Safely and irremovably packed into the schoolgirl's head, knowledge remains stable. If, for Arnold, Trollope, and Dickens, the examination room frames a stage for the display of intellectual labor, Ruskin, too, sets a frame around the anti-examination, but one that limits and controls pedagogical exchange rather than displaying it.[19]

At Winnington, wisdom is only gained through limits: obedient acceptance and identification. It is thus always *personified* wisdom. Bell disapproved of the piecemeal "accomplishment" style of education, instead exposing her students to great *men*—whether by having the girls memorize and copy their work, or enabling them to absorb their greatness in person. To "make it possible for her girls to be with them" (Burd 39–40), Bell played hostess not only to Ruskin, but to Burne-Jones, Bishop Colenso, and other literary, artistic, and musical celebrities. In *The Ethics*, a similar value is placed on the personification of knowledge. The Lecturer instructs his pupils in the historical narrative of the "characters" in which "heathen deities" appear. In their most primitive form they represent physical forces, in the next phase ethical forces: "Thus Apollo is first, physically, the sun contending with darkness; but morally, the power of divine life contending with corruption. Athena is, physically, the air; morally, the breathing of the divine spirit of wisdom." In the deity's third and final phase "it has, at last, a personal character; and is realised in the minds of its worshippers as a living spirit, with whom men may speak face to face, as a man speaks to his friend" (*Ethics* 348). The Lecturer directs his pupils' attention most forcefully to this final phase. Personification—in its relation to identification a kind of mirror image of the pathetic fallacy—contains and exceeds the earlier phases, because it grants to both the material and the abstract the psychic richness of the indefinably integrated personality. Personification, like the pathetic fallacy, produces a class of things which are and yet are not alive. It also locates for Ruskin the distinction between understanding a personality through empathy—a necessary and limited task—and the interpretation of an idea—a task that is dangerously infinite:

> EGYPT. But how you *do* puzzle us! Why do you say Neith [Egyptian goddess of wisdom] does it? You don't mean that she is a real spirit, do you?
>
> L. What *I* mean is of little consequence. What the Egyptians meant, who called her "Neith,"—or Homer, who called her "Athena,"—or Solomon, who called her by a word which the Greeks render as "Sophia," you must judge for yourselves. But her testimony is always the same, and all nations have received it....
>
> MARY. But is that not only a personification?
>
> LILY. If it be, what will you gain by unpersonifying it, or what right have you to do so? Cannot you accept the image given you, in its life; and listen, like children, to the words which chiefly belong to you as children; "I love them that love me, and those that seek me early shall find me"?
>
> (*They are all quiet for a minute or two; questions begin to appear in their eyes.*)
>
> I cannot talk to you any more to-day. Take that rose crystal away with you, and think. (231)[20]

The Ethics demonstrates the difference between personification and other less effective forms of representation by making an implicit comparison between two crystal plots: the transformation of the medieval fair into the Crystal Palace and a performance of crystallization by the girls in the school playground. Both "crystallizations" aim at the same goal: the reification and display of history and knowledge. But the Lecturer depicts the difference between the old fair and the new palace as trivial. While "the palace (as they call it)... is always there, instead of for three days only; and it shuts up at proper hours of night[,]... as for its teaching the people, it will teach them nothing but... hammer and tongs" (244). Learning—change of any kind— only happens through an identification that transforms students as well as object of study. The transformation of the old fair into the new is just history; "wooden poles" are simply transformed "into iron ones," and "all the little" canvas booths into "one great booth" of glass (243), without changing "the people" from medieval times to the present. Because identificatory personification is absent from this process, they learn nothing, and remain unredeemed even by death.

The playground experiment, however, teaches through its embodied reenactment of crystallization's disruption and return to stasis:

> L. ... However, the best—out and out the best—way of understanding the thing, is to crystallise yourselves.
> THE AUDIENCE. Ourselves!
> L. Yes; ... carefully and finely, out in the playground. You can play at crystallisation there as much as you please.
> KATHLEEN and JESSIE. Oh! how?—how? ...
> L. ... [Form a]ny figure you like, standing close together. You had better outline it first on the turf, with sticks, or pebbles ... then get into it and enlarge or diminish it at one side, till you are all quite in it, and no empty space left.
> DORA. Crinoline and all?
> L. The crinoline may stand eventually for rough crystalline surface, unless you pin it in; and then you may make a polished crystal of yourselves.
> LILY. Oh, we'll pin it in—we'll pin it in! (235–36)

Once they have mapped out their goal by embodying it, the girls are to scatter around the playground, and then "at a given signal, let everybody walk, at the same rate, towards the outlined figure in the middle. You had better sing as you walk; that will keep you in good time. And as you close in towards it, let each take her place, and the next comers fit themselves in beside the first ones, till you are all in the figure again" (236).[21] The girls' personification of formed, then unformed, then forming crystals blurs temporality, makes it go in more than one direction—a vast improvement, *The Ethics* implies, over the strict progression from "wood" to "iron" that is the Crystal Palace's version of history.

Like his pupils playing crystals, the Lecturer's coy preservation of uncertainty as to whether the crystals he describes are "really alive" makes the learning process utterly clear yet ultimately inexplicable, because stilled into personification:

> DORA. You know, you always talk as if the crystals were alive; and we never understand how much you are in play, and how much in earnest....
>
> L. Neither do I understand, myself, my dear, how much I am in earnest. The stones puzzle me as much as I puzzle you.... [A]ll questions of this sort lead necessarily to the one main question, which we asked, before, in vain, "What is it to be alive?" (340–41)

The rock formations that Ruskin praises in his art criticism and the girls he teases and idealizes in his social criticism are alike in that both represent arrested *motion*: in both, process is embodied, change is reified, narrative is personified—the cultural work done for many Victorians by the body of the child. Both mountains and pupils can be read as the "ethical history in things," which Ruskin's editors Cooke and Wedderburn describe him as so desiring in their introduction to the volume that contains *The Ethics* and *Sesame and Lilies* (xx). Rocks can thus offer an almost novelistic narrative richness to the stilled and identificatory gaze of schoolgirls, whom the Lecturer invites to "look at them, once understanding the surrounding conditions of their fate, with an endless interest," promising that they will see

> indulged crystals, who have had centuries to form themselves in, and have changed their mind and ways continually; and have been tired, and taken heart again; and have been sick, and got well again; and thought they would try a different diet, and then thought better of it; and made but a poor use of their advantages, after all. And others you will see, who have begun life as wicked crystals; and then have been impressed by alarming circumstances, and have become converted crystals, and behaved amazingly for a little while, and fallen away again, and ended, but discreditably, perhaps even in decomposition; so that one doesn't know what will become of them.... And sometimes you will see little child-crystals put to school like schoolgirls, and made to stand in rows; and taken the greatest care of, and taught how to hold themselves up, and behave: and sometimes you will see unhappy little child-crystals left to lie about in the dirt, and pick up their living, and learn manners, where they can. And some-

times you will see fat crystals eating up thin ones, like great capitalists and little labourers; and politico-economic crystals teaching the stupid ones how to eat each other, and cheat each other; and foolish crystals getting in the way of wise ones; and impatient crystals spoiling the plans of patient ones, irreparably; just as things go on in the world. (*Ethics* 334–35)

For Ruskin, the continuum between living and dead, between literal and figurative, is most powerfully characterized by this identification of schoolgirls with crystals. Rocks' histories, like schoolgirls' anti-exams, show that change inevitably results in "movelessness," and that the meaning of history is the end of history:

[T]he great laws which never fail, and to which all change is subordinate, appear such as to accomplish a gradual advance to lovelier order, and more calmly, yet more deeply, animated Rest.... For, through all the phases of [the dust's] transition and dissolution, there seems to be a continual effort to raise itself into a higher state; and a measured gain, through the fierce revulsion and slow renewal of the earth's frame, in beauty, and order, and permanence.... [D]uring countless subsequent centuries, declining, or, rather let me say, rising, to repose, [it] finishes the infallible lustre of its crystalline beauty, under harmonies of law which are wholly beneficent, because wholly inexorable. (357–58)

For the Victorians, argues Stephen Bann, historicism depends on the death of the past—its irrecoverable loss. Steedman suggests that the body of the child then proves a miraculous exception to this rule; it is where we find that which has been lost (80). For Ruskin, though, it is death itself that we find there, linking that body in its "animated Rest" to the living rock:

DORA and JESSE (*clapping their hands*). Then we really may believe that the mountains are living?

L. You may at least earnestly believe, that the presence of the spirit which culminates in your own life, shows itself in dawning, wherever the dust of the earth begins to assume any orderly and lovely state. You will find it impossible to separate this idea of gradated manifestation from that of the vital power. Things are not either wholly alive, or wholly dead. They are less or more alive. (*Ethics* 346)

Dora and Jesse are delighted to imagine an expansion of the living world to include mountains and jewels. But the Lecturer's gloss suggests that living rock does not expand, but contracts the learnable world, filling in a gap just as crystallization fills a fault in a rock. The formal principle of repetition, which for Arnold is life-giving and for Trollope gives life to the "mechanical," seems in Ruskin to be a principle of stasis rather than movement. Once again we are left with a zero-sum gain: if rocks and girls are ultimately metonymically related, then what girls know about rocks, rocks somehow lose, and when crystals are personified—persons are crystallized. Dora and Jesse seem to imagine a Disneyesque landscape of animate rocks, but the Lecturer seems to be imagining *in*animate girls.

It makes sense that there would be only one possible result to the anti-exam: failure. Despite his promises of a happy ending in stillness and rest, the crystal narratives that the girls are to read with "endless interest" all end in decay, frustration, injustice, sorrow. "This poor little book will sufficiently have done its work, for the present, if it engages any of its young readers in study which may enable them to despise it for its shortcomings," Ruskin claims pathetically in the preface to *Ethics* (202). Ruskin dedicates the book to the "little housewives" of Winnington, collapsing the distance between their youth and their destined tasks. But this very foreclosure is ostentatiously unsuccessful within the text itself. After the Lecturer defends the use of sewing as an illustration of the action of crystallization, he tells the girls:

> L. ... Wife means "weaver." You have all the right to call yourselves little "housewives," when you sew neatly.
>
> DORA. But I don't think we want to call ourselves "little housewives."
>
> L. You must either be house-Wives or house-Moths; remember that. In the deep sense, you must either weave men's fortunes,

and embroider them; or feed upon, and bring them to decay. You had better let me keep my sewing illustration, and help me out with it.

DORA. Well, we'll hear it, under protest. (336–37)

Despite their enjoyment of the crystallization game, when it comes to what the Lecturer sees as their proper *work* his pupils refuse the deadly identification. The erotic charge of Ruskin's writing to and about his Winnington pupils carries with it a remarkably open admission that their interests conflict. Writing to them, Ruskin likens his teaching to brushing out his pupils' hair—with the more usual disciplinary association of the hairbrush (not teasing but spanking) left unspoken:

> But I always will if I can, worry and teaze you, and pull your little ideas out of their knots—until—first you feel that there *are* knots in them—and secondly—know whether—when they are brushed out of the tangle—they are smooth and nice ideas—that can be pressed and made nice wreaths of—or only little broken bits of ideas—better cut or brushed away—knots & all. (to the students at Winnington Hall, 8 May 1864)

The domestic intimacy of hairbrushing—with its implicit sexual and punitive threats—results in ideas either "pressed" into the stillness of (mourning?) wreaths of hair, or "cut or brushed away." In *The Ethics*, the freedom to draw one's own conclusions is always associated with violent limits and the process of crystallization becomes a model for this process of purifying, clarifying violence, ending either in stasis or in chaos.

In *The Ethics of the Dust*, as in most of Ruskin's work, we are asked to equate his achievement with his pathos. Throughout his work, the establishment of identification, communication, and exchange inexorably leads to the blocking of identification, communication, and exchange. Like the story of history stilling into rock, his own youthful promise stilling into failure is a story Ruskin loves to tell and retell (it provides the only consistent narrative structure in *Praeterita*, for example). In "The Mystery of Life and Its Arts," Ruskin bases his authority as an observer and a teacher on "my own failure, and such success in petty things as in its poor triumph seemed to me worse than failure" (*Sesame* 152). The Winnington story turns out to have the same plot:

> I don't know any one who could do the sort of work I did at Winnington, the primal condition of it being my far-away sort of chivalrous devotion which enabled all the girls to trust me wholly—and say anything to me they wanted to say. But—I am sorry to add that I don't believe what I did was of the least use. There was great interest and excitement at the time,—but they did not go on with anything by themselves at home—Perhaps I am unjust and less might have been done otherwise—but I was wholly disappointed—they would all draw—or break stones, or do anything in the world, as long as I looked after them,—but it was only in affection, and ceased, when they were left to themselves. (to Mrs. John Simon, 19 March 1867)

Despite his efforts to still the examination process in the anti-exam, Ruskin reveals here that even his ruse to avoid it partakes of the examination's insistence on the display of intellectual labor—nullifying the difference between drawing and breaking stones, "as long as I looked on." Ruskin's anti-exam is, after all, not so different in its way from the alternative examinations proposed by Arnold, Trollope, and Dickens. Arnold's Inspectorial examination, displaying intellectual labor by bringing the working class to evaluation, Trollope's Chaffanbrass "working for money," collapsing the display of labor and labor itself, and Dickens's examinations of feminine ignorance that provide a professional ladder for masculine examiners, are all designed as "anti-exams," set against the Revised Code, the speculative promises of the Civil Service Commission, and the banking—or "self-betterment"—model of education. In other words, each of these authors uses one version of the examination to figure and contain the threat another poses to his pedagogical economy—whether that of making the exchange of meaning fall too readily into economic exchange or that of blocking it entirely, whether that of implying that intellectual work is just like other work—or that of implying it is not work at all.

Epilog:
Money for Nothing

> The property metaphor fits very nicely across education. Everything that is about schooling is about property, be it intellectual, social, or cultural, or be it about real property.
> —Gloria Ladson-Billings, quoted in Carlos Alberto Torres, *Education, Power, and Personal Biography*

> If it is virtually impossible now to imagine that particular objects and practices may be incommensurable, this fact goes a long way toward explaining why the pluralist or relativist discourse of value can so easily substitute for the analysis of objective social relations.
> —John Guillory, *Cultural Capital*

This book begins in the twentieth century, with an epigraph from Nabokov, and I'd like to return briefly to the present at its close. In recent years, literary critics have directed more and more attention to pedagogical issues and to their own workplaces as institutions within which value circulates. The Victorians were hardly the last educators to struggle with the competing claims of autonomy and accountability, or with accepting, adapting, or rejecting economic models for the school. Relationships between marketplace and classroom, work and education, money and cultural capital, still trouble us today. Indeed, debates on academic work seem to have advanced surprisingly little since the 1860s. More and more often lately, I find myself commenting (no doubt annoyingly), "Oh, that's what Arnold says," or "You should read Trollope," when colleagues complain about the absurdities involved in the academy's new quantification rituals or the emptiness of terms like "merit" or "excellence." We still use the figure of the examination as a way to think about these troubles, as demonstrated in recent controversies over the introduction of "standards-based" testing in public schools and over the spread in higher education of what Bill Readings calls the academic "discourse of excellence" (Readings 3). But we can also, like our Victorian predecessors, use the trope of the examination as a way to question our own dismay at the extension of market values and tactics into public schooling and university management.

The Victorian literary man's use of the examination trope can teach us that the opposition—and also the slippage—between the concept of an educational transaction and a financial transaction makes it surprisingly easy to lose track of the real relationship between the educational and economic systems in our society. Recent articulations of the question—What is literature's social function?—tend to end by admitting, or at least implying, that by now it has only one: it (sometimes) gives us work to do.[1] But rather than simply taking this fact for granted, perhaps we can use it to read literature's self-assertions as economic actions in this fundamental sense. If, like Victorian authors, we do this, we can use the test to test our conditions of labor. For example, we tend to think about the introduction of standards-based testing in public schools as a kind of twentieth-century payment by results, introducing "free trade" to the classroom by imposing arbitrary and culturally biased standards on students and teachers. I have to admit to a certain ambivalence about this position—in fact, I'd be thrilled if all (or even most) American high school graduates could write a coherent sentence and identify major historical events. But the issue becomes much clearer if we think about standards-based testing not in terms of its ideological impact but in terms of its economic infrastructure. Here, while schools all over the country are physically crumbling away, we find vast sums going to the private corporations who write and administer these tests and to the graders they hire, rather than to schools and teachers. Similarly, it helps to think of such trends as the distributing of funding within universities by competition, demands for the quantification of teaching and research, and attempts to raise individual universities' national rankings not as the "corporatizing" of the academy, but as making faculty add to their already growing workloads—without adding to their already shrinking salaries—a whole array of tasks for which they are not trained (obtaining funding for, quantifying, accounting for, and otherwise administering their own labor).

Readings notes that "such changes are hailed by conservatives"—and lamented by leftist academics—"as 'exposure to market forces,' whereas what is occurring is actually the highly artificial creation of a fictional market that presumes exclusive governmental control of funding" (36). When we resist attempts to "turn the University into a corporation," what exactly are we protecting, what exactly are we risking? There are, of course, obvious ways to exploit this rhetoric to our advantage: we can call on the myth of the extraeconomic to attack registration and funding cutoffs, for example. But it has a tendency to spill over into rhetoric on teaching and learning in ways that are less useful. For one thing, our resistance to the corporate organization of academic enclaves is becoming less and less effective. As university labor dispute after labor dispute shows us (including a current strike by maintenance workers at my own institution), clinging to the extraeconomic divides professionals from other workers, and allows money-capital plenty of opportunity for scapegoating intellectual workers in its own dealings with the working class. As a graduate student at Yale University in the early 1990s, the virulent resistance to graduate student unionization (and especially to affiliation with existing campus unions) by administrators, faculty, and other students taught me that figuring intellectual work as somehow extraeconomic can be used against, as well as for, intellectual workers themselves (see Nelson). This resistance was consistently couched in the same language—familial, sometimes even feudal—in which Victorians like Ruskin or Arnold celebrate their versions of the state. Figuring intellectual work as priceless inevitably brings it under the sway of alternatives to capitalism that are—like the Victorian home and the feudal manor—not extraeconomic, simply extracontractual. The priceless, as *Our Mutual Friend* and *The Three Clerks* teach us, can be hard to distinguish from the worthless.

University students and faculty tend to see "corporatizing" trends in education as merely interfering with what is essentially the academic family romance: identification, transmission, sublimation, and so on. In current battles between and among university faculty, graduate students, and administrators we continue to figure ideological production, exchange, and consumption as either an alternative to, or a replica of, the market. Insisting on this division, we become its victims: we become vulnerable to that special ambivalence toward that which is perceived to lie outside the "economic"—that which is worthless, beyond price, taboo. Academics are in increasing danger of depicting ourselves as getting money for nothing.

The nineteenth-century intellectual worker made sure that he knew what he was getting paid for, even if it was for inculcating the value of the priceless. Many academics in the humanities today also see themselves as self-conscious creators and managers of ideology once more, but without the same interest in placing a market value on ideology. As pedagogues in the twentieth century as well as students of the nineteenth century, we need to pay attention to the multiple, complicated, overdetermined uses of the examination trope in our culture. "Once excellence has been generally accepted as an organizing principle," warns Readings,

> there is no need to argue about differing definitions. Everyone is excellent, in their own way, and everyone has more of a stake in being left alone to be excellent than in intervening in the administrative process. There is a clear parallel here to the condition of the political subject under contemporary capitalism. Excellence draws only one boundary: the boundary that protects the unrestricted power of the bureaucracy. (33)

Being "left alone to be excellent" has been the goal of college and university faculty for too long. As teachers, as writers, as members of faculty senates, as administrators, as potential or actual members of labor unions, we already wield a good deal of power, ideological and economic. That power needs to be accepted, recognized, and made use of.

Reference Matter

Notes

Chapter One

1. Midcentury reforms in school architecture included the "gallery" formation described here, which, unlike earlier "monitorial" classrooms, emphasized the visibility of all students from the teacher's perspective (Hunter, *Culture* 59).

2. The roots of Western educational testing in religious rituals like the catechism and confession are well documented by Montgomery, Foucault (*Discipline* and *Sexuality*), and Hunter. Hunter notes that the nineteenth-century popular education system blends "the religio-philanthropic concern with the moral well-being of individuals, and the governmental concern with the 'moral and physical' condition of the population" (*Culture* 39). The result of this blend was inevitably a secularizing one: "The Christian care of the soul and the governmental administration of the populace converged in the techniques of moral supervision.... And it was precisely this convergence that sparked the opposition of those who wished the schools to remain wholly religious institutions" (Hunter, *Culture* 47).

3. The opening exam, as well as these closing set pieces, are clearly part of the paradoxical blending of "fact" and "fancy" noted in the novel by Catherine Gallagher in *The Industrial Reformation of English Fiction*.

4. One important exception is Byron Caminero-Santangelo's 1994 "Testing for Truth: Joseph Conrad and the Ideology of the Examination." However, Caminero-Santangelo focuses more on the ideological supports the examination offers turn-of-the-century social hierarchies, rather than on the

contradictions it raises. Recent critical and post-critical pedagogues have, for the most part, associated the examination either with the sterile "banking model" of education Paulo Freire critiques in *Pedagogy of the Oppressed* or with Foucauldian disciplinarity (see, for example, Carnoy and Levin, Hanson, Sosniski, Torres, and Trachsel, and the collections edited by Gallop, Giroux and McLaren, Stone, and Todd).

5. While China had long had a complex system of government examinations, the first written examinations took place in Europe in 1702 (N. Morris 27–30). The Cambridge Tripos, or Senate House exam, in mathematics only (moral and natural sciences were added in 1848), enjoyed a high reputation starting in the eighteenth century, and Oxford passed an Examination Statute in 1800 (Roach 12–13). Developing out of the clergyman's regular catechizing of local Church school pupils, the combination of government inspection and examination officially began in the factory school, and spread from there to working-class elementary schools and, eventually, middle-class secondary schools (Edmonds 67–70).

6. There is little doubt that there is some link between the growing power of the middle class in mid-nineteenth-century British culture and the examination revolution, just as the expansion of government involvement in education was related to expanding suffrage. Gordon and Lawton see the roots of this revolution in Utilitarian adaptations of classic political economy (179). Historians differ, however, as to the extent and nature of this link (see Roach, Simon, Gowan). Victorian educational reform was, after all, a thoroughly top-down phenomenon, which "came from the traditionally dominant classes—the landed gentry and aristocracy, assisted by the specific expertise of representatives of the professional groupings linked traditionally with these classes" (Simon 34). "There has been little overall evidence of social mobility through educational achievement" notes Eggleston (18–19). As local and national examination systems were established, they found themselves tied to Oxford and Cambridge, bastions of aristocratic power (Simon 35). In fact, the Education Committee's Balliol-bred reformers often saw state-supported education as a hedge against the inevitable extension of the franchise to portions of the working class in 1867 (Reeder 8).

7. If this fragile exchange between literal and cultural currencies is trusted too far, however, it falls apart. The examiner and the "consuming subject" might share an investment in judgment, taste, and an ideology of choice, but in a consumer culture, the test can reveal that one's choices are far

from free (Thomas Richards shows how the "consuming subject" was generated by the revolutionary semiotic structure of the Crystal Palace; see also Broadfoot 12, Watkins 181–82 and 187, and Baldick 67).

8. See Mary Poovey's *Making a Social Body* (5–6) for an account of the economic domain's gradual "disaggregation" from the social from the seventeenth through the nineteenth centuries.

9. An opposition between state and civil society nevertheless creeps back into the accounts of those historians most firmly devoted to critiquing such an opposition. Foucault is not disapproving of a liberalism that insists on an "incompatibility between the non-totalizable multiplicity which characterizes subjects of interest, and the totalizing unity of the juridical sovereign" (Gordon 22). One of the tasks Corrigan and Sayer assign to the state, the "legitimating of the illegitimate," involves enforcing a distinction between society and the state. For violence, say, must be figured first as illegitimate in society, and second as legitimate when wielded by the state. In Habermas's view (177), the late-nineteenth- and twentieth-century melding of state and society crush their traditional go-between, the bourgeois public sphere (which nevertheless, not least in Habermas, retains a nostalgic aura), leaving in its place the degraded space of leisure and consumption, ruled by mass culture rather than critical debate (160–61).

10. Jeff Hearn suggests that rather than reproducing separate spheres within itself, professionalization involves a competitive relationship between them. Arguing that "Capitalist development entails the shifting of control of different types of emotions or different bases of emotion from merely domestic labour into socialized labour," Hearn claims that law, medicine, and the Church have a historical basis in the transference of "the mediation of disputes and the management of life and death" from the domestic to the public sphere. Professional authority thus depends on men's takeover of traditionally female sources of power: "the traditional professions [law, medicine, the Church] ... operate close to and with jurisdiction over the various points of reproduction. They are concerned with the socialization of what were formerly private, emotional experiences around the points of reproduction" (Hearn 197). The uncertainty felt in the nineteenth century as now about the proper class placement of schoolteachers owes something to this profession's close association with feminine—and thus classless—nurturing. While earlier educators depicted the successful teacher as a strong father, in the mid–nineteenth century this image changed to that of a professionalized

nurturing mother, with an expertise in sympathy (P. Miller 139). Hunter writes of "the new pastoral teacher" of the nineteenth century; unlike the rod-wielding grammar-school teacher he is "sympathetic" (Hunter, *Rethinking* 73). The Foucauldian suspicion of this sympathy is allied to Arnoldian suspicion of the role of the bourgeois woman in the classroom.

11. As Herbert Sussman argues, the Victorian ideal of bourgeois masculinity was essentially that of "self-discipline, . . . the ability to control male energy and to deploy this power not for sexual but for productive purposes" (10). "Setting the intensity of discipline, then, becomes the crucial issue within the practice of the self. The formations of Victorian manhood may be set along a continuum of degrees of self-regulation" (Sussman 3).

12. See Kathy Psomiades' *Beauty's Body* on the significance for the Victorian gender system of the concept of a rich, complex, and self-contradictory interiority.

13. For another view of the work of "impersonation" in pedagogical exchanges, see Gallop "Im-Personation," who explores teacher/student interaction in the classroom (though not specifically the examination) as grounded in the trope of impersonation—as reproduction, as joke, as a meeting point between the personal and the impersonal in pedagogy.

14. See Baldick, Court, and especially Guillory *Capital* on the interaction between educational and literary institutions. This project is also deeply indebted to the essential work in this area by, among others, Nancy Armstrong, Catherine Gallagher, Thomas Richards, Regenia Gagnier, Ian Hunter, and Patrick Joyce.

Chapter Two

1. From T. S. Eliot and F. R. Leavis on, critics have noted that Arnold is "vulnerable in logic or semantics," and code it as a failure of rigor or an achievement of flexibility, depending on their sympathy with this style (see Robbins 14–16). See also Baldick, Graff, Hartman, Lambropoulos, Peltason "Function," and Riede.

2. The *Reports*, published by Sir Francis Sandford in 1889, "contain [Arnold's] nineteen General Reports to the Education Department on Elementary Schools . . . omitting matters of only local, personal, or temporary interest" (*Reports* v). They span most of the years of Arnold's tenure as an HMI, from 1851 to 1886. At first, he was responsible for visiting all non-Anglican

Voluntary schools in a broad swath of England and Wales, although his load was somewhat reduced in 1854, and grew smaller thereafter. The 1870 Education Act reorganized the Inspectorate and did away with denominational inspection. I cite the *Reports* by year. For more information on Arnold's bureaucratic career, see Tollers, Walcott, Connell, and Hopkinson.

3. In *Culture and Government*, Ian Hunter states that "Despite some recent claims concerning the ideological function of criticism, Arnold at no point advocated that it be deployed in the popular school . . . or that it be used in the training of teachers" (5), and that "literary subjects did not have an essential privilege" (114) for Arnold-as-inspector. Although it is true that Arnold advocates the memorizing and reciting of "good literature" in the Voluntary and teacher-training schools rather than writing or talking about it, it is nevertheless clear that he sees memorizing and reciting as different only in degree rather than kind from more elaborate forms of criticism. He quotes Wordsworth's equation of "a feeling of poetry" with "love of human nature and reverence for God," adding that "it is only through acquaintance with poetry, and with good poetry, that this "feeling of poetry" can be given (*Reports* 1880).

4. A Thatcherite version of payment by results continues to structure British government funding of universities: "The performance indicator is . . . an invented standard that claims to be capable of rating all departments in all British universities on a five-point scale. The rating can then be used to determine the size of the central government grant allocated to the department in question" (Readings 36). The result is one Arnold might have predicted: frantic "horse-trading" of faculty every five years, when departments are reviewed (Philip Rupprecht, personal communication, 12 January 1998). See also the treatment of the 1980s cuts in funding to British universities in David Lodge's novel *Nice Work*.

5. The recipient of the Newdigate and a postgraduate fellowship, he gained only a Second in his undergraduate examination. Significantly, Robert Lowe, the Code's creator, like most Civil Service advocates of examinations, had a brilliant examination record at university and in the Service.

6. Both the Anglican and the Nonconformist Societies use this flexibility to blur the boundary between secular and sectarian, naming themselves in ways that seem free of theological associations and yet emphasize subtly sectarian views of nationhood. The Anglican "National Schools Society" uses its name to tie the education of the poor to the existence of a national church, lo-

cating the universal in the institution and thus in its local manifestations. The Nonconformist "British and Foreign Schools Society" suggests a racial rather than an institutional definition of the nation, celebrating Britain's uniqueness as well as alluding to Nonconformist missionary ambitions.

7. Culler notes that, for Arnold, Homer is "a secular version of Scripture" (132) and "the supreme source of value standing at the head of the classical tradition, as revelation is at the head of the Christian tradition" (131).

8. Given what Ruth apRoberts calls his "wide-ranging and pretty steady novel habit" (277), Arnold's echo of the description of Bradley Headstone's dangerous brain-warehouse in *Our Mutual Friend* (see Chapter 4) seems likely to be intentional here.

9. For example, when he worries that "the bare power of reading" is "a most valuable power, yet capable, no doubt, like other good things, of being employed amiss later on in the pupil's life as well as of being employed for his good" (*Reports* 1878).

10. The rhetoric of the reform movements of the 1860s, for example, figured the working class as "children to your family" (Corrigan and Sayer 152) who "should not take their parents for their example" but be taught in school instead (Digby and Searby 127). Arnold extends this notion to the lower-middle-class pupils at the more expensive schools under his jurisdiction, where he complains of "the disposition of parents to interfere, and the diminished independence of the teacher" (*Reports* 1852).

11. Victorian working-class resistance to the education system often took the form of paying more to provide daughters with a private-school education, because small private schools, one step up from the dame school, did not insist on uniforms and regular attendance, and featured more refined varieties of needlework than the plain sewing required in the Society schools (Purvis 72 and Gomersall).

12. See Joyce and Simon (31) on the midcentury development of midlands Societies and Athenaeums, the philistine education against which Arnold is fighting.

Chapter Three

1 Trollope seems to have been particularly sensitive to this form of social geography. See not only *The Three Clerks* but also the difference between Adolphus Crosbie's prestigiously located Whitehall job and Johnny Eames's

less impressive private secretaryship at the Income Tax Office in *The Small House at Allington*.

2. From time to time, before examinations were uniformly adopted in 1870, the Civil Service Commissioners tried out full competition, as they do in the promotion exam at the Weights and Measures in *The Three Clerks*. For example, in 1857, competitions for four jobs in their own office produced candidates the majority of whom could be characterized as "gentlemen," and fully half of whom came from the universities (Roach 205). The Indian Civil Service, with its higher social status, adopted competitive examination before and more thoroughly than the Home Civil Service. From 1860 to 1874, 78 percent of ICS appointees had fathers who were members of the aristocracy, gentry, Army, Navy, the ICS itself, or one of the learned professions. Only 4 percent were sons of tradesmen (Roach 194). The separation of Oxbridge and the Civil Service came only with World War II and the democratization of the universities, when passing an exam was no longer a proof of gentility (Gowan 32). However, as Gowan emphasizes, "there is no evidence of a great beating on the doors of Whitehall by Oxbridge graduates before the Northcote–Trevelyan report.... Active pressure from [gentry-class-controlled] institutions did not precede the Report, but was articulated by and mobilized through it.... The ideas in the Report were in general far in advance of the thinking within the social groups the Report was designed to serve" (22–24).

3. Gowan includes both Arnold and Lowe in the group surrounding Jowett and Trevelyan. However, as we have seen in Chapter 2, Arnold was far more committed to expanding the provision of education by the state, admired such provision in Prussia and France, and worked closely with Lowe's predecessor, Kay-Shuttleworth, while Jowett's university-trained intellectuals in the Education Department put an end to "Kay-Shuttleworth's drive to expand the Department's budget in order to build a national system of working-class education" to "stress ... control and retrenchment" (Gowan 12).

4. James remarks that the Trollopian "story is always ... a love-story constructed on an inveterate system. There is a young lady who has two lovers, or a young man who has two sweethearts" (James 109). Kincaid *Novels* describes Trollope's participation in Victorian fiction's continual vacillation between closed and open form and spatial versus temporal plot structures. Kucich demonstrates how Trollope plays both sides of the division between morality and transgression. Riffaterre calls Trollope's metonymies paradigmatic of the central Trollopian contradiction: they point both to the "real"—

they consist of mundane, realistic details like chignons—and to the artificial—they draw attention to the narrator's/author's manipulation of the reader through humor and symbol (273–74).

5. "Yes. Let the devil take the hindmost; the three or four hindmost if you will; nay, all but those strong-running horses who can force themselves into noticeable places under the judge's eye. This is the noble shibboleth with which the English youth are now spurred on to deeds of—what shall we say?—money-making activity. Let every place in which a man can hold up his head be the reward of some antagonistic struggle, of some grand competitive examination. Let us get rid of the fault of past ages. With us, let the race be ever to the swift; the victory always to the strong. And let us always be racing, so that the swift and strong shall ever be known among us. But what, then, for those who are not swift, not strong? *Vae victis!* Let them go to the wall. They can hew wood probably; or, at any rate, draw water" (Trollope, *The Bertrams* 2).

6. The proliferation of Trollopian love triangles in the novel is also part of this pattern. Herbert shows that "comedy's all-pervading artificiality" in Trollope—his symmetrical pairings, substitutions, misunderstandings, cross-purposes, geometric arrangement of plots, etc.—owes much to his careful reading of early comedies. For example, he drew on Marston's "Eastward Ho" for *The Three Clerks* (Herbert 218).

7. There is evidence that Trollope, like Charley, was a lazy and careless worker in his early years at the Post Office, although the discipline was almost certainly less lax than it is portrayed as being in *The Three Clerks* (Super 3–4).

8. Arguing that Trollope's "public" view of authorship demands the exchange of "the same for the same" (*Ethics* 89) between author and reader, J. Hillis Miller claims that, for Trollope, "[t]he value of the most apparently heterogeneous items can be measured by the same standard: money. Everything of value enters into a circuit of production, purchase, and consumption within which nothing alien or unaccountable can ever be introduced" (87). But for Trollope, as for classical political economy, labor, not money, is the true measure of value. And thus, ultimately, it is *only* labor that can be exchanged.

9. During the 1850s and 1860s, "The mania for profit—combined with legal provisions that encouraged (but did not oversee) company formations and credit facilities that generated finance capital vastly in excess of gold reserves or even good debts—produced a concentration of financial abuses" in the wake of the 1844 Registration Act, the 1855 Limited Liability Act, the 1856 Joint Stock Companies Act, and the 1862 Companies Act (Poovey *Making* 160).

10. On Trollope's unfinished article on *Little Dorrit* and the Civil Service, see Booth.

11. The speculator as lover, ghost, disease, racial/sexual/cultural/class other, cliché villain, tragic suicide, and so on begins to provide rich figurative ground for nineteenth-century fiction from around the time of *The Three Clerks*. See Reed and Jaffe "Detecting."

12. Super quotes Trollope writing at the Post Office on 24 May 1863: "I feel very sure that the system of promotion by merit, as it is called, cannot in truth be carried out; and that it is injurious to the service.... No amount of excellence is safe, because a greater amount of excellence must always be possible.... To know whether a man be absolutely fit or unfit for certain duties is within the capacity of an observant and intelligent officer;—but it is frequently altogether beyond the capacity of any officer however intelligent and observant to say who is most fit. Zeal recommends itself to one man, intelligence to a second, alacrity to a third, punctuality to a fourth, and superficial pretense to a fifth. There can be no standard by which the excellence of men can be judged as is the weight of gold" (Super 53–54).

13. Sutherland has shown that Trollope did not, in fact, write his novels "mechanically" (472): "Trollope's secretarial exactitude and the aggressive account he gives of it in the *Autobiography* have masked the substantial creative effort which went into his fiction" (493). He would start with an original character plan—"to act as a trigger, releasing characters into an existence whose full complications could later emerge more or less spontaneously" (Sutherland 481), and wrote in "bursts, or spells of composition" rather than at a regular pace (Sutherland 476).

14. Though Trollope states in his *Autobiography* that he influenced Post Office style, in fact his reports are stylistically just like Post Office chief Freeling's—and like all the other surveyors (Lansbury 22–23). In fact, Lansbury argues that Trollope learned to write at the Post Office: "It was the conjunction and the conflict between the official factual report," written in the plain and straightforward style determined by Freeling, "and the realm of fiction that created the novels" (Lansbury 10).

15. E. B. Browning wrote to Trollope to report that her husband was delighted with the comparatively early *Three Clerks*: "[W]hat a thoroughly man's book it is!" On the other hand, the *Saturday Review* praises its almost feminine ability to depict domestic life: "But it is on the family, not the official, pictures that the reputation of the novel will be chiefly founded.... These girls

are like real girls.... The eldest and the youngest especially are capital—neither too good nor too bad, and with more freshness and life about them than is to be seen in the heroines of one novel out of a hundred," though they criticize its lack of a "matured knowledge of the beauties of character, and a skill in tracing the finer webs of human action" (vol. 4, 5 December 1857, 517–18).

16. "Working for Money" is one of the page titles added to *An Autobiography* by Trollope's son Henry on publication after Trollope's death. In the Oxford Classics edition, it heads page 107.

17. Trollope himself was, like Mr. Oldeschole, examined by the Civil Service Commission, and in Ireland, he had, like Undy, the experience of a witness "tortured" by a Chaffanbrass-like lawyer, with whom he engaged in a battle of wits at the trial of a postmistress caught stealing (Terry 39).

Chapter Four

1. In "Education, Print, and Paper in *Our Mutual Friend*," Richard Altick, noting the novel's interest in education in general as both "a moral theme" and "a social topic" (238), briefly discusses its examination motif, though he does not find it as important an element in the novel as I claim it is here. He argues that it achieves "three results": critiquing current "mechanical" modes of education in government-funded schools under the Revised Code, adding to the novel's "temporal immediacy;... and perhaps most importantly, by transferring the catechetical device to informal settings outside the schoolroom he managed a variety of comic effects.... Topicality, in a word, inspired technique" (246).

2. J. Fisher Solomon contrasts the novel's metaphorical reifications of many of its "comic villains" with its anti-reifying plot of escape from the market world. But such an escape, I will argue, is only very problematically endorsed by the novel.

3. The novel's introduction of Mr. Venus, articulator of bones, recalls this first view of his fellow-scavenger Gaffer: "His eyes are like the over-tired eyes of an engraver, but he is not that; his expression and stoop are like those of a shoemaker, but he is not that" (122). Like Gaffer, Venus traffics in the bodies of the dead; like most of the characters in the novel, he works at the border between the valuable and the valueless.

4. Aware of his daughter and co-worker Lizzie's disgust at their task, Gaffer chides her: "'As if it wasn't your living! As if it wasn't meat and drink

to you!'" (45). In "The Bioeconomics of *Our Mutual Friend*," Catherine Gallagher comments that "the shocking power of this metaphor . . . is its removal of all mediations between the girl's 'living,' her sustenance, and the corpse's moldering flesh, which becomes . . . her food" ("Bioeconomics" 53). The slippage between "a living" as means of subsistence and "a living" as "occupation" becomes a dangerous one here. Gallagher further argues that in *Our Mutual Friend* the derivation of value from the dead human body becomes synonymous with market exchange itself (57). Indeed, Gaffer's savage employment shocks because it typifies participation in the market economy. In doing so, however, it blurs the boundaries between the market, where value is at any rate fixed and exchangeable, and an extraeconomic sphere where it is much harder to locate.

5. For example, Miller cites Jenny's famous rooftop cry, "come up and be dead," as the novel's model of transcendence and David argues that "*Our Mutual Friend* both represents and transcends the social reality which is a pervasive determinant of the restlessness and dissatisfaction of its characters" (55). For Gallagher, the novel's "Bioeconomics" provide an escape from commodification for the novel's heroines. Jaffe (*Vanishing*) argues that the novel privileges a different kind of transcendence of reification for a male character, John Harmon, in the disembodied subjectivity of omniscience.

6. In "Detecting the Beggar," Jaffe examines a similar association between beggars and gentlemen (including financiers and authors) in Doyle and Mayhew, where they share a participation in an "illegitimate production" (109) of representation rather than products.

7. Cotsell notes that "despite the relative success of the Crimean War (1854–56), the British continued to mistrust the ambitions of the gigantic and illiberal Russian Empire" (58–59).

8. In *Reproduction*, Bourdieu and Passeron define "pedagogic action" (PA) as a form of "symbolic violence" that inculcates "cultural arbitraries," or culturally established categories of knowledge, through its command of "pedagogic authority" (PAu), an authority always granted by a particular political entity (such as a social class).

9. Lizzie's ineffectiveness is particularly striking when we compare her to another working-class angel, Sissy Jupe from *Hard Times*. The same qualities which cause nothing but trouble in *Our Mutual Friend* are seen as spectacularly redemptive in the earlier novel. Instead of encouraging an upper-class seducer, as Lizzie's goodness does, Sissy's allows her to defeat single-handedly

the ordinarily impervious James Harthouse (*Hard Times* 253). One reason for the difference in effectiveness between Sissy and Lizzie lies in the difference between the two novels' figuring of extraeconomic alternatives to the world of labor. Although, as Catherine Gallagher demonstrates, Sleary's circus is in fact just as subject to economic relations as Coketown is, it still functions as a positive alternative, a fantasy location from which working-class redemption can emerge, as Sissy does, to revivify bourgeois domesticity. As I have argued, however, Gaffer's similar location on the border between the economic and the extraeconomic provides an alternative to value-able labor which is sinister rather than redemptive. If, as in so many other Dickens novels, bourgeois domesticity does not work in *Our Mutual Friend*, this novel also lacks the cozily crowded working-class households his earlier fiction features.

10. Deirdre David calls attention to the oddity of a paper mill serving as a haven. Strangely enough, from the author of *Hard Times*, "In *Our Mutual Friend*, industrialism itself becomes a pastoral alternative" (84).

11. As Philip Collins shows in *Dickens and Education*, Dickens was not only one of the most outspoken critics of the Ragged Schools, but also one of their strongest supporters (86–92). And Dickens provides an equally stinging portrait of private working-class elementary education in the dame school run by Mr. Wopsle's great-aunt in *Great Expectations*: "Mr. Wopsle's great-aunt kept an evening school in the village; that is to say, she was a ridiculous old woman of limited means and unlimited infirmity, who used to go to sleep from six to seven every evening, in the society of youth who paid twopence per week each, for the improving opportunity of seeing her do it" (74). Rather than being presented with material which they are too wise to understand, Mr. Wopsle's great-aunt's students are (like Arnold's primary-school inspector) presented with nothing.

12. Clare Simmons pointed out to me in a personal communication that the Biblical Nicodemus is, like Mr. Boffin, an examiner who gets little out of his examination (see John 3:1–21).

13. Both the learning of ignorance and the suspension of cause and effect in narratives of female education suggest an ironic relation between the development of a feminine subjectivity and figurative or literal rites of formal education. Susan Winnett notes that in *Reading for the Plot*, Peter Brooks links the linearity of nineteenth-century plots—their temporal pull—to the structure of male sexual desire. Female development resists the linearity of the *bildungsroman*, which, Hirsch argues, depends on assumptions about the pur-

pose and temporal structure of education and the individual's involvement with society, with problematic applications for women: "'In song and story,' woman's role is to wait: her life is static, ahistorical, the course it enacts is the antithesis of the bildung" (23).

14. In *The Afterlife of Property*, Jeff Nunokawa demonstrates how women are assigned the role of property that does not circulate in Victorian fiction. Women ought to be "unportable property" (11). They can be the site of a threat of a "confusion ... of the zone of circulation and the zone of possession" (12). In *Our Mutual Friend*, I have argued, Dickens makes their inalienability dependent on a pedagogical economy that privileges midwife-exams over banking-exams.

CHAPTER FIVE

1. Ruskin confesses that "Queens' Gardens" was written for Rose La Touche, the most enduring of his teenaged passions. The 1882 preface to *Sesame and Lilies* is explicitly addressed to "girls." It is consequently girls rather than women that we may imagine as the most appropriate audience for the lecture in its written form—and perhaps as responsible for the volume's being Ruskin's most successful work in the nineteenth century.

2. In *Child-Loving*, James Kincaid explores the contradictory symbolism Victorians associated with children. They are at once development personified and wielders of unprecedented lightning bolts of moral power (66–67). The Victorian child personifies the blankness of a tabula rasa as well as the richness of race memory; she can epitomize savagery, purity, or original sin (70). Kincaid also suggests that childhood served the Victorians as a site for "resolving" contradictions in class and gender hierarchies, through its symbolic freedom from gender and class (78, 83).

3. Unless otherwise noted, my source for Ruskin's letters to and about Winnington is Van Akin Burd's collection of *The Winnington Letters*.

4. Ruskin had several romances with young girls. Adele Clothilde Domecq was fifteen when he fell in love with her in 1836. His attachment to Effie Gray, ending in their marriage in 1848 and annulment in 1854, began when she was twelve (when she was thirteen, he wrote *The King of the Golden River* for her). Ruskin's longest and most famous attachment of this kind was to Rose La Touche, whom he met in 1858 when she was nine, and to whom he proposed marriage (unsuccessfully) eight years later.

5. In *Ruskin: The Genesis of Invention*, Emerson shows Ruskin's rejection of maturity in favor of childhood and old age, and charts the lifelong intersection for Ruskin of obedience, intense sensual gratification, and girlishness. In "Ruskin's Womanly Mind" and "*Ethics of the Dust*: Ruskin's Authorities," Birch reads Ruskin's work as at once "protective" and "expressive" of his own gender ambiguity. In *Ruskin's Mythic Queen*, Sharon Weltman notes the creative, "styptic" power of femininity for Ruskin.

6. An anonymous review of *Unto This Last* in the *Saturday Review* of 10 November 1860 (582–84) describes the experience of reading Ruskin's prose as like "being preached to death by a mad governess," and the phrase nicely encapsulates Ruskin's problematic gender identifications, his ambivalence toward intellectual labor, and the insistent movement toward a deathlike stasis implicit (as I will argue) in the anti-exam.

7. On *Praeterita*'s resistance to teleology, see Austin "*Praeterita*"; Henderson; and Peltason "Ruskin's."

8. In *Pricing the Priceless Child*, Zelizer explores the relation between the economic and the extraeconomic by charting the changing market value of children from the nineteenth to the twentieth century. For example, she shows that in nineteenth-century America an adopted child of eight or nine was considered to be valuable, because of its potential labor power, while an infant would be nearly valueless. By the twentieth century, on the contrary, while the infant commands a high price on the black market in adoption, the older child is now worth nothing (170–71).

9. In *The Origin of the Family*, Friedrich Engels puts "the production of the means of subsistence, of food, clothing and shelter and the tools necessary for that production" on one side of this division and "on the other side, the production of human beings themselves" (35–36). Arguing in "Ideology and Ideological State Apparatuses" that "the production of human beings themselves" requires not only biological reproduction, but the reproduction of the subject within ideology, Louis Althusser maintains this distinction. But as Michelle Barrett points out, the distinction between the production of goods and the reproduction of subjects is a distinction gendered by ideology, not nature (27).

10. By contrast, in the *Grundrisse*, Marx envisions a progressive and dialectical relationship between consumption and production (Tucker 229). Richards cites Ruskin's celebration of the Gothic in *Modern Painters* as an early indication of his privileging of consumption (23). Crosby argues that while

Ruskin and his fellow revivalists felt that "the decorative accumulation of Gothic has nothing to do with the profane accumulation of the marketplace" (107), their work nevertheless contributed to the "Victorian production of history as some *thing* which is visible, palpable, and concrete" and hence subject to commodification (102). In *The Practical Ruskin*, Linda Austin argues that in the last decade of his writing life, Ruskin moved from a belief in value determined by production to value determined by consumption, or from "orthodox labor theory to marginal utility," a late-century theory that posits value as denoting "how much more one is willing to pay. It has become not only an individual but a comparatively invisible or psychological phenomenon, founded on demand rather than supply.... [W]hereas the orthodox economist had separated exchange- from use-value, [marginal utility theory] merged them" (11–12).

11. See Crosby and Culler. Girouard details the commercial and ideological associations of the Victorian Gothic movement. In its chapter on "Magical Narratives," Jameson's *Political Unconscious* introduces the concept of the reification of residual cultural meanings in the history of the romance. Ruskin is, of course, well known for his association with the Victorian Gothic revival. See Raymond Williams's *Culture and Society 1780/1950* for an account of Ruskin's problematic use of feudal values to critique capitalism in his political writing.

12. The spectacular failure of the Eglinton Tournament took place in August 1838 at Eglinton Castle; it was an elaborately planned event, complete with fully-armored aristocrats, a procession, and jousts. The expectations of its high-Tory participants and enormous popular audience were disappointed, however, by the rain, which started simultaneously with the procession to the lists (see Girouard, 88–110).

13. Margaret Homans suggests that another aspect of queenship in the 1860s—Queen Victoria's widely lamented and long-lasting seclusion after the death of Albert—gives Ruskin this freedom: "In the vacuum of Victoria's absence, Ruskin is free to invent his paradigm queen and her duplicates in any way he chooses" (72). Homans also provides an excellent overview of recent readings of Queen Victoria's role as an absent presence in "Of Queens' Gardens" (68–69).

14. Bourdieu and Passeron hint at the radical incongruity between these two pedagogical rituals when they remind us that the examination was "unknown to Antiquity, which saw only independent or even competing schools

and teachers" (144). Birch ("*Ethics*" 147) notes the significance of the erotic associations of the Socratic dialogue for *The Ethics*. Dowling's *Hellenism and Homosexuality at Oxford* documents the specific institutional processes by which these associations became current in the later nineteenth century. The form apparently attracted both Ruskin and Winnington: "I have your kind letter, and my children's about Plato and Socrates. Tell them I am so very glad they had the dialogues *so* read to them; they understand more of Plato from having *one* thus dramatically and feelingly & amusingly read, than perhaps great *mere* Greek scholars ever do in all their lives" (ltr. to Margaret Bell, 26 October 1862).

15. "Much of the joylessness and some of the violence behind Ruskin's passionate lectures in the mid-1860s arise from the unspoken assumption that their audiences will not respond to exhortation," notes Birch ("*Ethics*" 149). And while she shows how *The Ethics* lectures "comfortably incorporate their own audience," and that "giving voice to his [actual Winnington] pupils is a way of governing them" (150), she also notes the Lecturer's bullying and "Unlikeability" (150).

16. As in *The Ethics* itself, however, here too, the allegory is transferred to a literal level:

> *Sentence* out of letter from May, (who is staying with Isabel just now at Cassel,) dated 15th June 1877:—
>
> "I am reading the Ethics with a nice Irish girl who is staying here, and she's just as puzzled as I've always been about the fire-flies, and we both want to know so much.—Please be a very nice old Lecturer, and tell us, won't you?"
>
> Well, May, you never were a vain girl; so could scarcely guess that I meant them for the light, unpursued vanities, which yet blind us confused among the stars. One evening, as I came late into Sienna, the fire-flies were flying high on a stormy sirocco wind,—the stars themselves no brighter, and all their host seeming, at moments, to fade as the insects faded. (*Ethics* 355)

17. In the preface, Ruskin dismisses the allegory even more vehemently, retaining as valuable only its literal inclusion in the book: "[T]he imagery [of the first lecture] is stupid and ineffective throughout; and I retain this chapter only because I am resolved to leave no room for any one to say that I have

withdrawn, as erroneous in principle, so much as a single sentence of any of my books written since 1860" (*Ethics* 206). Richard Menke provides an excellent discussion of Ruskin's literalism in "Money Means Money: Literal Reading and Moral Currency in Ruskin."

18. Amirault suggests that this formulation allows for a teacher's identification with students that subsumes them (74).

19. Emerson identifies the elements of sexualized violence in Ruskin's need to have things filled up and fitting tight (130–31).

20. Excellent feminist discussions of the role of personification in Ruskin can be found in Helsinger, who discusses the commodification of women in "The Political Economy of Art"; Weltman, who discusses personification and the pathetic fallacy in *The Ethics* and *The Queen of the Air*; and especially Homans, who discusses the relationship between allegory and personification in "Of Queens' Gardens," noting that "the essay could be understood as a slow-motion narrative about how personification or pathetic fallacy come about, how meaning gets applied to a natural object" (87). Homans adds an important layer to our understanding of the anxiously bullying tone in both "Queens' Gardens" and *The Ethics* when she argues that, for Ruskin, "[w]omen and girls, it would seem, personify personification" (88), and thus "there is some necessary connection between anxiety about establishing referentiality and the anxious hope that women will do what he wants" (89).

21. The Winnington girls apparently never tried this experiment but were much taken with its depiction in *The Ethics*. In one of the few surviving letters to Ruskin from Winnington, two pupils write that they "were thinking in bed how delightful it would be if Miss Mary would invent us some crystal dances" (Lily Armstrong and Isabel Marshall to Ruskin, 26 November 1865).

Epilog

1. For the two most compelling of these articulations, see Evan Watkins's *Work Time* and John Guillory's "Literary Critics as Intellectuals." Both keep their eye solidly on the economic and institutional function of college English departments.

Works Cited

Adams, James Eli. *Dandies and Desert Saints: Styles of Victorian Manhood.* Ithaca, N.Y.: Cornell University Press, 1995.
Allen, Peter. "Masculinity and Novel-Writing in Trollope's *An Autobiography.*" *Prose Studies* 16, no. 2 (1993): 62–83.
Althusser, Louis. "Ideology and Ideological State Apparatuses." In *Lenin and Philosophy and Other Essays,* translated by Ben Brewster. New York: Monthly Review Press, 1971.
Altick, Richard. "Education, Print, and Paper in *Our Mutual Friend.*" In *Nineteenth-Century Literary Perspectives: Essays in Honor of Lionel Stevenson,* edited by Clyde de L. Ryals with the assistance of John Clubbe and Benjamin Franklin Fisher IV. Durham, N.C.: Duke University Press, 1974.
Amirault, Chris. "The Good Teacher, the Good Student: Identifications of a Student Teacher." In *Pedagogy: The Question of Impersonation,* edited by Jane Gallop. Bloomington: Indiana University Press, 1995.
apRoberts, Ruth. *Arnold and God.* Berkeley: University of California Press, 1983.
Arac, Jonathan. *Commissioned Spirits: The Shaping of Social Motion in Dickens, Carlyle, Melville, and Hawthorne.* New Brunswick, N.J.: Rutgers University Press, 1989.
Armstrong, Frances. *Dickens and the Concept of Home.* Ann Arbor: UMI Research Press, 1990.
Armstrong, Nancy. *Desire and Domestic Fiction: A Political History of the Novel.* New York: Oxford University Press, 1987.

Arnold, Matthew. *Culture and Anarchy*. 1869. Edited by Samuel Lipman. Commentary by Maurice Cowling, Gerald Graff, Samuel Lipman, and Steven Marcus. New Haven, Conn.: Yale University Press, 1994.
———. "A French Eton" and "The Twice-Revised Code." In *Matthew Arnold and the Education of the New Order: A Selection of Arnold's Writings on Education*, edited by Peter Smith and Geoffrey Summerfield. Cambridge: Cambridge University Press, 1969.
———. "The Function of Criticism at the Present Time." In *The Complete Prose Works of Matthew Arnold*. Vol. 3: *Lectures and Essays in Criticism*. Edited by R. H. Super with the assistance of Sister Thomas Marion Hoctor. Ann Arbor, Mich.: University of Michigan Press, 1962.
———. *Reports on Elementary Schools, 1852–1882*. Edited by Sir Francis Sandford. London: Macmillan and Co., 1889.
Austin, Linda M. *The Practical Ruskin: Economics and Audience in the Late Work*. Baltimore: Johns Hopkins University Press, 1991.
———. "*Praeterita*: In the Act of Rebellion." *Modern Language Quarterly* 48, no. 1 (1987): 42–58.
Avery, Gillian. *The Best Type of Girl: A History of Girls' Independent Schools*. London: Deutsch, 1991.
Baker, Robert S. "Imagination and Literacy in Dickens' *Our Mutual Friend*." *Criticism* 18 (1976): 57–72.
Baldick, Chris. *The Social Mission of English Criticism: 1848–1932*. Oxford: Clarendon Press, 1983.
Bann, Stephen. *The Clothing of Clio: A Study of the Representation of History in Nineteenth-Century Britain and France*. Cambridge: Cambridge University Press, 1984.
Barbour, Judith. "Euphemism and Paternalism in *Our Mutual Friend*." *Sydney Studies in English* 7 (1981–1982): 55–68.
Bareham, Tony. "Patterns of Excellence: Theme and Structure in *The Three Clerks*." In *Anthony Trollope*, edited by Tony Bareham. London: Vision, 1980.
Barrett, Michele. *Women's Oppression Today: Problems in Marxist Feminist Analysis*. London: Verso Editions, 1980.
Barthes, Roland. "Writers, Intellectuals, Teachers." In *Image, Music, Text*, translated by Stephen Heath. New York: Hill and Wang, 1977.
Baudrillard, Jean. *Selected Writings*. Edited by Mark Poster. Cambridge: Polity, 1988.

Belenky, Mary Field, Blythe McVicker Clinchy, Nancy Rule Goldberger, and Jill Mattuck Tarule. *Women's Ways of Knowing: The Development of Self, Voice, and Mind*. New York: Basic Books, 1986.
Bersani, Leo. *A Future for Astyanax: Character and Desire in Literature*. Boston: Little, Brown, 1976.
Birch, Dinah. "*The Ethics of the Dust*: Ruskin's Authorities." *Prose Studies* 12 (1989): 147–58.
———. "Ruskin's 'Womanly Mind.'" *Essays in Criticism* 38 (1988): 308–24.
Bizup, Joseph. "Walter Pater and the Ruskinian Gentleman." *English Literature in Transition* 38 (1995): 51–69.
Block, Fred, and Larry Hirschhorn. "New Productive Forces and the Contradictions of Contemporary Capitalism." *Theory and Society* 7 (1979): 363–95.
Booth, Bradford A. "Trollope and *Little Dorrit*." *The Trollopian* (March 1948): 237–40.
Bourdieu, Pierre, with the collaboration of Monique de Saint Martin. *The State Nobility: Elite Schools in the Field of Power*. Foreword by Loic JD Wacquant; translated by Lauretta C. Clough. Stanford, Calif.: Stanford University Press, 1996.
Bourdieu, Pierre, and Jean-Claude Passeron. *Reproduction in Education, Society, and Culture*. Translated by Richard Nice. London: Sage Publications, 1990.
Bradley, Alexander. "Ruskin at Oxford: Pupil and Master." *Studies in English Literature* 32 (1992): 747–64.
Bradley, J. L., ed. *Ruskin: The Critical Heritage*. London: Routledge & Kegan Paul, 1984.
Broadfoot, Patricia. *Assessment, Schools, and Society*. London: Methuen, 1979.
Brooks, Peter. *Reading for the Plot: Design and Intention in Narrative*. New York: Vintage Books, 1984.
Burd, Van Akin, ed. *The Winnington Letters: John Ruskin's Correspondence with Margaret Alexis Bell and the Children at Winnington Hall*. Cambridge, Mass.: Harvard University Press, 1969.
Burstyn, Joan. *Victorian Education and the Ideal of Womanhood*. New Brunswick, N.J.: Rutgers University Press, 1984.
Butler, Judith. *Gender Trouble: Feminism and the Subversion of Identity*. London and New York: Routledge, 1990.
Caminero-Santangelo, Byron. "Testing for Truth: Joseph Conrad and the Ideology of the Examination." *Clio* 23, no. 3 (1994): 271–84.

Carnoy, Martin, and Henry M. Levin. *Schooling and Work in the Democratic State.* Stanford, Calif.: Stanford University Press, 1985.

Chester, Sir Norman. *The English Administrative System: 1780–1870.* Oxford: Clarendon Press, 1981.

Cohen, Monica F. *Professional Domesticity in the Victorian Novel: Women, Work, and Home.* Cambridge: Cambridge University Press, 1998.

Collins, Philip, ed. *Dickens: The Critical Heritage.* London: Routledge & Kegan Paul, 1971.

———. *Dickens and Education.* London: Macmillan, 1963.

Connell, W. F. *The Educational Thought and Influence of Matthew Arnold.* London: Routledge & Kegan Paul, 1950.

Corrigan, Philip, and Derek Sayer. *The Great Arch: English State Formation as Cultural Revolution.* Oxford: Basil Blackwell, 1985.

Cotsell, Michael. *The Companion to "Our Mutual Friend."* London: Allen & Unwin, 1986.

Court, Franklin E. *Institutionalizing English Literature: The Culture and Politics of Literary Study, 1750–1900.* Stanford, Calif.: Stanford University Press, 1992.

Crosby, Christina. "Reading the Gothic Revival: 'History' and *Hints on Household Taste.*" In *Rewriting the Victorians: Theory, History, and the Politics of Gender,* edited by Linda M. Shires. New York: Routledge, 1992.

Culler, A. Dwight. *The Victorian Mirror of History.* New Haven, Conn.: Yale University Press, 1985.

David, Deirdre. *Fictions of Resolution in Three Victorian Novels: "North and South," "Our Mutual Friend," and "Daniel Deronda."* New York: Columbia University Press, 1981.

Dickens, Charles. *Great Expectations.* Harmondsworth: Penguin, 1965.

———. *Hard Times for These Times.* Harmondsworth: Penguin, 1969.

———. *Our Mutual Friend.* Harmondsworth: Penguin, 1971.

Dickstein, Morris. *Double Agent: The Critic and Society.* New York: Oxford University Press, 1992.

Digby, Anne, and Peter Searby. *Children, School, and Society in Nineteenth-Century England.* London: Macmillan, 1981.

Donajgrodzki, A. P. "New Roles for Old: The Northcote–Trevelyan Report and the Clerks of the Home Office, 1822–48." In *Studies in the Growth of Nineteenth-Century Government,* edited by Gillian Sutherland. London: Routledge & Kegan Paul, 1972.

Dowling, Linda. *Hellenism and Homosexuality in Victorian Oxford*. Ithaca, N.Y.: Cornell University Press, 1994.

Duncan, Ian. *Modern Romance and Transformations of the Novel: The Gothic, Scott, Dickens*. Cambridge: Cambridge University Press, 1992.

Eagleton, Terry. *Literary Theory: An Introduction*. Oxford: Basil Blackwell, 1983.

Edmonds, E. L. *The School Inspector*. New York: Humanities Press, 1962.

Eggleston, John. "School Examinations—Some Sociological Issues." In *Selection, Certification, and Control: Social Issues in Educational Assessment*, edited by Patricia Broadfoot. London: Falmer Press, 1984.

Ehrenreich, Barbara, and John Ehrenreich. "The Professional-Managerial Class." In *Between Labor and Capital*, edited by Pat Walker. Boston: South End Press, 1979.

Elliott, Dorice Williams. "The Female Visitor and the Marriage of Classes in Gaskell's *North and South*." *Nineteenth-Century Fiction* 49, no. 1 (1994): 21–49.

Ellsworth, Elizabeth. "Why Doesn't This Feel Empowering? Working Through the Repressive Myths of Critical Pedagogy." In *The Education Feminism Reader*, edited by Lynda Stone. New York: Routledge, 1994.

Emerson, Sheila. *Ruskin: The Genesis of Invention*. Cambridge: Cambridge University Press, 1993.

Engels, Friedrich. *The Origin of the Family, Private Property, and the State*. Harmondsworth: Penguin Books, 1985.

Ermarth, Elizabeth Deeds. *Realism and Consensus in the English Novel*. Princeton, N.J.: Princeton University Press, 1983.

Felman, Shoshana. "Psychoanalysis and Education: Teaching Terminable and Interminable." In *Learning Desire: Perspectives on Pedagogy, Culture, and the Unsaid*, edited by Sharon Todd. New York: Routledge, 1997.

Feltes, N. N. *Modes of Production of Victorian Novels*. Chicago: University of Chicago Press, 1986.

Fielding, K. J. "Carlyle's Unpublished Comments on the Northcote–Trevelyan Report." *Carlyle Annual* 10 (1989): 5–13.

Fletcher, Joseph. Evidence to the Committee of Council on Education. *Parliamentary Papers* (1847) XLV, 299-300.

Foucault, Michel. *Discipline and Punish: The Birth of the Prison*. Translated by Alan Sheriden. New York: Vintage, 1995.

———. *The History of Sexuality*. Vol. 1: *An Introduction*. Translated by Robert Hurley. New York: Vintage Books, 1980.

———. "Politics and the Studies of Discourse." In *The Foucault Effect: Studies in Governmentality*, edited by Graham Burchell, Colin Gordon, and Peter Miller. Chicago: University of Chicago Press, 1991.

———. "Questions of Governmentality." In *The Foucault Effect: Studies in Governmentality*, edited by Graham Burchell, Colin Gordon, and Peter Miller. Chicago: University of Chicago Press, 1991.

Freire, Paulo. *Pedagogy of the Oppressed*. Translated by Myra Bergman Ramos. New York: Continuum, 1997.

Fuss, Diana. *Identification Papers*. New York: Routledge, 1995.

Gagnier, Regenia. *Subjectivities: A History of Self-Representation in Britain, 1832–1920*. New York: Oxford University Press, 1991.

Gallagher, Catherine. "The Bioeconomics of *Our Mutual Friend*." In *Subject to History: Ideology, Class, Gender*, edited by David Simpson. Ithaca, N.Y.: Cornell University Press, 1991.

———. *The Industrial Reformation of English Fiction: Social Discourse and Narrative Form, 1832–1867*. Chicago: University of Chicago Press, 1985.

Gallop, Jane. "Im-Personation: A Reading in the Guise of an Introduction." In *Pedagogy: The Question of Impersonation*, edited by Jane Gallop. Bloomington: Indiana University Press, 1995.

Gallop, Jane, ed. *Pedagogy: The Question of Impersonation*. Bloomington: Indiana University Press, 1995.

Gardner, Phil. *The Lost Elementary Schools of Victorian England: The People's Education*. London: Croom Helm, 1984.

Gilead, Sarah. "Trollope's *Autobiography*: The Strategies of Self-Production." *Modern Language Quarterly* 47, no. 3 (1986): 272–90.

Gilmour, Robin. *The Idea of the Gentleman in the Victorian Novel*. London: Allen & Unwin, 1981.

Girouard, Mark. *The Return to Camelot: Chivalry and the English Gentleman*. New Haven, Conn.: Yale University Press, 1981.

Giroux, Henry, and Peter McLaren, eds. *Critical Pedagogy, the State, and Cultural Struggle*. Albany: State University of New York Press, 1989.

Gomersall, Meg. "Ideals and Realities: The Education of Working-Class Girls, 1800–1870." *History of Education* 17, no. 1 (1988): 37–53.

Gordon, Colin. "Governmental Rationality: An Introduction." In *The Foucault Effect: Studies in Governmentality*, edited by Graham Burchell, Colin Gordon, and Peter Miller. Chicago: University of Chicago Press, 1991.

Gordon, Peter, and Denis Lawton. *Curriculum Change in the Nineteenth and Twentieth Centuries*. London: Hodder and Stoughton, 1978.

Gowan, Peter. "The Origins of the Administrative Elite." *New Left Review* 162 (March–April 1987): 4–34.

Graff, Gerald. "Arnold, Reason, and Common Culture." In *Culture and Anarchy*, edited by Samuel Lipman. New Haven, Conn.: Yale University Press, 1994.

Gramsci, Antonio. *An Antonio Gramsci Reader*. Edited by David Forgacs. New York: Schocken Books, 1988.

Guillory, John. *Cultural Capital: The Problem of Literary Canon Formation*. Chicago: University of Chicago Press, 1993.

———. "Literary Critics as Intellectuals: Class Analysis and the Crisis of the Humanities." In *Rethinking Class: Literary Studies and Social Formations*, edited by Wai Chee Dimock and Michael T. Gilmore. New York: Columbia University Press, 1994.

Gully, Anthony Lacy. "Sermons in Stone: Ruskin's Geology." In *John Ruskin and the Victorian Eye*, edited by Harriet Whelchel. New York: Harry N. Abrams, 1993.

Habermas, Jürgen. *The Structural Transformation of the Public Sphere: An Inquiry into a Category of Bourgeois Society*. Translated by Thomas Burger with the assistance of Frederick Lawrence. Cambridge, Mass.: MIT Press, 1991.

Hanson, F. Allan. *Testing Testing: Social Consequences of the Examined Life*. Berkeley: University of California Press, 1993.

Hardy, Barbara. *The Moral Art of Dickens*. New York: Oxford University Press, 1970.

Hart, Jenifer. "The Genesis of the Northcote–Trevelyan Report." In *Studies in the Growth of Nineteenth-Century Government*, edited by Gillian Sutherland. London: Routledge, 1972.

Hartman, Geoffrey. *Criticism in the Wilderness*. New Haven, Conn.: Yale University Press, 1980.

Hearn, Jeff. "Notes on Patriarchy, Professionalization, and the Semi-Professions." *Sociology* 16 (1982): 184–202.

Helsinger, Elizabeth. "Ruskin and the Politics of Viewing: Constructing National Subjects." *Nineteenth-Century Contexts* 18 (1994): 125–46.

Henderson, Heather. *The Victorian Self: Autobiography and Biblical Narrative*. Ithaca, N.Y.: Cornell University Press, 1989.

Herbert, Christopher. *Trollope and Comic Pleasure.* Chicago: University of Chicago Press, 1987.
Hirsch, Marianne. "Spiritual *Bildung*: The Beautiful Soul as Paradigm." In *The Voyage In: Fictions of Female Development,* edited by Elizabeth Abel, Marianne Hirsch, and Elizabeth Langland. Hanover, N.H.: University Press of New England, 1983.
Hobsbawm, Eric. *Industry and Empire.* Harmondsworth: Penguin, 1969.
Holloway, John. *The Victorian Sage: Studies in Argument.* London: Macmillan, 1953.
Homans, Margaret. *Royal Representations: Queen Victoria and British Culture, 1837–1876.* Chicago: University of Chicago Press, 1998.
Hopkinson, David. "Matthew Arnold's School Inspections," parts 1 and 2. *History Today* 29 (1979): 29–37, 98–105.
Hughes, Edward. "Notes and Documents: Sir Charles Trevelyan and Civil Service Reform, 1853–5," parts 1 and 2. *English Historical Review* 64 (1949): 53–88, 206–34.
Hunter, Ian. *Culture and Government: The Emergence of Literary Education.* London: Macmillan, 1988.
———. *Rethinking the School: Subjectivity, Bureaucracy, Criticism.* New York: St. Martin's Press, 1994.
Ingham, Patricia. *Dickens, Women, and Language.* London: Harvester Wheatsheaf, 1992.
Irigaray, Luce. *Speculum of the Other Woman.* Translated by Gilian C. Gill. Ithaca, N.Y.: Cornell University Press, 1985.
Jaffe, Audrey. "Detecting the Beggar: Arthur Conan Doyle, Henry Mayhew, and 'The Man with the Twisted Lip.'" *Representations* 31 (1990): 96–117.
———. *Vanishing Points: Dickens, Narrative, and the Subject of Omniscience.* Berkeley: University of California Press, 1991.
Jakobson, Roman. "Two Aspects of Language and Two Types of Aphasic Disturbances." In *Language in Literature/Roman Jakobson.* Edited by Krystyna Pomorska and Stephen Rudy. Cambridge, Mass.: Harvard University Press, 1987.
James, Henry. "Anthony Trollope." In *Partial Portraits.* London: Macmillan and Co., 1888.
Jameson, Fredric. *The Political Unconscious: Narrative as a Socially Symbolic Act.* Ithaca, N.Y.: Cornell University Press, 1981.

Johnson, Barbara. "Teaching Ignorance: L'Ecole des Femmes." *Yale French Studies* 63 (1982): 165–82.

Joyce, Patrick. *The Self and the Social in Nineteenth-Century England*. Cambridge: Cambridge University Press, 1994.

Kendrick, Walter M. *The Novel-Machine: The Theory and Fiction of Anthony Trollope*. Baltimore: Johns Hopkins University Press, 1980.

Kincaid, James. *Child-Loving: The Erotic Child and Victorian Culture*. New York: Routledge, 1992.

———. *The Novels of Anthony Trollope*. Oxford: Clarendon Press, 1977.

———. "Trollope's Fictional Autobiography." *Nineteenth-Century Fiction* 37, no. 3 (1982): 340–49.

Kucich, John. "Transgression in Trollope: Dishonesty and the Antibourgeois Elite." *ELH* 56 (1989): 593–616.

Lambropoulos, Vassilis. "Violence and the Liberal Imagination: The Representation of Hellenism in Matthew Arnold." In *The Violence of Representation*, edited by Nancy Armstrong and Leonard Tennenhouse. London: Routledge, 1989.

Lansbury, Coral. *The Reasonable Man: Trollope's Legal Fiction*. Princeton, N.J.: Princeton University Press, 1981.

Larson, Magali Sarfatti. *The Rise of Professionalism: A Sociological Analysis*. Berkeley: University of California Press, 1977.

Levine, George. *The Realistic Imagination: English Fiction from Frankenstein to Lady Chatterley*. Chicago: University of Chicago Press, 1981.

Lodge, David. *Nice Work*. Harmondsworth: Penguin, 1988.

Macleod, Roy. Introduction to *Government and Expertise: Specialists, Administrators, and Professionals: 1860–1919*, edited by Roy MacLeod. Cambridge: Cambridge University Press, 1988.

Marx, Karl. *Capital*. Vol. 1: *A Critical Analysis of Capitalist Production*. Edited by Frederick Engels. Translated by Samuel Moore and Edward Aveling. New York: International Publishers, 1967.

———. *The Eighteenth Brumaire of Louis Bonaparte*. New York: International Publishers, 1984.

Menke, Richard. "Money Means Money: Literal Reading and Moral Currency in Ruskin." Paper presented at the Conference of the Victorians Institute, held at the University of Virginia in Charlottesville, Virginia, October 1996.

Midwinter, Eric. *Nineteenth-Century Education: Seminar Studies in History.* Edited by Patrick Richardson. London: Longman, 1970.

Miller, D. A. *The Novel and the Police.* Berkeley: University of California Press, 1988.

Miller, J. Hillis. *Charles Dickens: The World of His Novels.* Cambridge, Mass.: Harvard University Press, 1958.

———. *The Ethics of Reading: Kant, de Man, Eliot, Trollope, James, and Benjamin.* New York: Columbia University Press, 1987.

Miller, Paula. "History of Compulsory Schooling: What Is the Problem?" *History of Education* 18, no. 2 (1989): 122–44.

Miller, Sue. "*In Loco Parentis*: Addressing (the) Class." In *Pedagogy: The Question of Impersonation,* edited by Jane Gallop. Bloomington: Indiana University Press, 1995.

Montgomery, R. J. *Examinations: An Account of Their Evolution as Administrative Devices in England.* Pittsburgh: University of Pittsburgh Press, 1965.

Morris, Norman. "An Historian's View of Examinations." In *Examinations and English Education,* edited by Stephen Wiseman. Manchester, U.K.: Manchester University Press, 1961.

Morris, Pam. *Dickens's Class Consciousness: A Marginal View.* London: Macmillan, 1991.

Nabokov, Vladimir. *Strong Opinions.* New York: McGraw Hill, 1973.

Nelson, Cary, ed. *Will Teach for Food: Academic Labor in Crisis.* Minneapolis: University of Minnesota Press, 1997.

Northcote, Sir Stafford, and Charles Trevelyan. *Papers on the Re-Organisation of the Civil Service.* Presented to Both Houses of Parliament by Command of Her Majesty. London: George E. Eyre and William Spottiswoode, for Her Majesty's Stationery Office, 1855.

Nunokawa, Jeff. *The Afterlife of Property: Domestic Security and the Victorian Novel.* Princeton, N.J.: Princeton University Press, 1994.

Osborne, Thomas. "Bureaucracy as a Vocation: Governmentality and Administration in Nineteenth-Century Britain." *Journal of Historical Sociology* 7, no. 3 (1994): 289–313.

Peltason, Timothy. "The Function of Matthew Arnold at the Present Time." *College English* 56, no. 7 (1994): 749–65.

———. "Ruskin's Finale: Vision and Imagination in *Praeterita.*" *ELH* 57 (1990): 665–84.

Perkin, Harold. *The Rise of Professional Society: England since 1880*. London: Routledge, 1989.

Pollard, Arthur. "Trollope and the Idea of the Gentleman." In *Trollope: Centenary Essays*, edited by John Halperin. New York: St Martin's Press, 1982.

Poovey, Mary. *Making a Social Body: British Cultural Formation, 1830–1864*. Chicago: University of Chicago Press, 1995.

———. *Uneven Developments: The Ideological Work of Gender in Mid-Victorian England*. Chicago: The University of Chicago Press, 1988.

Psomiades, Kathy Alexis. *Beauty's Body: Femininity and Representation in British Aestheticism*. Stanford, Calif.: Stanford University Press, 1997.

Purvis, June. *Hard Lessons: The Lives and Education of Working-Class Women in Nineteenth-Century England*. Minneapolis: University of Minnesota Press, 1989.

Reader, W. J. *Professional Men: The Rise of the Professional Classes in Nineteenth-Century England*. New York: Basic Books, 1966.

Readings, Bill. *The University in Ruins*. Cambridge, Mass.: Harvard University Press, 1996.

Reed, John R. "A Friend to Mammon: Speculation in Victorian Literature." *Victorian Studies* 27, no. 2 (1984): 179–202.

Reeder, David, ed. *Educating our Masters*. Leicester, U.K.: Leicester University Press, 1980.

Richards, Thomas. *The Commodity Culture of Victorian England: Advertising and Spectacle, 1851–1914*. Stanford, Calif.: Stanford University Press, 1990.

Richardson, Alan. *Literature, Education, and Romanticism: Reading as Social Practice, 1780–1832*. Cambridge: Cambridge University Press, 1994.

Riede, David G. *Matthew Arnold and the Betrayal of Language*. Charlottesville: University Press of Virginia, 1988.

Riffaterre, Michael. "Trollope's Metonymies." *Nineteenth-Century Fiction* 37, no. 3 (1982): 272–92.

Riley, Denise. *"Am I That Name?": Feminism and the Category of "Women" in History*. Minneapolis: University of Minnesota Press, 1988.

Roach, John. *Public Examinations in England, 1850–1900*. Cambridge: Cambridge University Press, 1971.

Robbins, William. *The Arnoldian Principle of Flexibility*. Victoria, B.C.: English Literary Studies, 1979.

Rogers, Henry N., III. "Trollope's Fourth Clerk: 'Crinoline and Macassar' in *The Three Clerks*." *Publications of the Arkansas Philological Society* 13, no. 2 (1987): 81–99.

Ruskin, John. *The Ethics of the Dust*. In *The Works of John Ruskin*, edited by E. T. Cook and Alexander Wedderburn. Vol. 18. London: George Allen, 1905.

———. *Praeterita*. Oxford: Oxford University Press, 1989.

———. *Sesame and Lilies*. In *The Works of John Ruskin*, edited by E. T. Cook and Alexander Wedderburn. Vol. 18. London: George Allen, 1905.

———. *Unto this Last*. In *Unto this Last and Other Writings*, edited by Clive Wilmer. Harmondsworth: Penguin, 1985.

Sawyer, Paul. "Ruskin and the Matriarchal Logos." In *Victorian Sages and Cultural Discourse: Renegotiating Gender and Power*, edited by Thais E. Morgan. New Brunswick, N.J.: Rutgers University Press, 1990.

Sedgwick, Eve Kosofsky. *Between Men: English Literature and Male Homosocial Desire*. New York: Columbia University Press, 1985.

Simon, Brian. *The State and Educational Change: Essays in the History of Education and Pedagogy*. London: Lawrence and Wishart, 1994.

Slakey, Roger L. "Anthony Trollope, Master of Gradualness." *VIJ* 16 (1988): 27–35.

Smalley, Donald, ed. *Trollope: The Critical Heritage*. London: Routledge & Kegan Paul, 1969.

Smelser, Neil. *Social Paralysis and Social Change: British Working-Class Education in the Nineteenth Century*. Berkeley: University of California Press, 1991.

Solomon, J. Fisher. "Realism, Rhetoric, and Reification: Or the Case of the Missing Detective in *Our Mutual Friend*." *Modern Philology* 86, no. 1 (1988): 34–45.

Sosnoski, James J. "Examining Exams." In *Knowledges: Historical and Critical Studies in Disciplinarity*, edited by Ellen Messer-Davidow, David R. Shumway, and David J. Sylven. Charlottesville: University Press of Virginia, 1993.

Spear, Jeffrey. *Dreams of an English Eden: Ruskin and His Tradition in Social Criticism*. New York: Columbia University Press, 1984.

Steedman, Carolyn. *Strange Dislocations: Childhood and the Idea of Human Interiority, 1780–1930*. Cambridge, Mass.: Harvard University Press, 1995.

Stone, Lynda. "Toward a Transformational Theory of Teaching." In *The*

Education Feminism Reader, edited by Linda Stone. New York: Routledge, 1994.

Stone, Lynda, ed. *The Education Feminism Reader*. New York: Routledge, 1994.

Super, R. H. *Trollope in the Post Office*. Ann Arbor: University of Michigan Press, 1981.

Sussman, Herbert. *Victorian Masculinities: Manhood and Masculine Poetics in Early Victorian Literature and Art*. Cambridge: Cambridge University Press, 1995.

Sutherland, John A. "Trollope at Work on *The Way We Live Now*." *Nineteenth-Century Fiction* 37, no. 2 (1982): 472–93.

Terry, R. C., ed. *Trollope: Interviews and Recollections*. London: Macmillan, 1987.

Thompson, Nicola. "'Something Both More and Less Than Manliness': Gender and the Literary Reception of Anthony Trollope." *Victorian Literature and Culture* 22 (1994): 151–71.

Tillotson, Geoffrey. "Matthew Arnold's Prose: Theory and Practice." In *The Art of Victorian Prose*, edited by George Levine and William Madden. New York: Oxford University Press, 1968.

Todd, Sharon, ed. *Learning Desire: Perspectives on Pedagogy, Culture, and the Unsaid*. New York: Routledge, 1997.

Tollers, Vincent L. "A Working Isaiah: Arnold in the Council Office." *Essays and Studies* 41 (1988): 108–24.

Torres, Carlos Alberto. *Education, Power, and Personal Biography: Dialogues with Critical Educators*. New York: Routledge, 1998.

Trachsel, Mary. *Institutionalizing Literacy: The Historical Role of College Entrance Examinations in English*. Carbondale: Southern Illinois University Press, 1992.

Trollope, Anthony. *An Autobiography*. Oxford: Oxford University Press World's Classics, 1980.

———. *The Bertrams*. London: The Folio Society, 1993.

———. "The Civil Service." *Dublin University Magazine*, October 1855. Reprinted in *Miscellaneous Essays and Reviews by Anthony Trollope* (New York: Arno Press, 1981).

———. "The Civil Service." *Fortnightly Review*, October 15, 1865. Reprinted in *Miscellaneous Essays and Reviews by Anthony Trollope* (New York: Arno Press, 1981).

———. *The Small House at Allington*. Edited by James R. Kincaid. New York: Oxford University Press, 1989.

———. *The Three Clerks*. Edited by Graham Handley. Oxford: Oxford University Press, 1989.

———. *The Vicar of Bullhampton*. Edited by David Skilton. Oxford: Oxford University Press, 1988.

———. "The Young Women at the London Telegraph Office." In *Miscellaneous Essays and Reviews by Anthony Trollope*. New York: Arno Press, 1981. First published in *Good Words* (June 1877).

Tucker, Robert C., ed. *The Marx–Engels Reader*. 2d edition. New York: Norton, 1978.

Vallance, Elizabeth. "Hiding the Hidden Curriculum: An Interpretation of the Language of Justification in Nineteenth-Century Education Reform." In *The Hidden Curriculum and Moral Education*, edited by Henry Giroux and David Purpel. Berkeley, Calif.: McCutchen, 1983.

Viswanathan, Gauri. *Masks of Conquest: Literary Study and British Rule in India*. New York: Columbia University Press, 1989.

Walcott, Fred G. *The Origins of Culture and Anarchy: Matthew Arnold and Popular Education in England*. Toronto: University of Toronto Press, 1970.

Walford, Geoffrey, ed. *The Private Schooling of Girls: Past and Present*. London: Woburn Press, 1993.

Watkins, Evan. *Work Time: English Departments and the Circulation of Cultural Value*. Stanford, Calif.: Stanford University Press, 1989.

Weiss, Barbara. *The Hell of the English: Bankruptcy and the Victorian Novel*. Lewisburg, Pa.: Bucknell University Press, 1986.

Welsh, Alexander. *The City of Dickens*. Oxford: Clarendon Press, 1971.

———. *From Copyright to Copperfield: The Identity of Dickens*. Cambridge, Mass.: Harvard University Press, 1987.

Weltman, Sharon Aronofsky. *Ruskin's Mythic Queen: Gender Subversion in Victorian Culture*. Athens: Ohio University Press, 1998.

Williams, Raymond. *Culture and Society, 1780/1950*. New York: Columbia University Press, 1958.

Winnett, Susan. "Coming Unstrung: Women, Men, Narrative, and Principles of Pleasure." *PMLA* 105 (1990): 505–18.

Yeazell, Ruth Bernard. "Podsnappery, Sexuality, and the English Novel." *Critical Inquiry* 9 (1982): 339–57.

Zelizer, Viviana A. *Pricing the Priceless Child: The Changing Social Value of Children*. New York: Basic Books, 1985.

INDEX

Adams, James Eli, 23
Agnew, Joan, 203
Althusser, Louis, 31, 147, 232
Altick, Richard, 155, 228
Amirault, Chris, 235
apRoberts, Ruth, 224
Arac, Jonathan, 145–46
Armstrong, Frances, 137
Armstrong, Nancy, 222
Arnold, Matthew, 20–21, 29–75,
    81–82, 107, 113, 144–47 passim, 167,
    174, 196–97, 210, 222–25; on
    teaching of literature, 29–34,
    53–60, 72–73, 222, 223. See also
    Culture and Anarchy; "A French
    Eton"; "The Function of Criticism
    at the Present Time"; Reports on
    Elementary Schools 1852–1882; Revised
    Code of 1862 exam
Austen, Linda, 233
An Autobiography (Trollope), 21, 25,
    74–78 passim, 88, 93–98 passim,
    106–8, 114–19, 227–28

Bann, Stephen, 209
Bareham, Tony, 92, 96

Barrett, Michelle, 232
Barthes, Roland, 176
Baudrillard, Jean, 188
Beale, Dorothea, 177
Bell, Margaret, 176–79, 182, 190, 205.
    See also Winnington Hall School
The Bertrams (Trollope), 4, 86, 226
Birch, Dinah, 174, 232, 234
Bourdieu, Pierre, 6–8, 16, 18, 143–47
    passim, 156–59, 229, 233–34
British and Foreign Schools Society,
    223–24. See also Voluntary schools
Browning, Robert, 227
Browning, Elizabeth Barrett, 227
Burd, Van Akin, 190, 203, 205, 231
Burstyn, Joan, 159–60
Butler, Judith, 24

Caminero-Santangelo, Byron, 219–20
Carlyle, Thomas, 22, 172, 174
Childhood, 172–75, 178, 184, 208–9,
    231, 232
Civil Service: office work in, 79, 101–7,
    111–15; reform of, 77–82, 109–10,
    225; social status and, 52–53, 78–82,
    89–96, 101–6, 111–14, 224–25

251

"The Civil Service" (1855) (Trollope), 78–80, 82–86, 111, 114–15
"The Civil Service" (1865) (Trollope), 86
Civil Service Examinations, 56, 73, 89–94, 105–8, 119–20, 212. *See also* Northcote–Trevelyan Report
Class system, and education system, 61–73, 149–52, 159–64, 224. *See also* Civil Service, social status and
Cohen, Monica F., 17, 24
Corrigan, Philip, 15, 48, 221
Cotsell, Michael, 229
Critical pedagogy, 157–60, 197, 220
Crosby, Christina, 186, 232–33
Crystal Palace, 206–7, 221
Culler, Dwight, 192, 224
Culture and Anarchy (Arnold), 48, 49, 50, 54–55, 58–59, 66

dal Bagno, Pannuccio, 193–94
Dame schools, 62, 230
David, Dierdre, 229, 230
David Copperfield (Dickens), 125
Dickens, Charles, 21–23, 123–69, 171, 174, 182. *See also David Copperfield*; *Dombey and Son*; *Great Expectations*; *Hard Times*; *Little Dorrit*; *Our Mutual Friend*
Dombey and Son (Dickens), 139
Domesticity, 132–33, 139–44, 210–11, 229–30; institutions and, 66–70, 107, 144–47, 181–82
Dowling, Linda, 234

Eglinton tournament 192, 233
Ehrenreich, Barbara, 18, 33
Ehrenreich, John, 18, 33
Elliott, Dorice Williams, 16
Emerson, Sheila, 174, 232, 235

Engels, Friedrich, 232
Ermarth, Elizabeth Deeds, 133
The Ethics of the Dust (Ruskin), 170–73, 181–82, 189–90, 197–211, 234–35
Examination breakdown, 1–4, 56, 83, 90–91
Excellence, 213–16, 227
Exchange, economic, 13–15, 213–16; 220–21; in Arnold, 35–37, 42–48, 62–63; in Dickens, 126–28, 153–57, 161–69; and the extraeconomic, 128–35, 184, 212, 215–16, 228, 229–30; in Ruskin 182–85, 197–99; in Trollope, 97–109, 226

Felman, Shoshana, 170
Fitzgerald, Edward, 192–3
Foucault, Michel, 6–8, 219, 221; and theory of governmentality, 10–11, 89
Freire, Paulo, 158, 202, 220; "banking model" of education, 158–69, 197, 220, 231
"A French Eton" (Arnold), 36–37, 40, 65–66
Freud, Sigmund, 173, 175
"The Function of Criticism at the Present Time" (Arnold), 29, 46–47, 55
Fuss, Diana, 173–75, 201

Gagnier, Regenia, 222
Gallagher, Catherine, 219, 222, 228–29
Gallop, Jane, 222
Gender, 52–53, 105, 116–18, 135–40, 174–78 *passim*, 188–89, 232; and education, 157–69, 189–97, 230–31; and intellectual labor, 22–24, 221–22, 227–28; and narrative structure, 160, 190–97

Index

Girouard, Mark, 233
Gladstone, William Ewart, 10, 77, 80–81, 108, 110
Gowan, Peter, 79, 110–11, 225
Gramsci, Antonio, 17, 29–30
Gray, Effie, 231
Great Expectations (Dickens), 139, 230
Guillory, John, 213, 222, 235

Habermas, Jurgen, 221
Hard Times (Dickens), 3, 139, 229–30
Hardy, Barbara, 164
Hearn, Jeff, 221
Helsinger, Elizabeth, 235
Herbert, Christopher, 87–88, 226
Hirsch, Marianne, 230–31
Holloway, John, 30
Homans, Margaret, 233, 235
Humphreys, E. R., 107
Hunter, Ian, 15–16, 31, 48, 72–73, 219, 222, 223

Ideology, 19, 29–34, 55–73, 147, 216
Ingham, Patricia, 139
Intellectual labor, 9, 15–28, 33; in Arnold 58, 69–71; containment of 204–5; in Dickens 124–28, 135–38, 148, 152–53; display of, 23–25, 64–65, 68–73, 93–94, 118–22, 212; and "mechanical" labor 111–18, 127–28, 210, 227; in Ruskin, 184, 214; in Trollope 96–101, 108, 114–19
Inspection, government, 48–53, 100–101, 123; in Education Department, 29–75, 222–23; in Post Office, 74–6, 79
Interiority, 6, 23–24, 87–89, 93–96, 122, 157–69, 222
Irigaray, Luce, 169

Jaffe, Audrey, 229
James, Henry, 84, 116–18, 225
Jameson, Fredric, 233
Johnson, Barbara, 160
Jowett, Benjamin, 77–78, 90, 108–11, 115, 225. *See also* Northcote–Trevelyan Report
Joyce, Patrick, 222

Kay-Shuttleworth, James, 14–16, 67, 225
Kekewich, G. W., 154
Kincaid, James, 85, 87–88, 225, 231
Kucich, John, 70, 84, 225

labor system, relation to education system, 2–3, 107–14
labor unions, 215–16
Ladson-Billings, Gloria, 213
Lansbury, Coral, 101–2, 227
Larson, Magali Sarfatti, 18, 96
La Touche, Rose, 173, 231
Lawyers, 120–21, 143, 163–64
Levine, George, 87–88
Little Dorrit (Dickens), 99, 114, 227
Lowe, Robert, 14, 51, 223, 225. *See also* Revised Code of 1862 exam

Marian Fay (Trollope), 78–79
Marx, Karl, 129–30, 194, 232
Maurice, Frederick, 190
Mayhew, Henry, 133–34, 229
Menke, Richard, 235
Mill, John Stuart, 12
Miller, J. Hillis, 106, 117, 125, 130, 226, 229
Morris, Pam, 132
"Mystery of Life and Its Arts" (Ruskin), *see Sesame and Lilies*

Nabokov, Vladimir, 1–3, 213
National Schools Society, 31, 223–24.
    See also Voluntary schools
Neith, Egyptian Goddess, 206
Northcote–Trevelyan Report, 8,
    10–12, 21–22, 76–89, 99–100,
    108–15, 127, 225
Nunokawa, Jeff, 231

"Of Kings' Treasuries" (Ruskin),
    see Sesame and Lilies
"Of Queens' Gardens" (Ruskin),
    see Sesame and Lilies
Orley Farm (Trollope), 121
Osborne, Thomas, 82, 108–9
Our Mutual Friend (Dickens), 44, 63,
    123–69, 215, 224, 228–31; classification of labor in, 123–35; gender
    and labor in, 131–33; literacy in, 125,
    150–53; pedagogic authority and,
    140, 147–57, 229; scavengers in,
    132–35, 168–69, 228

Passeron, Claude, *see* Bourdieu, Pierre
Patmore, Coventry, 193–94
Payment by results exam, *see* Revised
    Code of 1862 exam
Peltason, Timothy, 34, 202
Perkin, Harold, 16, 18–19
physical education, 177–78
political economy, 179–81, 185–90,
    226, 233
Poovey, Mary, 22–23, 221
Praeterita (Ruskin), 174–75, 201, 211,
    232
Professionalization, *see* intellectual
    labor
Psomiades, Kathy Alexis, 222

Ragged schools, 63, 151–52

Readings, Bill, 214–16
Religion, 3, 49–51, 178–79, 201, 219,
    220
Repetition: in Arnold 34, 46; in
    Ruskin, 199, 210; in Trollope 84–85
Reports on Elementary Schools 1852–1882
    (Arnold), 26, 29–75, 113
Revised Code of 1862 exam, 13, 14, 105,
    214, 223, 228; Arnold on, 37–47,
    60–63, 73; in *Our Mutual Friend*
    (Dickens), 153–57
Richards, Thomas, 221, 222, 232
Riede, David G., 33
Riffaterre, Michael, 225–26
Riley, Denise, 11–12
Roach, John, 10, 13, 77, 225
Rogers, Henry N., III, 94
Ruskin, John, 21–22, 24, 169–212, 215,
    231–35; on failure, 175, 210–12; on
    history, 180–82, 189, 206–10; and
    identification: 172–75, 201–9; on
    personification, 201, 205–10, 235;
    and Victorian Gothic, 192–97,
    232–33. *See also The Ethics of the Dust*;
    Praeterita; *Sesame and Lilies*; *Unto this
    Last*
Ruskin, John, Sr., 182–83

Sandford, Sir Francis, 222
Sawyer, Paul, 23
Sayer, Derek, 15, 48, 221
Sedgwick, Eve Kosofsky, 143, 150
Separate spheres, doctrine of: in
    Trollope, 103–7; in Dickens,
    135–44; in Ruskin, 138–39, 180–81,
    187–88
Sesame and Lilies: 1882 Preface, 174, 192,
    195, 231; "Mystery of Life and Its
    Arts" 171, 179–82, 211–12; "Of
    Kings' Treasuries," 188–89, 195–96;

Index

"Of Queens' Gardens," 171, 181, 185, 187–97, 231
Sewing, 52–53, 67–69, 174–75, 195, 210–11
Simmons, Clare, 230
Simon, Brian, 12
The Small House at Allington (Trollope), 74, 224–25
Socratic dialogue, 197–98, 233–34
Solomon, J. Fisher, 228
State and civil society, 15–17, 99–101, 221; and education, 10–15, 47–48, 72–73, 107–11; and intellectual labor, 17–21, 144–47; relations with subject, 48–52, 65, 89, 195–97
Steedman, Carolyn, 173, 209
Stone, Lynda, 158
Super, R. H., 105–6, 227
Sussman, Herbert, 222
Sutherland, John, 227

Teachers, 1–2, 213–16; in Arnold, 38–39, 43, 47; in Dickens, 127–28, 153–59, 162–64; pupil-teachers, 32, 58–61, 64, 67, 159–60; in Ruskin, 197–99, 202–5
Thompson, Nicola, 116
The Three Clerks (Trollope), 24, 78–105 passim, 109–11, 115, 119–21, 215; financial speculation in, 92, 94, 98–101, 226, 227; genre in, 89–94; names in, 94–96; scholastic imagery in, 109–11
Trevelyan, Sir Charles, 77–78, 225. *See also* Northcote–Trevelyan Report
Trollope, Anthony, 73–122, 213, 224–28; and Dickens, 144–47; and the London telegraph office, 107, 121–22; and the Post Office, 73–76, 105–6, 119, 226–27; realism in, 87–92; and Ruskin, 174, 210, 212. *See also An Autobiography*; *The Bertrams*; "The Civil Service" (1855); "The Civil Service" (1865); *Marian Fay*; *Orley Farm*; *The Small House at Allington*; *The Three Clerks*; *The Vicar of Bullhampton*; "The Young Women at the London Telegraph Office"
Trollope, Frances, 116–17
Trollope, Henry, 228

Unto this Last (Ruskin), 185–87, 232

The Vicar of Bullhampton (Trollope), 87–88
Victoria, Queen, 233
Voluntary schools, 29–73, 146, 223–24; architecture of, 62–63, 219

Watkins, Evan, 2, 14, 29–30, 57, 235
Welsh, Alexander, 139
Weltman, Sharon, 174, 232, 235
Winnett, Susan, 230
Winnington Hall School, 172–79, 181–85, 190–91, 199, 203, 210–12, 234, 235
Wollstonecraft, Mary, 137
Women's Ways of Knowing (Belenky), 158–59
Wordsworth, William, 53–54, 191, 223

Yeazell, Ruth Bernard, 140, 160, 169
"The Young Women at the London Telegraph Office" (Trollope), 107, 121–22

Zelizer, Viviana A., 184, 232